AN INTRODUCTION TO THE MAKING AND MEANING OF THE BIBLE

AN INTRODUCTION
TO THE MAKING AND MEANING
OF THE BIBLE

Michael B. Shepherd

WILLIAM B. EERDMANS PUBLISHING COMPANY
GRAND RAPIDS, MICHIGAN

Wm. B. Eerdmans Publishing Co.
4035 Park East Court SE, Grand Rapids, Michigan 49546
www.eerdmans.com

Book design by Lydia Hall

Printed in the United States of America

30 29 28 27 26 25 24   1 2 3 4 5 6 7

ISBN 978-0-8028-8393-3

Library of Congress Cataloging-in-Publication Data

A catalog record for this book is available from the Library of Congress.

To Esther

CONTENTS

TABLES

PREFACE

This book is written for those who want to learn more about how comprehension of the making of the Bible informs interpretation of the meaning of the Bible. The first chapter features an introduction to biblical composition designed to show how the Bible is built to interpret itself from the level of individual verses, chapters, and sections to the level of whole books and canonical divisions. This introduction includes a treatment of the variety of literary forms and genres that go into the making of the Bible. Chapter 2 discusses the various textual witnesses to the Bible known from its earliest history of transmission. Here the goal is to raise awareness of textual plurality in antiquity and of the availability of the different witnesses in English translation for the modern readers in order that they might see the value of these witnesses not only for the establishment of the original text of the Bible but also for the early history of interpretation. The conclusion to this chapter traces the history of Bible translation from the ancient versions to the plethora of modern English versions to show that the differences between translations are due not only to differing translation techniques but also to differing source texts.

The third and fourth chapters are not intended to be a survey of the books of the Bible, nor are they a discussion of introductory issues such as authorship and date. Rather, these chapters take the material from the first chapter on the making of the Bible to demonstrate how this informs biblical interpretation. These two chapters show that each of the biblical compositions has a macrostructural strategy that communicates a theological message applicable to every generation of faithful readers. The fifth chapter looks at the Bible holistically via the extensive system of intertextuality among the books. This final chapter invites readers to enter the textual world of the Bible by faith, allowing it to define, explain, and represent reality. The goal of this chapter is to reorient readers to the principal concerns of the biblical authors.

Special thanks to Andrew Knapp (acquisitions editor), Laurel Draper (project editor), and the Eerdmans team for their support of this project. I would also like to thank my colleagues and students at Cedarville University for their encouragement and willingness to interact with the material included in this book. As always, I could not do what I do without the love and care of my wife, Esther, and my four daughters Abbi, Anna, Audrey, and Ava.

ABBREVIATIONS

Alex	Alexandrian text
ANEM	Ancient Near East Monographs
ApOTC	Apollos Old Testament Commentary
b. B. Bat.	Babylonian Baba Batra
b. Ber.	Babylonian Berakot
BCOTWP	Baker Commentary on the Old Testament Wisdom and Psalms
b. Menaḥ.	Babylonian Menaḥot
b. Qidd.	Babylonian Qiddušin
Byz	Byzantine text
ca.	circa
CBET	Contributions to Biblical Exegesis and Theology
CBQ	*Catholic Biblical Quarterly*
Contempl.	Philo, *De vita contemplativa*
CRINT	Compendia Rerum Iudaicarum ad Novum Testamentum
DCH	*Dictionary of Classical Hebrew*. Edited by David J. A. Clines. 9 vols. Sheffield: Sheffield Phoenix Press, 1993–2014
EBC	Expositor's Bible Commentary
11QMelch	Cave 11, Qumran, Melchizedek
11QPsᵃ	Cave 11, Qumran, Psalms manuscript A
FAT	Forschungen zum Alten Testament
1 En.	1 Enoch
4QCantᵃ	Cave 4, Qumran, Canticles manuscript A
4QCantᵇ	Cave 4, Qumran, Canticles manuscript B
4QCommGen A	Commentary on Genesis A
4QFlor	Florilegium
4QJerᵇ	Cave 4, Qumran, Jeremiah manuscript B
4QJudgᵃ	Cave 4, Qumran, Judges manuscript A
4QMMTᵈ	Miqṣat Maʿaśe ha-Torah

4QSam^a	Cave 4, Qumran, Samuel manuscript A
Frg. Tg.	Fragmentary Targum of the Pentateuch
FRLANT	Forschungen zur Religion und Literatur des Alten und Neuen Testaments
Hen	*Henoch*
HS	*Hebrew Studies*
JBL	*Journal of Biblical Literature*
JSOT	*Journal for the Study of the Old Testament*
JSOTSup	Journal for the Study of the Old Testament Supplement Series
Jub.	Jubilees
KEL	Kregel Exegetical Library
LHBOTS	The Library of Hebrew Bible/Old Testament Studies
LXX	Septuagint
MT	Masoretic Text
NETS	New English Translation of the Septuagint
nonn Mss	some medieval Masoretic manuscripts
NovT	*Novum Testamentum*
OG	Old Greek
1QIsa^a	Cave 1, Qumran, Isaiah manuscript A
1QIsa^b	Cave 1, Qumran, Isaiah manuscript B
OTL	Old Testament Library
Pal. Tgg.	Palestinian Targumim
p967	Chester Beatty papyrus 967
REJ	*Revue des études juives*
SBLMS	Society of Biblical Literature Monograph Series
Sir	Sirach
SP	Samaritan Pentateuch
StBibLit	Studies in Biblical Literature
STI	Studies in Theological Interpretation
Syr.	Syriac Peshitta
Syr. Josh	Syriac Joshua
TCSt	Text-Critical Studies
Tg. Jon.	Targum Jonathan
Tg. Neof.	Targum Neofiti
Tg. Onq.	Targum Onqelos
Tg. Ps.-J.	Targum Pseudo-Jonathan
Them	*Themelios*

TLOT	*Theological Lexicon of the Old Testament.* Edited by Ernst Jenni, with assistance from Claus Westermann. Translated by Mark E. Biddle. 3 vols. Peabody, MA: Hendrickson, 1997
t. Meg.	Tosefta Megillah
TrinJ	*Trinity Journal*
VT	*Vetus Testamentum*
VT Sup	Supplements to Vetus Testamentum
Vulg.	Latin Vulgate
WTJ	*Westminster Theological Journal*
ZAW	*Zeitschrift für die alttestamentliche Wissenschaft*

INTRODUCTION

How did we get the Bible? Why are there so many different translations? How do we interpret the Bible? How does the Bible apply to our lives? These are the kinds of questions that this book is designed to address. Before getting started, it is important to lay some groundwork for the following discussion. This introduction will disclose the assumptions held in this book about the nature of Scripture. It will also clarify what is meant by the "Old Testament," the "New Testament," and the "canon" of Scripture. These assumptions and clarifications will provide a basic foundation for the subsequent chapters.

ASSUMPTIONS ABOUT THE NATURE OF SCRIPTURE

The present volume accepts the claims that the Bible makes for itself. In many ways the books of the Bible are like other works of world literature. They are written in human languages and composed according to human literary conventions. On the other hand, the biblical books are unique in two very important ways. First of all, the text of Scripture is "God-breathed." In 2 Timothy 3:15–17, Paul refers to the holy writings that Timothy has known since his youth (i.e., the Hebrew Scriptures). These writings are able to make a person wise "for salvation through faith in Christ Jesus."[1] All such Scripture is "God-breathed" and beneficial for teaching, rebuking, correcting, and training in righteousness in order that "the man of God" might be complete, fully equipped for every good work. This status of divine revelation for the Hebrew Bible eventually extends to the New Testament documents (see John 14:26; 1 Tim 5:18; 2 Pet 3:16). Second, the prophetic authors of Scripture are said to be carried along by the Holy

---

1. Scripture translations are the author's own unless otherwise indicated.

Spirit in their work.[2] The Holy Spirit superintended the composition of the biblical books in such a way that what was produced was exactly what God wanted, nothing more and nothing less.

THE OLD AND NEW TESTAMENTS

It is not uncommon for readers of the Bible to work under the assumption that the so-called Old Testament is the law, and the New Testament is the gospel. Or, that the Old Testament is the old covenant, and the New Testament is the new covenant. These assumptions are problematic for a number of reasons. While it is true that the Old Testament reveals some of the laws that were given through Moses on Mount Sinai, these laws are primarily located in Exodus 20–Leviticus 27 and in Deuteronomy 12–28. What about the rest of the Old Testament? It is surely reductionistic to characterize the entire composition of the Hebrew Bible as law.[3] Furthermore, the New Testament itself says repeatedly that the message of the gospel is already revealed in the Hebrew Scriptures (e.g., Luke 24:25–27, 44–47; Rom 3:21–22; 16:25–27; 1 Cor 15:3–5; 2 Tim 3:15–17). It is equally reductionistic to refer to the whole of the Hebrew Bible as the old covenant (i.e., the Sinai covenant), as if it were one long covenant document. There are five major divine-human covenants in the Hebrew Bible: the Noahic covenant (Gen 9), the Abrahamic covenant (Gen 15), the Mosaic covenant (also known as the old covenant or the Sinai covenant; Exod 24), the Davidic covenant (2 Sam 7), and the new covenant (Jer 31:31–34). The writings of the Hebrew Bible assume either that the old covenant will be broken (e.g., Deut 31:16) or that the old covenant has been broken (e.g., Jer 11:10). Thus, the Hebrew Bible for the most part looks forward to the hope of a new

---

2. "And we have even more surely the prophetic word, to which you do well paying attention as to a light shining in a murky place until day dawns and morning star rises in your hearts; knowing this first, that every prophecy of Scripture does not come by one's own interpretation, but men carried by the Holy Spirit spoke from God" (2 Pet 1:19–21).

3. This problem is partly due to the translation history of the Hebrew term *torah*. In ancient Greek translation, this term was rendered as *nomos* (law), and this practice has continued in modern English translation, but the Hebrew term *torah* does not mean law. It means instruction, and as such it can refer to things such as law codes (e.g., Deut 4:44–45) or parental instruction (e.g., Prov 1:8), but it can also refer to the book of Moses (i.e., Genesis through Deuteronomy; e.g., Neh 8:1) or to the entire Hebrew Bible (e.g., Rom 3:19 where *nomos* stands for *torah*).

covenant relationship. Indeed, the writer to the Hebrews does not quote Jesus or Paul to tell readers about the new covenant. Rather, the writer quotes the prophet Jeremiah (Heb 8:8–12). It is therefore somewhat of a misnomer to call the Hebrew Bible the "Old Testament."

Another common assumption that readers often bring to the Bible is that the Hebrew Bible is the history and religion of ancient Israel and Judaism, and the New Testament is the history and religion of the early Christian church. The Hebrew Bible certainly has its fair share of historical narratives, but these are framed and interpreted in such a way that they function as more than documentaries of past events. The mainstream religious practice of ancient Israel was idolatrous and syncretistic as attested by prophets like Isaiah, Jeremiah, Ezekiel, Hosea, and Amos. This is not the religion advocated by the Hebrew Scriptures. Furthermore, the religion of Judaism is a postbiblical phenomenon best represented by the Mishnah and the Talmud. It is anachronistic to equate the Hebrew Bible with Judaism. Likewise, while the New Testament does provide an account of the early church (see Acts), this is not its sole purpose; nor does it seek to create a new religion. The New Testament authors are primarily concerned with establishing continuity with the Hebrew Scriptures. They want to explain the life, death, and resurrection of Jesus, the coming of the Holy Spirit and the birth of the early church, and the hope of Christ's eventual return from the Bible that they already have.

In the end, it is best to describe the Bible the way the texts describe themselves. The Hebrew Scriptures are variously known as the Law/Torah (e.g., Rom 3:19); the prophetic writings (e.g., Rom 1:2); Moses and the Prophets (e.g., Luke 24:25–27); the Law/Torah of Moses and the Prophets and Psalms (Luke 24:44–47); simply as the Scriptures (1 Cor 15:3–5); or Scripture (2 Tim 3:16). On the other hand, the New Testament documents are the apostolic writings produced either by the apostles themselves or by those in close association with the apostles.

THE CANON OF THE HEBREW BIBLE

Scholars often say that the term "canon" (meaning reed, or standard of measure) is used anachronistically with reference to the biblical writings. The term first came into use in the early church for the norm or rule of faith and only later referred to the definitive list of biblical books. If by "canon" one means a closed list of authoritative books determined by an official body and universally agreed upon, then the term is not only anachronistic but also completely useless. The biblical canon is not merely about what books are included or excluded, nor is it something decided by authorities who pass their decision down to the general populace. Organic acceptance of the canon by the community of faith is important. Nothing is ever universally agreed upon, however, and thus such a notion cannot possibly or realistically be a determining factor. For the purposes of the present introduction, the focus will be on making a distinction between books that were shaped in light of one another and books that were produced primarily as exegetical works that assumed a fixed body of scriptural literature.[4]

For the extent and order of the Hebrew canon, the original language tradition holds primary importance. The later fourth- and fifth-century CE Greek codices (Vaticanus, Sinaiticus, and Alexandrinus) do not agree with one another, nor do they appear to represent any known Hebrew tradition.[5] The earliest external evidence from the historical record for the basic shape of the Hebrew canon appears in the prologue to a book known as the Wisdom of Jesus ben Sirach, a work that was originally composed in Hebrew around 200 BCE. The prologue was added by the author's grandson to the Greek translation of the book around 130 BCE. This prologue refers three times to the Hebrew Scriptures as they were known in the time of Jesus ben Sirach: "the Law and the Prophets" and a third division variously called "the others that followed them," "the other ancestral books," and "the rest of the books." This does not provide great detail, but it does speak of a threefold structure recognizable from later Hebrew tradition. While it is possible to guess that the designations "the Law and the Prophets" refer at the very least to Moses (Genesis–Deuteronomy)

4. See Stephen B. Chapman, *The Law and the Prophets: A Study in Old Testament Canon Formation*, FAT 27 (Tübingen: Mohr Siebeck, 2000), 105; Julius Steinberg and Timothy J. Stone, "The Historical Formation of the Writings in Antiquity," in *The Shape of the Writings*, ed. Julius Steinberg and Timothy J. Stone, Siphrut: Literature and Theology of the Hebrew Scriptures 16 (Winona Lake, IN: Eisenbrauns, 2015), 5, 9.

5. See E. Earle Ellis, "The Old Testament Canon in the Early Church," in *Mikra: Text, Translation, Reading and Interpretation of the Hebrew Bible in Ancient Judaism and Early Christianity*, ed. Martin Jan Mulder and Harry Sysling (Philadelphia: Fortress, 1988; repr., Peabody, MA: Hendrickson, 2004), 678. The earliest reference to Greek translation of a particular shape of the Hebrew canon occurs in the prologue to Sirach: "for what was originally expressed in Hebrew does not have the same force when it is in fact rendered in another language. And not only in this case, but also in the case of the Law itself and the Prophets and the rest of the books the difference is not small when these are expressed in their own language" (NETS).

and the Latter Prophets (Isaiah, Jeremiah, Ezekiel, and Hosea–Malachi), the third division seems at first glance to be ambiguous at best. It has been suggested that such an undefined reference to this third division reveals either uncertainty about its contents or an assumption that it is still open and developing. It is possible, however, to understand this another way. A precise listing of books for the third division would presuppose that readers need to be told what occupies it. A simple reference to the other books or the rest of the books presupposes that readers know exactly what books occupy the third division and do not need to be told.

One of the fragmentary sectarian documents from the Qumran community, 4QMMT[d] (first century BCE),[6] also refers to the threefold shape of the Hebrew Bible: "the book of Moses [and] the book[s of the pr]ophets and Davi[d . . .]." The book of Moses and the books of the prophets correspond to the Law and the Prophets in the prologue to Sirach. The name David is given for the third division, which the prologue to Sirach simply calls the other books. This name could signify a single book (e.g., Psalms) or a collection of books (e.g., 1–2 Samuel, 1–2 Kings, 1–2 Chronicles) associated with David. It is possible that such a book or collection of books constitutes the entirety of this third division, but the reference in the prologue of Sirach to a plurality of books here suggests that this book or collection merely stands at the beginning of a larger body of literature.

In Luke 24:27 (first century CE), the designation "Moses" and "the Prophets" is given for the Hebrew Scriptures. Later in verse 44 of the same chapter, Jesus refers to the same literature as "the Law of Moses and the Prophets and Psalms." The first two divisions correspond to the evidence of the prologue to Sirach and 4QMMT[d]. The designation of the third division as "Psalms" corresponds to the name David in 4QMMT[d], and the indication in the prologue to Sirach of a plurality of books here makes it likely that the book of Psalms stands at the head of a larger section. Because the book of Psalms was received as prophetic literature in the early church (see, e.g., Acts 2:29–30), it has been suggested that "Psalms" in Luke 24:44 is simply part of "the Prophets." The problem is that this fails to recognize that not all prophetic books in the Hebrew canon fall within the Prophets

6. This document was discovered in what is known as Cave 4 near the Qumran settlement in the Judean wilderness. 4QMMT[d] is considered one of the Dead Sea Scrolls because of the proximity of the place of its discovery to the Dead Sea. The abbreviation MMT stands for a phrase in Hebrew that means *Some of the Works of the Law*. It appears to be a letter that was sent to the priestly authorities in Jerusalem to express a difference of opinion about more than twenty legal issues.

division. Moses is a prophet (Deut 18:15, 18; 34:10), but his book (i.e., the Pentateuch) is not among the Prophets. Daniel is a prophet (Matt 24:15), but his book is not among the Prophets. Thus, it appears that there are multiple ways in the New Testament to refer to the same threefold structure of the Hebrew Bible: (1) "the Law/Torah" (John 10:34; Rom 3:19); (2) "prophetic writings" (Rom 1:2; 16:26); (3) "Moses and the Prophets" (Luke 24:27); and (4) "the Law of Moses and the Prophets and Psalms" (Luke 24:44). The uses of "the Law/Torah" and "prophetic writings" in these examples are not references to single divisions to the exclusion of the others. Likewise, the designation "Moses and the Prophets" does not exclude the third division. Sometimes the Hebrew Bible is simply called "Scripture" (2 Tim 3:16) or "the Scriptures" (1 Cor 15:3–5).

The first-century Jewish philosopher Philo describes the Scriptures to which an ascetic group known as the Therapeutae devoted themselves as "the laws, the oracles uttered by the prophets, and hymns and the other [books]" (*Contempl.* 1f., 25). This agrees with the earlier references to the Law of Moses and the Prophets as the first two divisions of the canon. It also agrees with the conclusion drawn from the other witnesses that the third division not only begins with the book of Psalms but also contains other books.

In order to fill in the books that occupy the three divisions of the Hebrew canon, it will be necessary to consult a variety of witnesses. There is no debate about the first division, the Law/Torah of Moses, which includes Genesis, Exodus, Leviticus, Numbers, and Deuteronomy. There is also little debate, at least in Hebrew tradition, about the Prophets division, which consists of the Former Prophets (Joshua, Judges, 1–2 Samuel, 1–2 Kings) and the Latter Prophets (Isaiah; Jeremiah; Ezekiel; and Hosea, Joel, Amos, Obadiah, Jonah, Micah, Nahum, Habakkuk, Zephaniah, Haggai, Zechariah, and Malachi). The placement of Ruth among the Former Prophets between Judges and Samuel comes from Greek tradition (Vaticanus, Alexandrinus). The decision to do this was likely motivated by Ruth 1:1 ("In the days of the judges . . .") and possibly also by the connection between Ruth 4:15b ("she is better to you than seven sons") and 1 Samuel 1:8b ("Am I not better to you than ten sons?"). The church father Jerome put Ruth between Judges and Samuel in his listing of books according to the threefold structure of the Hebrew Bible, but in doing this he was likely influenced more by Greek tradition than by any known Hebrew tradition. As for the Latter Prophets, the earliest known arrangement—Isaiah, Jeremiah, Ezekiel, and Hosea–Malachi (Sir 46–49)—appears consistently in

Hebrew tradition (e.g., the medieval witnesses of the Aleppo Codex, the Leningrad Codex, and the Cairo Codex). The strange order for the Latter Prophets (Jeremiah, Ezekiel, Isaiah, Hosea–Malachi) found in the Babylonian Talmud (b. B. Bat. 14b), a major body of rabbinic literature from around 600 CE, has no manuscript support, despite the rationale provided there. The placement of Hosea–Malachi (the Twelve) prior to Isaiah, Jeremiah, and Ezekiel in the Greek codices Vaticanus and Alexandrinus has no support from Hebrew tradition, nor does the inclusion of other books (Baruch, Lamentations, Epistle of Jeremiah, Daniel, Susanna, Bel and the Dragon). Likewise, there is no support from Hebrew tradition (or the earliest Greek tradition) for the placement of the Latter Prophets last among the Hebrew Scriptures as in Codex Vaticanus.

The third division, the Writings, experiences the most fluctuation of the three within Hebrew tradition. Nevertheless, there is an observable consistency: (1) b. Baba Batra 14b: Ruth, Psalms, Job, Proverbs, Ecclesiastes, Song of Songs, Lamentations, Daniel, Esther, Ezra(-Nehemiah), and 1–2 Chronicles; (2) the Leningrad Codex: 1–2 Chronicles, Psalms, Job, Proverbs, Ruth, Song of Songs, Ecclesiastes, Lamentations, Esther, Daniel, and Ezra-Nehemiah; and (3) Rabbinic Bibles: Psalms, Proverbs, Job, Song of Songs, Ruth, Lamentations, Ecclesiastes, Esther, Daniel, Ezra-Nehemiah, and 1–2 Chronicles. It appears from this evidence that 1–2 Chronicles can be either at the beginning or at the end of the list. The books of 1–2 Chronicles, which form a single composition in the Hebrew Bible, presuppose a canon before it that stretches from the account of Adam in the book of Genesis (1 Chr 1:1) to the version of the decree of Cyrus in Ezra 1:1–4 (2 Chr 36:22–23).[7] Placement of 1–2 Chronicles at the conclusion of the Writings is confirmed by the early witness of Matthew 23:34 and Luke 11:51 where Jesus's words presuppose a canon that extends from Abel in the book of Genesis to Zechariah in 2 Chronicles 24:20–21.

All three of the above witnesses to the order of the Writings have either Psalms-Job-Proverbs (two witnesses) or Psalms-Proverbs-Job (one witness) either at the beginning or near the beginning. In the traditional, rabbinic text of the Hebrew Bible (the Masoretic Text, which will be abbreviated MT hereafter in references), the books of Psalms, Job, and Proverbs have their own system of accentuation separate from the other books. The earliest witnesses to the threefold shape of the Hebrew Bible all indicate

7. See Hendrik J. Koorevar, "Chronicles as the Intended Conclusion to the Old Testament Canon," in Steinberg and Stone, *Shape of the Writings*, 207–35.

that the book of Psalms should stand at the beginning of the Writings (4QMMTᵈ; Luke 24:44; Philo *Contempl.* 1f., 25). The placement of Ruth at the head of the Writings in the Talmud might have been motivated by the appearance of David's name at the end of the book, perhaps as a fitting introduction to the Psalter. The problem with this line of reasoning is that the genealogy at the end of Ruth presupposes that the reader already knows who David is. Furthermore, the book of Psalms already has its own introduction in Psalms 1 and 2. The Psalms-Job-Proverbs order likely has priority over the Psalms-Proverbs-Job order, given some of the intertextual connections between Psalms and Job.[8] More importantly, the book of Proverbs has a close relationship to the following five books of the Megilloth (festival scrolls) to be discussed later in the present volume.

Two of the three orders mentioned above have the Megilloth together: the Leningrad Codex (Ruth, Song of Songs, Ecclesiastes, Lamentations, Esther) and Rabbinic Bibles (Song of Songs, Ruth, Lamentations, Ecclesiastes, Esther). The Talmud (b. B. Bat. 14b), however, separates Ruth and Esther from Ecclesiastes, Song of Songs, and Lamentations. It has been thought that the grouping of these books together is a secondary one motivated by the later liturgical tradition of reading these books during the major festivals: Passover (Song of Songs), Pentecost (Ruth), Temple Destruction (Lamentations), Tabernacles (Ecclesiastes), and Purim (Esther). It should be noted, however, that only the order of the books in the Rabbinic Bibles follows the chronological order of these festivals. The order found in the Leningrad Codex predates the liturgy and appears to be the result of compositional activity.[9]

The last three books of the Writings in Rabbinic Bibles are Daniel, Ezra-Nehemiah, and 1–2 Chronicles. This is probably the best option once all of the above factors have been taken into consideration. The Talmud order interrupts this arrangement with the book of Esther: Daniel, Esther, Ezra-(-Nehemiah), and 1–2 Chronicles. The Leningrad Codex begins the Writings with 1–2 Chronicles and places Daniel and Ezra-Nehemiah at the end. John Sailhamer notes well the significance of these competing orders:

> There thus appears to have been at least two contending final shapes of the Tanak. The one closes with the book of Ezra/Nehemiah. In that version, the edict of Cyrus finds its fulfillment in the historical return

---

8. See Will Kynes, "Reading Job following the Psalms," in Steinberg and Stone, *Shape of the Writings*, 131–45.

9. See Steinberg and Stone, "Historical Formation of the Writings," 50–51.

from exile. The other shape of the Tanak closes with Chronicles and a repetition of the edict of Cyrus. In this arrangement, the edict of Cyrus has been shortened from that in Ezra/Nehemiah (Ezra 1:2–4), so that it concludes with the clause "Let him go up" (2 Chron 36:23). In the book of Chronicles, the subject of that clause is identified as he "whose God is with him." For the Chronicler this is possibly also a messianic image (cf. 1 Chron 17:12).[10]

The term "Tanak" is an acronym that represents the three divisions of the Hebrew Bible: Torah, Nevi'im (Prophets), and Ketuvim (Writings). The arrangement of the books within these divisions is suggested here as follows: Torah (Genesis–Deuteronomy), Nevi'im (Joshua-Judges-Samuel-Kings, Isaiah, Jeremiah, Ezekiel, Hosea–Malachi), and Ketuvim (Psalms-Job-Proverbs, Ruth-Song of Songs-Ecclesiastes-Lamentations-Esther, Daniel-Ezra/Nehemiah-Chronicles).[11]

Apocryphal (hidden) works like Sirach or the books of the Maccabees and pseudepigraphal (falsely ascribed) works like 1 Enoch appear inconsistently in some early lists of canonical books and in witnesses to the Greek Bible. Most of these books were produced by Jews in Hebrew or Aramaic but later preserved by Christians in translation. These books have no recognizable position or role in the composition of the Hebrew Bible.[12] The apocrypha and pseudepigrapha assume a fixed and authoritative Hebrew canon to which they relate exegetically. Thus, they are valuable today for their insight into the early history of interpretation of the Hebrew Bible.

THE CANONICAL SEAMS

Since the books of the Hebrew Bible could not fit on a single scroll, and since the codex was not invented until the first century CE and did not

---

10. John H. Sailhamer, "Biblical Theology and the Composition of the Hebrew Bible," in *Biblical Theology: Retrospect and Prospect*, ed. Scott J. Hafemann (Downers Grove, IL: InterVarsity, 2002), 35. Sailhamer continues, "The central role of the edict of Cyrus at the conclusion of the Tanak appears to be motivated by the expectation injected into the end of the Tanak by Daniel 9. In Daniel 9, Jeremiah's expectation of a return to Jerusalem is projected beyond the immediate return from Babylonian captivity" ("Biblical Theology," 36).

11. The Scripture references in this book are provided following the order provided here instead of the order used in English Bibles.

12. See Roger T. Beckwith, "Formation of the Hebrew Bible," in Mulder and Sysling, *Mikra*, 83–84.

come into common use until the fourth century, guides to the canonical reading order of the books had to be built into the books themselves at key junctures. These guides helped readers to form a conceptual framework for the threefold shape of the Hebrew Bible. In particular, there are texts between Moses (Deut 34:5–12) and the Prophets (Josh 1:1–9) on the one hand, and between the Prophets (Mal 4:4–6) and the Writings (Pss 1–2) on the other hand, that serve as canonical seams.[13] These seams determine the arrangement of the canon and also indicate at the highest macrostructural level what the theological message of the Hebrew Bible is. This indication influences reading of the texts at lower levels of composition.

The first canonical seam begins with the death account of Moses (Deut 34:5–12), which for obvious reasons has traditionally not been attributed to Moses by conservative Jews and Christians. Nevertheless, this piece of text is considered part of the inspired book of Moses. The text shows that the person responsible for it was a careful student of the Torah. For instance, in Deuteronomy 34:9, the reader learns that Joshua was filled by the Spirit of wisdom (cf. Gen 41:38; Exod 31:3) because Moses had put his hand(s) on him to be his successor (cf. Josh 1:17). This is an interpretation of what is said in Numbers 27:18: "Take Joshua the son of Nun, a man in whom is the Spirit, and put your hand on him." Likewise, when Deuteronomy 34:10 says that never again did a prophet arise in Israel like Moses whom the LORD knew face to face (cf. Exod 33:11), it is an interpretation of the prophecy in Deuteronomy 18:15, 18, which anticipates that the LORD will raise up a prophet like Moses. In other words, the expectation in Deuteronomy 34:10 is that this prophet is still yet to come. While the traditional view attributes Deuteronomy 34:5–12 to Joshua (b. B. Bat. 14b), the language of Deuteronomy 34:10 ("never again did a prophet arise in Israel like Moses") suggests the perspective of someone living at a much later time—someone like Ezra in the postexilic period who was able to look back over the history of Israel's prophets.[14] There had been prophets like Moses in the sense that there had been genuine prophets (e.g., Jer 1:4–9), but the one particular prophet like Moses had not come. This is the perspective

---

13. See Joseph Blenkinsopp, *Prophecy and Canon: A Contribution to the Study of Jewish Origins* (Notre Dame: University of Notre Dame Press, 1977), 85–95, 120–23; John H. Sailhamer, *Introduction to Old Testament Theology: A Canonical Approach* (Grand Rapids: Zondervan, 1995), 239–52.

14. See Michael Fishbane, *Biblical Interpretation in Ancient Israel* (Oxford: Clarendon, 1985), 36. See also b. Sanhedrin 21b.

that the New Testament authors adopted when they claimed that Jesus was the long-awaited prophet like Moses (e.g., John 6:14; Acts 3:22; 7:37).

The second part of the first canonical seam stands at the beginning of the Prophets in Joshua 1:1–9. This text takes up the references to Moses and Joshua in Deuteronomy 34:9–10 and features an address from the Lord to Joshua that precedes the main narrative of the book. Here the Lord urges Joshua to be firm and to be strong to be careful to do according to all the torah (i.e., the law) that Moses commanded in order to be wise (Deut 4:6; 34:9). He then speaks separately of the necessity of Joshua's devotion to the study of the book of the Torah (i.e., the Pentateuch): "This book of the Torah should not depart from your mouth, but you ought to murmur in it daily and nightly in order to be careful to do according to all that is written in it, for then you will make your way prosperous, and then you will be wise" (Josh 1:8). This reflects the perspective of a Torah scholar like Ezra (Ezra 7:6, 10). Murmuring in the Torah day and night describes reading the text of the Torah aloud quietly to oneself in private study every waking hour (as opposed to public reading of the Torah [e.g., Neh 8]). The result of such textual activity is wisdom or insight. The Hebrew verb *taskil* at the end of Joshua 1:8 is often translated as "have success," but the primary sense is "be wise" or "have insight." This wisdom or insight leads to success. Thus, Joshua 1:8 explains the source of Joshua's wisdom—the book of the Torah.[15] Joshua, who is filled by the Spirit of wisdom (Deut 34:9), is to wait on the coming prophet like Moses (Deut 34:10) by studying the text of the Torah day and night (Josh 1:8).

The second canonical seam (Mal 4:4–6 and Pss 1–2) connects the Prophets to the Writings and corresponds to the first and appears to be the product of the same person who produced the first canonical seam. Malachi 4:4–6 features two short appendixes—4:4 and 4:5–6—that stand apart from the main content of the book, which consists of six disputations: 1:2–5; 1:6–2:9; 2:10–16; 2:17–3:5; 3:6–12; 3:13–4:3.[16] Likewise, Psalms 1 and 2 both lack superscriptions and together form a separate introduction

---

15. The Torah itself is called wisdom in Deuteronomy 4:6. The wisdom literature defines wisdom as the fear of the Lord (Prov 1:7; 9:10; Job 28:28). It is worth noting then that the purpose given for the regular reading of the Torah is to learn the fear of the Lord (Deut 31:13; see also Ps 19:9, where the Torah is called the fear of the Lord).

16. The appendixes in Malachi 4:4–6 appear in a different order in the Septuagint (the Greek translation of the Hebrew Bible), with 4:4 occurring after 4:5–6. This is most likely a secondary arrangement motivated either by a concern not to conclude with the abrasiveness of 4:6b or by an effort to connect the Torah of 4:4 with the Torah of Psalm 1.

to the Psalter (see b. Ber. 9b–10a). Malachi 4:4 begins the second seam by referring the reader back to the first seam: "Remember the Torah of Moses my servant whom I commanded at Horeb concerning all Israel statutes and judgments." Moses is called the LORD's servant at the beginning of the first canonical seam (Deut 34:5). Furthermore, Malachi 4:4 features language that is distinctive to the book of Deuteronomy in particular: "Horeb" (for "Sinai"; e.g., Deut 29:1) and the combination "statutes and judgments" (Deut 4:5, 8, 14).

Just as the first seam (Deut 34:9–10) draws upon material from earlier in the book (Num 27:18; Deut 18:15, 18), so the second seam is based on exegesis of previous content. Malachi 3:1a combines language from Exodus 23:20 and Isaiah 40:3 to announce the coming of a forerunner who will prepare the way of the Lord (cf. Mark 1:2–3): "Look, I am about to send my messenger, and he will prepare a way before me." Malachi 4:5 revisits this text and identifies the messenger as a prophet like Elijah: "Look, I am about to send to you Elijah the prophet before the coming of the great and terrible Day of the LORD." This prophet will restore the hearts of the fathers in addition to those of the sons (Mal 4:6; Luke 1:17). The New Testament authors identify the prophet like Elijah as John the Baptist (Matt 11:10, 14; 17:9–13; Mark 1:2–8; 9:9–13; Luke 1:15–17; John 1:19–28).[17]

The second half of the second canonical seam (Pss 1–2) quotes from the second half of the first canonical seam (Josh 1:8): "Blessed is the person who does not walk in the counsel of the wicked . . . but in the Torah of the LORD is his delight, and in his Torah he murmurs daily and nightly . . . and all that he does he makes prosperous" (Ps 1:1a, 2, 3b). The blessed/righteous/wise person is the one who lives in expectation of the future work of God by reading the text of the Torah day and night. Psalm 1:3–6 features the same contrast between the righteous and the wicked as Jeremiah 17:5–8 but in the opposite order. In Jeremiah 17:7–8, the person who trusts in the LORD is blessed and comparable to a tree planted by water. Psalm 1:3a gives this trust concrete expression: Torah study. The text of the Torah provides the spiritual nourishment necessary for the believer to grow and to bear spiritual fruit. Thus, the one responsible for the canonical seams has once again demonstrated his devotion to Torah study (Ezra 7:6, 10) and his careful attention to the composition of the books being incorporated

---

17. The passage in John 1:19–28 shows that there was confusion about whether Elijah himself would come (see 2 Kgs 2:11) or a prophet like Elijah. The New Testament authors understood the prophecy in the latter sense.

into the canon. The second canonical seam meets the same criteria as the seams connecting the individual parts of the Book of the Twelve (Hosea–Malachi): (1) distinctive material (Mal 4:4–6; Pss 1–2); (2) development of the program of the Twelve in Hosea 3:4–5—coming judgment followed by messianic salvation in the last days (Mal 4:5–6); and (3) citation from the book of Jeremiah (Ps 1:3a).[18]

THE NEW TESTAMENT CANON

The canonicity of a New Testament writing depends not only upon apostolic authority (John 14:26) but also upon continuity with the Hebrew Scriptures (1 Tim 5:18; 2 Pet 3:16).[19] Thus, the apocryphal Gospel of Thomas, for example, does not qualify. Both the Hebrew Bible and the Greek New Testament derive their ultimate authority from Jesus whose historical resurrection vindicated his claims not only about himself but also about the Scriptures (Luke 24:44–47). Three major arrangements of the New Testament documents emerged from church history in the fourth century CE and beyond: (1) Athanasius (Festal Letter, 367): Matthew, Mark, Luke, John, Acts, James, 1–2 Peter, 1–3 John, Jude, Romans, 1–2 Corinthians, Galatians, Ephesians, Philippians, Colossians, 1–2 Thessalonians, Hebrews, 1–2 Timothy, Titus, Philemon, Revelation; (2) Codex Sinaiticus: Matthew, Mark, Luke, John, Romans, 1–2 Corinthians, Galatians, Ephesians, Philippians, Colossians, 1–2 Thessalonians, Hebrews, 1–2 Timothy, Titus, Philemon, Acts, James, 1–2 Peter, 1–3 John, Jude, Revelation; and (3) Latin Vulgate (Jerome): Matthew, Mark, Luke, John, Acts, Romans, 1–2 Corinthians, Galatians, Ephesians, Philippians, Colossians, 1–2 Thessalonians, 1–2 Timothy, Titus, Philemon, Hebrews, James, 1–2 Peter, 1–3 John, Jude, Revelation.

Unlike the Hebrew Bible, there are no canonical seams designed to dictate a reading order. Nevertheless, it has been suggested that these orders reflect deliberate arrangement of the material. For instance, it is possible that Matthew always precedes Mark due to the connection between the

---

18. See Michael B. Shepherd, *A Commentary on the Book of the Twelve: The Minor Prophets*, KEL (Grand Rapids: Kregel Academic, 2018), 23–36, 506–10.

19. See Christopher R. Seitz, "Two Testaments and the Failure of One Tradition History," in *Biblical Theology: Retrospect and Prospect*, ed. Scott J. Hafemann (Downers Grove, IL: InterVarsity, 2002), 205.

genealogies in 1 Chronicles 1–9 and the genealogy in Matthew 1. It is also possible that John interrupts the two-volume work of Luke-Acts in order to anticipate the coming of the Spirit (John 14–16). If these arrangements are intentional, then it is not clear who was responsible for them or how early they were made. Furthermore, there is nothing built into the texts themselves to ensure a particular order. Therefore, statements about the meaning of any given order, which could conceivably vary from interpreter to interpreter, must remain speculative. The conclusion to the New Testament canon, however, does appear to show signs of canon consciousness. Revelation 22:18–19 issues a warning to anyone who would add or take away from the words of the book's prophecy (cf. Deut 4:2; Prov 30:6). Given the late date of the book of Revelation and its consistent placement at the end of the canon, it is quite probable that this warning was intended not only for the book but also for the entire New Testament canon (perhaps even the entire Christian canon, the Hebrew Bible and Greek New Testament).

THE MAKING OF THE BIBLE | 1

The Bible is a self-interpreting book made of many books.[1] In order to see this self-interpretation, the reader needs only to learn the clues that are built into the biblical texts themselves. Such clues are found at multiple levels: clauses, sections, books, and between books. Biblical authors provide guidance to the reading of their own books. They also read one another and establish an extensive system of citation. The present chapter highlights some of the clues to interpretation found within biblical books, including a discussion of literary form and genre. Chapters 3 and 4 will build upon this foundation and look at the Hebrew Bible and Greek New Testament in greater depth. Chapter 5 will explore examples of interpretation between biblical books.

MICROLEVEL SELF-INTERPRETATION

At the lowest level of the text, there are explanatory comments for individual words, phrases, and clauses. Here it is important to distinguish between authorial comments and scribal comments. Authorial comments are part of the original text and are well attested by the available textual witnesses. Scribal comments, on the other hand, are comments that have been added secondarily during the transmission process and are typically absent from one or more of the major textual witnesses. Genesis 14 provides several examples of authorial comments (Gen 14:2b, 3b, 7a, 8a, 17b), which English translators usually flag with parentheses. For instance, Genesis 14:3a refers to the Valley of Siddim, which 14:3b explains with the following parenthetical comment: "that is, the Salt Sea." English translators often

---

1. See Gerald Bruns, "Midrash and Allegory," in *The Literary Guide to the Bible*, ed. Frank Kermode and Robert Alter (Cambridge, MA: Belknap, 1987), 626–27.

take this particular example a step further and render "the Salt Sea" as "the Dead Sea."

Another example of an authorial comment occurs in Judges 5:5 (cf. Ps 68:8): "Mountains flowed [shook] before the LORD, (This is Sinai.), before the LORD the God of Israel." Here the comment "this is Sinai" interrupts the poetic parallelism between parts A ("Mountains flowed [shook] before the LORD") and B ("before the LORD the God of Israel").[2] Some understand this not as a comment but as a description of the LORD as "this one of Sinai," but such a description for the LORD is not a well-established one.[3] Judges 5 is the song of Deborah and Barak in celebration of their victory over the Canaanite king Jabin and his military commander Sisera (Judg 5:1–3). The song begins in Judges 5:4–5 by depicting the LORD coming from the south in a storm as he did when he delivered the people from Egypt and brought them to Sinai (see Exod 19:16) before he led them to the land of the covenant. The authorial comment in Judges 5:5 makes this connection explicit and ensures that the reader understands the present deliverance from the Canaanites to be a kind of new exodus comparable to the original one. It is worthwhile to note then that Judges 4–5 shows the same pattern of narrative followed by poetic interpretation as that found in Exodus 14–15 (see also Isa 11–12).

A similar example involving the use of the demonstrative ("this") appears in Ezra 3:12a: "And many of the priests and the Levites and heads of the fathers (and) the elders who saw the former house/temple in its founding (This is the house/temple.) with their eyes were weeping loudly." This example, however, is usually smoothed over in English translations. The referent of "its" in the phrase "in its founding" is ambiguous and might be taken as a reference to Solomon's temple when its foundation was laid. Of course, it would have been impossible for anyone who saw the founding of Solomon's temple to be alive in the postexilic period. Thus, the authorial

2. There are many examples of authorial comments either interrupting or standing outside poetic parallelism. In 1 Sam 2:2, Hannah prays, "There is no one holy like the LORD, (Indeed, there is no one apart from you.), and there is no rock like our God." The comment "indeed, there is no one apart from you" comes between parts A ("There is no one holy like the LORD") and B ("and there is no rock like our God") to explain that there is not only no one holy like the LORD but also no other gods apart from him. Everyone owes their existence to him. The Septuagint (minus Codex Alexandrinus) has this comment at the end of the verse. One witness to the Old Latin lacks the comment altogether.

3. See Michael Fishbane, *Biblical Interpretation in Ancient Israel* (Oxford: Clarendon, 1985), 51–55.

comment "this is the house/temple" clarifies that "its" refers to the present temple (i.e., the Second Temple).

Some authorial comments explain outdated terms or customs. For example, the comment in 1 Samuel 9:9 explains the term "seer" that follows in 1 Samuel 9:11: "Formerly in Israel, thus the man said when he went to seek God, 'Come and let us go to the seer,' for the prophet today was formerly called the seer." Likewise, Ruth 4:7 explains the custom of the sandal removal narrated in Ruth 4:8 (see Deut 25:5–10): "And this was formerly in Israel concerning the redemption and concerning the exchange to confirm every matter: A man removed his sandal and gave (it) to his neighbor. And this was the testimony in Israel." Some English translations put both 1 Samuel 9:9 and Ruth 4:7 in parentheses.

Sometimes an explanation is required for a foreign term. In Genesis 15:2b the phrase "the son of the possession [*mesheq*] of my house" (= heir) appears. The word *mesheq* (possession) is Aramaic. Abram is saying that his childless status leads him to believe that his household servant will be his heir: "and the son of the possession of my house is Eliezer." There is a comment, however, inserted between the phrase "the son of the possession of my house" and the name "Eliezer": *hw' dmsq*. The traditional Hebrew text has vocalized this so that it is a reference to "Damascus" (*hu' dammeseq*; see Gen 14:15b). English translations thus render the text to say "Eliezer of Damascus," but such a rendering is not very natural according to the Hebrew syntax. It is possible that the text should be translated, "and the son of the possession of my house is from Damascus, namely, Eliezer," but it is not clear what the point of saying this would be in the immediate context. A more plausible alternative is to re-vocalize *dmsq* as *demesheq*, which is a combination of the Aramaic relative *de* (which) and the Aramaic noun *mesheq* (possession). The resulting translation shows this to be a comment on the previous phrase: "and the son of possession [*mesheq*] of my house—that is, the one of possession [*hu' demesheq*]—is Eliezer." This authorial comment clarifies that the phrase "the son of possession of my house" means "the one of possession" (= heir).

English translations do not always recognize or mark authorial comments with parentheses or by other means. Micah 3:8 is an example of this. The prophet is contrasting himself with the false prophets, and, according to the ESV, he says, "But as for me, I am filled with power, with [*'eth*] the Spirit of the LORD, and with justice and might, to declare to Jacob his transgression and to Israel his sin." This rendering gives no indication of the presence of an authorial comment. The ESV translates the Hebrew word *'eth* as a preposition (with) in the phrase "with the Spirit of the LORD." The problem with this is that the preposition *'eth* does not ordinarily mean "with" in the sense "by means of" but in the sense "in association with." The Hebrew *'eth* can also be an untranslated definite direct object marker, but this would not work in the present context. A third option is to take it as a marker of an authorial comment, which would result in the following translation: "But as for me, I am filled with power (that is, the Spirit of the LORD) and justice and might to declare to Jacob his transgression and to Israel his sin." The comment serves to explain that the prophet is filled with the power of the Spirit and not physical strength (see Num 11:29).

Authorial comments also appear in the New Testament documents (e.g., Matt 24:15). John is especially fond of making parenthetical statements to help his readers understand the narrative (e.g., John 1:24, 38, 41, 44; 4:9; 6:6, 64, 71; 7:5; 8:6, 20, 27; 11:13, 30, 38, 51–52, 57; 12:6, 33; 13:11, 28–29; 18:2, 5, 9, 14, 18, 32; 19:35). The comments in John 11:51–52 and 18:14 are particularly intriguing because they explain that the high priest Caiaphas spoke better than he knew, which is something that the reader would not know without the author's guidance. Caiaphas reckoned that it would be better for one man (Jesus) to die than for the whole nation (Israel) to perish (John 11:50), by which he meant that Jesus ought to be killed before he made all the Jews culpable to the Roman authorities. John, however, explains that Caiaphas unwittingly prophesied as high priest about the substitutionary death of Jesus not only for the nation of Israel but also in order to gather the scattered children of God as one (John 11:51–52).

In contrast to authorial comments, scribal comments are comments that have been added during the transmission process. They are not part of the original text, and their secondary nature is usually evident from their absence in one or more of the major textual witnesses. These comments provide insight into the early history of interpretation and thus have the potential to be very valuable. The textual history of Jeremiah 25:1 provides an illustration of a scribal comment. According to the Hebrew source behind the Greek translation of Jeremiah, the shorter, more original text of the verse is as follows: "The word that came to Jeremiah concerning all the people of Judah in the fourth year of Jehoiakim the son of Josiah, the king of Judah." The traditional Hebrew text has added a comment to the end of this verse: "that is, the first year of Nebuchadrezzar, the king of Babylon." This addition is similar to other additions made throughout the revised edition of the book of Jeremiah represented by the traditional

Hebrew text.[4] The differences between the two editions of Jeremiah will be discussed in more detail in chapter 3.

Like the book of Jeremiah, the book of Ezekiel has a shorter edition, which is represented by its Greek version, and a longer edition, which is represented by the traditional Hebrew text (MT).[5] Here is a translation of the Hebrew source behind Greek Ezekiel 2:3–4 with the exegetical expansions of the traditional Hebrew text in brackets:

> And he said to me, "Son of man, I am sending you to the house [MT: sons] of Israel, [MT adds: to nations], the rebels who have rebelled against me, they and their fathers [MT adds: have transgressed against me] to this very day. [MT adds: And the sons are hard of face and firm of heart. I am sending you to them.] And you will say to them, 'Thus says the LORD [MT: the Lord GOD].'"

The addition "to nations" in Ezekiel 2:3a presumably comes from the account of Jeremiah's call in which the LORD says that he has appointed Jeremiah a prophet "to the nations" (Jer 1:5b). The added description of the children of Israel as those who are "hard of face and firm of heart" in Ezekiel 2:4a is consistent with what the reader finds in Ezekiel 3:7b ("firm of forehead and hard of heart"). Thus, these scribal comments draw upon other biblical texts both inside and outside the book of Ezekiel for their content.

Some scribal comments are especially intrusive to the context not only because of their content but also because of their failure to fit into the syntax. The traditional Hebrew text of Haggai 2:5a furnishes an example of this kind. In the immediate context, the LORD is encouraging Zerubbabel, Joshua, and the remnant through the prophet Haggai to act despite the disappointing appearance of the Second Temple (Hag 2:3–4; cf. Ezra 3:12; Zech 4:10). The shorter, more original Hebrew text of Haggai 2:5 is represented by the Greek version and includes only the second half of the verse. If this shorter text is read with the end of the previous verse (2:4b), then the result is very smooth: "'and work, for I am with you,' the prophetic ut-

4. See J. Gerald Janzen, *Studies in the Text of Jeremiah* (Cambridge: Harvard University Press, 1973); Emanuel Tov, *Textual Criticism of the Hebrew Bible*, 3rd ed. (Minneapolis: Fortress, 2012), 286–94.

5. Tov, *Textual Criticism*, 299–301.

terance of the LORD of hosts, 'and my Spirit remains in your midst. Do not fear.'" When the scribal comment is added at the beginning of Haggai 2:5 in the traditional Hebrew text, the result is very awkward: "'and work, for I am with you,' the prophetic utterance of the LORD of hosts—'the word that I made with you when you came out of Egypt—and my Spirit remains in your midst. Do not fear.'" English translations try to smooth this out by adding a preposition (e.g., ESV: "according to the covenant that I made with you when you came out of Egypt"), but the marker 'eth in the Hebrew text does not mean "according to" even if it is interpreted as a preposition. Furthermore, the covenant that was made when the people came out of Egypt has long since been broken (Jer 11:10), and the people have suffered the consequences of that broken covenant relationship.

Beyond explanatory comments at the lowest level of the biblical text, the Bible is also built to interpret itself at higher levels, such as whole sections and chapters. The multiple retellings of a story in chapters like Genesis 24 and 41 are often designed to introduce interpretive elements into the repetition.[6] Abraham's sending of his servant to find a wife for Isaac begins with Abraham's instructions (Gen 24:1–9), which anticipate how the story will unfold, and with the servant's own anticipation of what will happen (24:10–14). The story of the servant's encounter with Rebekah is then narrated (24:15–27), and this is followed by the servant's retelling of the story to Rebekah's family (24:28–49). The conclusion narrates the success of the mission (24:50–67). In each section, the providence of God is highlighted in a different way (24:7, 12, 21, 27, 40, 42, 50, 56). This is an important aspect of the author's worldmaking in which he seeks to depict the real world as one whose events the God of the Bible providentially oversees and orchestrates. Likewise, the account of Pharaoh's dream in Genesis 41 is given in three panels. There are the two versions of Pharaoh's dream (41:1–13). Then there are the retellings of the two versions of the dream to Joseph (41:14–24). The third panel is Joseph's interpretation of the dream (41:25–32). According to Joseph, the two versions of the dream have the same meaning: God has revealed to Pharaoh what he is about to do (41:25). The repetition indicates that the matter is established by God

6. This sort of retelling happens on a large scale in the interpretation of Samuel-Kings found in the book of Chronicles. The genre of Rewritten Bible represented by postbiblical literature like Jubilees and the Genesis Apocryphon carries on the tradition of interpreting the Bible by retelling the Bible. See Louis H. Feldman, James L. Kugel, and Lawrence H. Schiffman, eds., *Outside the Bible: Ancient Jewish Writings Related to Scripture*, vol. 1 (Philadelphia: The Jewish Publication Society, 2013), 211–666.

and that God is hastening to do it (41:32). Again, this illustrates that God is in control of his own world.

One of the hallmarks of apocalyptic literature is the built-in interpretation of visions and dreams (e.g., Ezek 37:1–14; Zech 1–6; Dan 2; 4; 7; 8; Rev 17:1; 21:9). Without the presence of an angelic guide or an inspired interpreter like Daniel, there would be no way to understand the meaning of these revelations (Zech 4:5, 13). This is not unlike what happens when Jesus explains a parable like the parable of the sower (Matt 13:1–23). Jesus says that he teaches in parables because knowledge of the mysteries of the kingdom of heaven has been granted to his disciples but not to the crowds (13:11). Thus, he interprets the parable for his disciples but not for the crowds. The meaning of the parable would not be apparent apart from Jesus's exposition. The reader does not need to debate the validity of such built-in interpretation. Rather, the reader's task is to identify the interpretation and to accept it as a gift from the author.

MACROLEVEL SELF-INTERPRETATION

Above the levels of individual clauses and sections are the levels of whole books and canonical divisions. The Bible is built to interpret itself even at the highest levels of composition. To understand how this works, it is necessary to listen to the way the biblical authors talk about their process of composition. The biblical texts are composite works. This does not mean that the books ought to be disassembled according to the tenets of historical-critical scholarship for the purpose of examining their hypothetical prehistory. It does mean, however, that the books cannot be read contrary to their own presentation as if they were made of whole cloth. The biblical authors themselves testify to the fact that their works are made of different literary forms and genres of various sizes and shapes from a variety of times and places. The reader must learn how to navigate these literary complexes in a manner that is consistent with the deliberate techniques employed by the authors to put their texts together in a meaningful way. The strategy of the juxtaposition of manifold pieces of material communicates a cohesive, coherent, and unified theological message.[7]

---

7. This method of composition is well known from the ancient Near East. See Jeffrey H. Tigay, *The Evolution of the Gilgamesh Epic* (Philadelphia: University of Pennsylvania Press, 1982; repr., Wauconda, IL: Bolchazy-Carducci, 2002), 42.

The first clue to the composite nature of the biblical texts is the consistent reference to source material. That is, the biblical authors have incorporated preexisting material into their new, revelatory compositions. For instance, Numbers 21:14–15 cites from The Book of the Wars of the LORD. This is a source that is no longer extant and otherwise unknown, but its citation here serves to illustrate the fact that the author has put his book together using source material intentionally selected for his purpose. In other words, the selection process itself suggests deliberate design. Another example of source citation is "The Book of Jashar" or "The Book of the Upright" cited in Joshua 10:13 (not in LXX) and 2 Samuel 1:18. Because this book appears to have been a collection of poetry (see Josh 10:12–13; 2 Sam 1:17–27), it has been suggested that "The Book of Jashar" (*sepher hayyashar*) should be "The Book of Song" (*sepher hashshir*) (cf. Syr. Josh 10:13: "The Book of Praises"). Indeed, the Greek text of 3 Kingdoms 8:53a (= 1 Kgs 8:12–13) appears to include a citation from the same book and calls it "The Book of Song."

The most well-known source citations in the Bible are the ones found in Kings and Chronicles. There are three main sources cited in Kings from which the author selects his material: (1) The Chronicles of Solomon (1 Kgs 11:41); (2) The Chronicles of the Kings of Israel (1 Kgs 14:19); and (3) The Chronicles of the Kings of Judah (1 Kgs 14:29). The first of these sources provides the material for the stories about Solomon in 1 Kings 1–11. The latter two are consistently cited throughout the remainder of the book in the conclusions to the accounts of the kings as the author alternates between accounts of northern kings and accounts of southern kings. On the other hand, the book of Chronicles cites a greater number of sources with more specificity, even though the Chronicler is essentially working with the same material.[8] Many of these sources are attributed to prophets (1 Chr 29:29; 2 Chr 9:29; 12:15; 13:22; 26:22; 32:32; 33:19),[9] which reflects a

---

8. See 1 Chr 9:1 ("The Book of the Kings of Israel"); 29:29; 2 Chr 9:29; 12:15; 13:22; 16:11 ("The Book of the Kings of Judah and Israel"); 20:34 ("The Book of the Kings of Israel"); 24:27; 25:26 ("The Book of the Kings of Judah and Israel"); 26:22; 27:7 ("The Book of the Kings of Israel and Judah"); 28:26 ("The Book of the Kings of Judah and Israel"); 32:32; 33:18–19; 35:25–27; 36:8 ("The Book of the Kings of Israel and Judah").

9. Only the Chronicler includes a source citation for the stories of David, which he attributes to the prophets Samuel, Nathan, and Gad, corresponding to the beginning (1 Samuel), middle (2 Sam 1–12), and end (2 Sam 13–24) of the stories. Several of the Chronicler's citations mention the prophet Iddo (2 Chr 9:29; 12:15; 13:22), the unidentified prophet from 1 Kgs 13.

prophetic view of history.[10] The term *midrash* is used in 2 Chronicles 13:22 and 24:27 to refer to a type of interpretation or "commentary" (NLT).

The account of Jeremiah 36 provides remarkable insight into the composition process of a biblical book. According to this story, the prophet Jeremiah received instruction from the LORD to write all the words that he had spoken to him over a period of more than twenty years (Jer 36:1–3). This would have involved collection and arrangement of messages of various lengths from different times and places. Likely, some of these messages had been preserved in writing, while others had been preserved in memory. Jeremiah summoned his scribe Baruch to whom he dictated the words and to whom he entrusted the tasks of textualizing the prophecies and of giving a public reading of the new scroll (36:4–8). When news of this reading reached the royal officials (36:9–13), they requested a private reading for themselves (36:14–18). Upon hearing the words of the scroll, the officials advised both Baruch and Jeremiah to go into hiding before the words were reported to the king (36:19–20). When the king received the report, he sent for the scroll itself and had it destroyed sheet by sheet as it was being read (36:21–26). This then led to the rewriting of the original scroll (36:27–31), which, because of its implied content, many believe to have been some form of what is now found in Jeremiah 1:1–25:13. The conclusion to the story, however, indicates that not only were the words of the original scroll rewritten but also many more words like them were added to them (36:32). This reveals the process of growth that eventually led to the final form of the book of Jeremiah. Thus, the account of Jeremiah 36 shows the relationship between a prophet and his scribe both in the making of a biblical book and in its literary development.

The epilogue to the book of Ecclesiastes provides yet another example of conscious reflection on the composition process (Eccl 12:9–14). Here the author notes that Qoheleth "weighed and sought, he arranged many proverbs" (12:9b). Qoheleth carefully considered and sought the material that he selected from what was available, and he arranged his material in a meaningful way. His purpose was to find pleasing words (12:10). The author then either warns his son that there is no end to the "making" or "composing" of many books (12:12b) or, perhaps more likely, urges his son to be careful to make or compose many books without end, which is the interpretation of the Hebrew text provided by the ancient Aramaic translation

10. See William M. Schniedewind, *The Word of God in Transition: From Prophet to Exegete in the Second Temple Period*, JSOTSup 197 (Sheffield: Sheffield Academic, 1995), 228.

known as the Targum. In light of the final judgment to come, the author concludes by commending to his son the fear of the LORD (12:13–14).

The New Testament documents also bear witness to their process of composition. Luke notes in his prologue how many have undertaken to "compile" an account of recent events (Luke 1:1). Such written compilations are comparable to the traditions passed down by those who were eyewitnesses (1:2). Thus, Luke has taken it upon himself to compose an orderly account of things in order that Theophilus may know the truth (1:3–4). Once again, a biblical author has collected preexisting material and purposefully arranged it so as to make his own unique contribution. John's purpose statement also speaks of deliberate selection of material: "Jesus performed many other signs in the presence of his disciples, which are not written in this book; but these things are written that you may believe that the Christ, the Son of God, is Jesus, and that by believing you may have life in his name" (John 20:30–31).

The Bible not only attests to the compositional process of its individual books but also shows an awareness of the shaping of its canonical divisions. This canon consciousness, as it were, is first of all evident in the prohibitions against adding or taking away from the text:

> Do not add to the word that I am commanding you and do not take away from it to keep the commands of the LORD your God that I am commanding you. (Deut 4:2a; cf. Deut 12:32)

> Every saying of God is refined; he is a shield to those who take refuge in him. Do not add to his words, lest he rebuke you, and you be found a liar. (Prov 30:5–6; cf. Pss 2:12; 12:6; 18:30; 119:140)

> I testify to every person who hears the words of the prophecy of this book: if anyone adds to them, God will add to him the plagues that are written in this book; and if anyone takes away from the words of this book of prophecy, God will take away his portion from the tree of life and from the holy city that are written in this book. (Rev 22:18–19)

It is important to note the strategic placement of these warnings. Deuteronomy 4:2 appears in the preface to the last of the five books of Moses. Proverbs 30:5–6 appears in the final two chapters of the book of Proverbs and also in the final two chapters of the Psalms-Job-Proverbs sequence of books. Revelation 22:18–19 appears not only at the end of the book of

Revelation and at the end of the New Testament canon but also at the conclusion of the biblical canon.

Other texts highlight the relationship between Moses and the Prophets and their mutual formation. Texts like 2 Kings 17:13 and Daniel 9:10 speak of the transmission of the Torah via the prophets. Despite the fact that transmission of the Torah was entrusted to the priests (Deut 31:9–13), this responsibility ultimately fell to the prophets (see 2 Kgs 22–23). Thus, even Ezra the priest acknowledges his indebtedness to the prophets for the Torah that he received (Ezra 9:10–11). Still other texts speak of a combination of Moses and the Prophets in anticipation of the use of these two pillars to refer to the entire Hebrew Bible (e.g., Matt 5:17; Luke 24:27, 44; John 1:45; Acts 28:23): "the Torah and the words that the LORD of hosts sent by his Spirit through the agency of the former prophets" (Zech 7:12a; cf. Isa 1:10; 2:3; 8:16, 20). This presupposes the formation of a prophetic corpus.[11] Awareness of such a corpus is evident from texts like Daniel 9:2 (cf. Ezek 38:17; Zech 1:4; 7:7): "In year one of his reign, I, Daniel, observed in the books the number of years that was the word of the LORD to Jeremiah the prophet to fulfill the desolations of Jerusalem—seventy years." It is apparent that Daniel is reading the prophecy of seventy years from the book of Jeremiah (Jer 25:11; 29:10), but it is important to note that he has the book of Jeremiah among other presumably prophetic books. The book of Jeremiah now belongs to a plurality of books.

The New Testament also shows early signs of canon formation. Second Peter 3:2 puts together the prophets and the apostles. Peter later mentions a circulating corpus of Paul's letters, "as in all letters speaking in them about these things, in which there are some things difficult to understand, which the untaught and unstable twist as also the other Scriptures to their own destruction" (2 Pet 3:16). Here Paul's letters appear to be known as a collection to churches other than the so-called original recipients (cf. Col 4:16; Rev 2–3; see also Papyrus manuscript 46, a collection of Paul's letters from 200 CE). According to Peter, Paul speaks in these letters about "these things"—that is, the prophecies of the last days (2 Pet 3:3–13; see, e.g., 1–2 Thessalonians). There are some things difficult to understand in the letters, which some twist "as also the other Scriptures." By comparing Paul's letters to the Hebrew Scriptures and by referring to the Hebrew Scriptures as "the other Scriptures," Peter assumes the scriptural status of Paul's writings.

---

11. See Stephen B. Chapman, *The Law and the Prophets: A Study in Old Testament Canon Formation*, FAT 27 (Tübingen: Mohr Siebeck, 2000), 212–13.

LITERARY FORM AND GENRE

The composition of the biblical books involves a complex combination of a variety of different literary forms and genres: narrative, speech, poetry, genealogy, law, epistle, and so on. Biblical interpretation entails the ability to navigate these individually and also the ability to understand their interaction. For instance, how do the major poetic units of the Pentateuch punctuate and interpret the narratives that precede them? How do the major speeches of the Former Prophets guide the reader through the narratives to see the theological message of the whole? In this section, the focus will be on the rules of the hermeneutical game to be played in each of the major literary forms and genres. Chapters 2 and 3 will discuss their interplay in the biblical compositions.

The study of literary form and genre may be compared to playing a sport. If someone comes to a basketball game expecting to play according to the rules of a football game, then there will be a serious failure for the person to function properly as a player. The same is true of reading literature. If someone comes to a poem expecting to read according to the rules of a narrative, then there will be a serious failure to understand the words properly. This failure is unfortunately all too common in Bible reading, especially in popular Bible reading where there is a tendency to read the whole Bible as if it were all one type of literature—a manual or set of instructions for life. The different literary forms and genres of the Bible require the reader to make the appropriate adjustments for the ever-changing textual landscape. This is essentially a matter of knowing the right kinds of questions to ask when reading a particular text. The fundamental problem that readers must overcome in interpretation is not the lack of answers or the incorrectness of answers but the wrong questions. If readers are asking the wrong questions of the text, then the answers cannot possibly be right for the task of interpretation.

Narrative

The predominant form of literature in the Bible is narrative. The default mode of operation in the genre of historical narrative is for literal words to depict real events. This does not mean that metaphors and other figures of speech never occur in narrative. It only means that the reader should assume a literal depiction unless there is a clear indication that the language is figurative. For example, the narrative of Exodus 7 says that all the water that was in the Nile turned into blood (Exod 7:20b). Some commentators suggest that the water only looked like blood, and they refer to the simile of 2 Kings 3:22 or to the image of Joel 2:31 to make their case.[12] The problem with this suggestion is twofold. First, it assumes a figure of speech (a simile) without clear indication from the narrative. Second, the references to 2 Kings 3:22 and Joel 2:31 are not sound comparisons. The text of 2 Kings 3:22 features an explicit simile that signals a figure of speech to the reader. The light of the morning sun made the water look "like blood." This is not a feature of Exodus 7:20b. The text of Joel 2:31 is poetry, not narrative. Thus, when the text says that the moon will turn into blood before the Day of the LORD, the thought is parallel to the previous clause, which says that the sun will be turned into darkness. That is, the blood is a metaphor for the darkness that symbolizes coming judgment. It is precisely this use of metaphor that readers should expect to occur consistently in poetry, but not in narrative. To compare a narrative text like Exodus 7:20b to a poetic text like Joel 2:31 is like comparing apples to oranges.

Biblical authors have a number of different techniques at their disposal in the making of their narratives. Readers often interpret the biblical narratives in an ad hoc fashion in order to formulate moral principles, but it is important to recognize that there are identifiable patterns in these texts that enable interpreters to make legitimate claims about the author's activity. Many resources are available to readers of the Bible to help them develop the skill of following an author's work in a narrative.[13] The development of this skill will give readers the exegetical warrant that they need to make decisions about the meaning of the text. The narrative techniques briefly discussed here include selectivity, setting, characterization, plot, and point of view.

Selectivity means an author does not include everything in the narrative that could possibly be said about a given event. Rather, the author selects those things that will help to accomplish the stated purpose in writing (John 20:30–31). Thus, an understanding of why certain things

---

12. Walter C. Kaiser Jr., "Exodus," in *Genesis–Leviticus*, ed. Tremper Longman III and David E. Garland, EBC rev. ed. (Grand Rapids: Zondervan, 2005), 402–3.

13. E.g., Shimon Bar-Efrat, *Narrative Art in the Bible* (London: T&T Clark, 2004); Adele Berlin, *Poetics and Interpretation of Biblical Narrative* (Winona Lake, IN: Eisenbrauns, 1994); J. P. Fokkelman, *Reading Biblical Narrative: An Introductory Guide*, trans. Ineke Smit (Louisville: Westminster John Knox, 1999); Meir Sternberg, *The Poetics of Biblical Narrative: Ideological Literature and the Drama of Reading* (Bloomington: Indiana University Press, 1985).

are included while others are not goes a long way toward grasping what the author is trying to communicate to readers through the presentation of the narrative. It is not the reader's job to fill in the perceived gaps in the narrative but to understand why the author has deliberately left such gaps. The reader may be curious about what is not included in the narrative, but these questions must not be allowed to distract the reader from the author's work. Pursuit of questions not being raised by the author directly only obscures the specific textual depiction already provided by the author. Each kind of text has a set of questions that the author raises and answers. The reader's task is to identify those questions, not to raise questions independently in such a way as to make the text do something that it was never intended to do.

Biblical narratives feature both geographical and temporal settings. The manipulation of these settings is often crucial to the author's work. For example, the alternation in Job 1–2 between Job's situation on earth and the heavenly assembly makes all the difference for the reader's understanding of what happens behind the scenes of Job's suffering. Without this knowledge it would be difficult to make sense of what the remainder of the book has to say. Another example is the relationship between narration time (the time that it takes to read a narrative) and narrated time (the time that it takes for the actual events to occur) in a narrative like the flood story of Genesis 7:11–8:14. The narration time (about five minutes) is drastically less than the narrated time (a whole year). Thus, an author can provide a more scenic presentation or a more cursory one, depending upon what suits his purposes. An author can also manipulate the ordering of the narrative sequence. He can flash back to previous events that were withheld from the earlier narrative until the appropriate time (e.g., 1 Kgs 11:14–25), or he can flash forward to future events before they unfold in an effort to group those events with things that are currently happening in the narrative (e.g., Ezra 4:6–23). Failure to recognize these techniques inevitably results in confusion for the reader.

Characterization in narrative has several different facets. There is the role that a character plays in the narrative, whether major or minor. Then there is the extent of a character's development in the narrative, whether round (fully developed, multidimensional, complex) or flat (underdeveloped, one-dimensional, simple). There is also the quality of a character to consider, whether good or bad—or something in between. A character like David plays a major role in the biblical narrative and is fully developed. Readers see David in multiple stages of life and from a variety of different angles. Readers are allowed to see David's flaws, which gives them the sense that they really know David. Despite David's failures, however, he receives an overall positive evaluation from the narrative (e.g., 1 Kgs 15:5), which presents him as exemplary in many ways. On the opposite end of the spectrum is a character like Bathsheba (2 Sam 11) who is both minor and flat to the point that it is very difficult to make a judgment about the quality of her character. She only briefly emerges from her one-dimensional presentation in 1 Kings 1–2. Of course, there are other characters who are a mixture of these two extremes. There are major protagonists such as Joseph or Daniel who are more or less underdeveloped as characters due to the absence of a major flaw. This does not make characters like Joseph or Daniel uninteresting. Rather, it presents them to the reader as examples of Spirit-filled lives (Gen 41:38; Dan 4:8, 18; 5:11). There are also examples of characters who play a relatively minor role in the narrative yet are very fully developed, complex characters. Both Joab in 2 Samuel (and at the beginning of 1 Kgs) and Peter in the Gospels would qualify for this category. Joab is not a major character, but he appears in the narrative in both a positive and a negative light. Likewise, Peter plays a minor role in the Gospels compared to Jesus, but the reader comes to know Peter very intimately through the things that he says and does.

Characterization can be a very effective means of communicating a theological interpretation of a story to the readership. Since authors of narratives normally do not speak directly to their readers, they require some other way to send their message. It is not uncommon for major protagonists to function as an author's mouthpiece at critical junctures of a narrative. For instance, Joseph's comments at the climax (Gen 45:7) and the conclusion (50:20) of his story reflect the author's own viewpoint and serve to highlight the fact that God is moving the events of the story toward a particular goal. Sometimes an author will use a major character as a literary foil to set up another major character. Both Saul (1 Sam 11) and his likely successor Jonathan (14), for example, look very promising at first, but they only serve to set up David, who surpasses them both (16–17). This makes David look even better than he otherwise would and helps the reader focus on him as the one through whom the messianic hope of the people of God will come (2 Sam 7).

Some biblical authors exploit the relationship between a character's physical appearance and his or her virtue (or lack thereof).[14] This is not

---

14. See Sternberg, *Poetics of Biblical Narrative*, 342–64.

unlike what happens in modern film when a handsome actor is cast as the good guy or an actor with a scar is cast as the bad guy. Thus, characters like the wives of the patriarchs, Joseph, Moses, David, Abigail, Esther, and Daniel are all described as good looking, and this generally fits with their roles in their respective narratives. An example of how this might serve the development of a narrative occurs in the stories of Saul and David. According to 1 Samuel 9:2, there was no one "better than" (*tov min*) Saul among the sons of Israel, which is usually taken to mean that there was no one more handsome than he was. Saul is subsequently chosen as the first king of Israel. After Saul's failures in 1 Samuel 13 and 15, Samuel informs Saul that the kingdom will be given to someone who is "better than" (*tov min*) he is (1 Sam 15:28; cf., Esth 1:19). This person turns out to be David, who is not only "good" (*tov*) in appearance (1 Sam 16:12) but also one whose heart is acceptable to the Lord (13:14; 16:7).

Rarely, if ever, does an author highlight a character's physical appearance for its own sake. For instance, the kind of association that is made between Abigail's beauty and her wisdom (1 Sam 25:3; cf. Joseph [Gen 39:6b; 41:39] and Daniel [Dan 1:4]) is consistent enough within biblical narrative to influence the way a reader encounters the threefold description of the Shulammite woman's beauty in the Song of Songs (Song 4:1–7; 6:4–9; 7:1–9). Her outward appearance directs the reader to her words of wisdom (2:7, 16; 3:5; 6:3; 7:10; 8:4; cf. Prov 31:10–31). Sometimes, however, the expected association between good looks and good character (or bad looks and bad character) is deliberately subverted for a certain effect. Absalom, for example, has all the outward qualities of his father David (2 Sam 14:25), and he initially appears as his sister Tamar's vindicator (13) and as potential successor to his father's throne (3:2–5), but his rebellion against his father and his attempt to usurp his father's throne lead to his ultimate demise (15–18). Sometimes a character's attractiveness can distract a reader from personal flaws. Readers typically think of a character like the matriarch Rachel as a good character, but this is likely because they are blinded by her beauty (Gen 29:17) and Jacob's love for her (29:18, 30). Her appearances in the narrative are not all that flattering when it comes to her virtue (see, e.g., 30:1–3, 14–15; 31:19, 34–35).

There are other ways to help readers either to identify with a character or to distance themselves from a character. Readers are able to identify with a character when they know that character intimately by name and when they are able to see things from that character's perspective. On the other hand, when a character like Goliath is primarily known not by name but merely as "the Philistine," it creates a distance between the reader and the character so that the reader sees Goliath as nothing more than the antagonist. The story of 1 Samuel 17 is not told from Goliath's perspective at all. Characterization is thus an important tool that biblical authors can employ to communicate indirectly with their readers.

Another technique available to authors of biblical narratives is plot development. A typical plot structure begins with the author establishing a setting and then introducing a problem that becomes the main catalyst for the story. Without a major problem to resolve, a story holds little interest for its readers. The main body of a narrative is usually devoted to the search for a solution to the problem. Once the problem is resolved, a new setting is established and the story concludes. Readers' ability to identify the plot structure is critical to their chances of staying on track with what the author is trying to develop in the narrative. Acknowledging plot structure prevents readers from isolating parts of the story from one another and enables them to see how the parts of the story fit into the whole.

The book of Esther is a good example of plot structure because it develops a single plot from beginning to end. The setting is established in the first two chapters. King Ahasuerus's feasts in Susa during the third year of his reign over the Persian empire serve as the initial backdrop for the story (Esth 1:1–9). When Queen Vashti refuses Ahasuerus's request to be displayed before the king and his guests (1:10–15), the suggestion is made that Vashti ought to be replaced (1:16–22). This leads to the introduction of Mordecai and his cousin Hadassah (i.e., Esther), who is among those taken to the king as potential replacements for Vashti (2:1–8). When Esther wins the king's favor, she becomes queen (2:9–20), and all the key elements of the setting are in place for the main problem of the story to be introduced in the following chapter. Before this occurs, however, a subplot emerges in Esther 2:21–23 that briefly describes Mordecai uncovering an attempt to assassinate the king. The recording of the details of this event in the king's chronicles allows for the later merging of this subplot with the main narrative in Esther 6.

It is premature to suggest that the problem of the story already appears in Esther 2. Some modern interpreters have viewed the taking of Esther to the king as a moment of great distress for both Mordecai and Esther, but there is no indication of this in the narrative itself. Some have even gone so far as to say that Esther's willingness to go to the king and to become his wife is morally reprehensible (as if she had much of a choice in the matter). This is similar to what is sometimes said about the actions of the midwives in Exodus 1:15–22 or the actions of Rahab in Joshua 2, despite the fact that Rahab's actions are praised by multiple biblical authors (Heb 11:31; Jas 2:25). It is not the reader's job, however, to make independent judgments of the characters. It is the reader's job to follow the author's presentation and evaluation of the characters in the narrative. When the author wants the reader to see a character or a character's action in a particular light, the author will let the reader know (e.g., 2 Sam 11:27b; 1 Kgs 11:6). This is an instance where understanding plot structure can help a reader to avoid an error in interpretation. If the reader knows that the main problem of the story does not appear until chapter 3, then she knows not to look for it in the setting of chapters 1 and 2.

The major problem in the story of the book of Esther is the decree issued by Haman against the Judeans. Haman the Agagite is introduced in chapter 3 as the king's new right-hand man who feels slighted by Mordecai and thus becomes opposed not only to him but also to the people whom he represents (Esth 3:1–7). Since Mordecai is a descendant of King Saul's father Kish (2:5), this renews an old conflict between King Saul and King Agag of the Amalekites (1 Sam 15). Haman leverages the king's trust in him to set a date for the destruction of the Judeans (Esth 3:8–15). The king unwittingly gives his consent and appears unaware of the details of what Haman now has his permission to do.

Now the search for the solution to the problem begins, and this search occupies the next several chapters of the book. Mordecai learns of Haman's decree, and news of Mordecai's distress in response to the decree reaches Esther who subsequently finds out about the decree herself (Esth 4:1–9). The narrative makes clear that both the king and the queen have been sheltered from what has become common knowledge among the general populace. Mordecai's report, which comes only indirectly to Esther, also arrives with a plea for Esther to go to the king on behalf of her people. Esther sends back word to Mordecai that she can only do so at the risk of her life (4:10–12), yet Mordecai insists that now is the time to act (4:13–14). Thus, Esther concedes that she must prepare to go to the king (4:15–17).

Mordecai initially instructed Esther not to reveal her identity (Esth 2:10). Indeed, the name "Esther" (*'sthr*), which is Persian for "star," appears transliterated in Hebrew as if it were from the root *sthr* (to hide). Ironically, Mordecai's refusal to conceal his own identity leads to the major problem of the narrative (3:4). Now Esther must make herself known in order to save her people. Some interpreters think that Esther should have been "feasting instead of fasting" during the Passover month (3:7), but this overlooks the fact that the old covenant was broken at this point (Jer 11:10). Such a criticism of Esther is based on the reader's independent evaluation apart from any warrant provided by the author's own presentation of her in the narrative itself.

When Esther is granted an audience with the king, she requests the presence of the king and Haman at the banquet that she has prepared (Esth 5:1–5). During this banquet, the king invites Esther to ask for virtually anything that she might want, which seems to be a golden opportunity to expose Haman and to intercede for her people. However, Esther only requests again the presence of the king and Haman at a banquet that she will prepare for them on the following day (5:6–8). It is not clear why Esther makes this delay, but it does create an opportunity for the subplot from Esther 2:21–23 to reemerge. In the period of time between the two banquets, Haman decides that he cannot wait for the day of destruction for the Judeans to see the end of Mordecai, and his wife suggests to him that he should have a gallows or pole constructed on which to hang or to impale Mordecai (5:9–14). Precisely at this point the king has a sleepless night during which the chronicles are read to him—the very chronicles in which Mordecai's efforts to prevent the king's assassination are recorded (6:1–2; cf. Esth 2:21–23). When the king finds out that nothing has been done to reward Mordecai, he asks who might be available in the court to advise him about this. And, as it turns out, Haman is waiting in the wings to ask permission to execute Mordecai (6:3–4). The king asks Haman what should be done for the man whom the king seeks to honor; and Haman, thinking that the honor must be for him, suggests an elaborate procession (6:5–9). When the king then instructs Haman to have this done for Mordecai, it is not only one of the most striking examples of dramatic irony in all of biblical narrative but also a foreshadow of things to come in the following chapters (6:10–13).

Haman is finally exposed at Esther's second banquet, and he is subsequently executed on the very gallows or pole constructed for Mordecai (Esth 6:14–7:10). The king gives the house of Haman to Esther who then appoints over that house her cousin Mordecai whose relation to Esther is now known and who has received authority from the king (8:1–2). It would seem that the story has now reached a point of resolution, but not all is well quite yet. According to the law of the Medes and Persians (see Dan 6:8, 15), the king cannot revoke his own authorized decree. Thus, the best that he can do in response to Esther's request for the reversal of Haman's day of destruction determined for the Judeans is to have another decree issued that might offset the prior one in some way (Esth 8:3–8). The word goes out to the Judeans to defend themselves against their enemies; and, because the Judeans have the support of the king, many people join their side instead (8:9–17).

The story finally comes to a resolution in chapter 9 when the Judeans successfully defend themselves against their enemies. Note how the three-fold reference to the people's refusal to take any of the plunder (Esth 9:10, 15, 16) despite having permission to do so (8:11) reverses the earlier failure of the people to resist the plunder when they were forbidden to take it (1 Sam 15:9). The feast of Purim (lots) is established to commemorate how the Judeans overcame Haman's casting of lots to determine the day of their destruction (Esth 3:7). The new setting is established in Esther 10 with a brief description of what was happening in the kingdom and a description of Mordecai's status within it, including a source citation for further reference. The author has successfully navigated all the key components of a good narrative: setting (chapters 1–2), problem (3), search for a solution (4–8), resolution (9), and new setting (10).

There is one other narrative technique to consider: point of view. Much of biblical narrative naturally comes from the viewpoint of the narrator himself, but the perspective of the biblical narrator often has an extraordinary quality about it. For instance, in the narrative of Job 1–2, the narrator knows not only about Job and his family and friends on earth but also about God and the heavenly assembly. The narrator appears to be omniscient. This is no doubt related to the revelatory nature of the text and its ability to present a God's-eye view of things.[15] On the other hand, there are many times in biblical narrative when the point of view is that of a particular character. The Hebrew word *hinneh* (look/behold) often signals a shift from the narrator's perspective to the perspective of a character: "And the LORD appeared to him [Abraham] by the oaks of Mamre, and he was sitting at the entrance of the tent during the heat of the day. And he lifted up his eyes and saw, and look [*hinneh*], three men standing nearby him. And he ran to meet them from the entrance of the tent, and he prostrated himself to the ground" (Gen 18:1–2).

This technique is similar to the use of a different camera angle in film to move from a panoramic viewpoint to a perspective that enables the viewer to see things through the eyes of a specific character and to be drawn into the narrative itself. Sensitivity to the use of this technique in narrative can

---

15. See Sternberg, *Poetics of Biblical Narrative*, 87.

help the reader to follow what is happening in the narrative and to understand the relationship between the point of view of the narrative and that of the author himself, which may or may not be the same. Sometimes an author will provide alternative viewpoints in order to bring the author's own perspective into relief. Now that we have looked at some of the techniques of biblical narrative, it is time to turn to another major literary form in the Bible—poetry.

Poetry

The interaction between narrative and poetry is very important for biblical composition, and this interaction will be explored in the survey of biblical composition in chapter 3. For now it is necessary to note some of the key differences between narrative and poetry for interpretation. If the primary mode of operation for narrative is to use literal words to depict real events, then the primary mode of operation for poetry is to use figurative language to cast images of real events. This does not mean that literal language never appears in poetry. It only means that readers ought to expect a greater density of figurative language in poetry by default. If readers skip the intermediary step of image casting and try to draw a straight line from the figurative language to the real events, then they are very likely to make serious errors in interpretation.

Some people claim that the Bible ought to be read "literally," but this cannot mean that readers should disregard metaphors and other figures of speech. Rather, the Bible should be read according to the letters and words. That is, it should be read according to the author's intent or verbal meaning.[16] Sometimes the words are literal words, and sometimes they are figurative words. The reader here needs only to think of the poetic descriptions of the woman in the Song of Songs (Song 4:1–7; 6:4–9; 7:1–9). A literalistic reading of these poems would result in a rather grotesque picture, but it is obviously not the intent of the poet to insult the woman.[17]

A comparison of Exodus 14 and Exodus 15 makes for a good illustration of the difference between narrative and poetry. Exodus 14 is a narrative account of the exodus event, and Exodus 15 is a poetic account of the same

---

16. See E. D. Hirsch Jr., *Validity in Interpretation* (New Haven: Yale University Press, 1967), 18.

17. See E. W. Bullinger, *Figures of Speech Used in the Bible: Explained and Illustrated* (London: Eyre and Spottiswoode, 1898; repr., Grand Rapids: Baker, 1968).

event. According to the narrative account, the LORD made the sea into dry land by means of a strong east wind so that the water was like a "city wall" on opposite sides of the path (Exod 14:21–22). The Israelites went into the sea on dry ground to pass safely to the other side (14:29–30), and the Egyptians willfully pursued them there (14:22–23). The LORD shook the Egyptians into the sea and covered them with water (14:26–28). According to the poetic account, however, it was by the blast of God's nostrils (an anthropomorphism) that the water of the sea was piled up like a heap (15:8). God threw the Egyptians into the sea (15:1, 4) where they sank like a stone (15:5). If readers attempt to read these two accounts as literal words depicting real events, then they are likely to reach the conclusion that the two accounts are contradictory. Such a reading only works with the first account. The second account uses figurative language to cast images of the events depicted in the first account. Thus, the strong east wind is characterized poetically as the blast of God's nostrils. The Egyptians' pursuit of the Israelites into the sea where they were covered with water is characterized poetically as God picking up the Egyptians and throwing them into the sea. In each case the interpretation of the narrative account in the poetic rendition is a theological one. The imagery highlights the fact that God was fighting for the Israelites (14:14; 15:3). Another good illustration of the relationship between a narrative account and its poetic rendition can be found in Judges 4 and 5.

Hebrew poetry features a consistency of three main characteristics: parallelism, terseness of expression, and figurative language.[18] A parallelistic line typically consists of two clauses, which English translations usually format as one on top of the other so that readers can see the parallelism. The relationship between the two clauses is such that the second clause always gives something more—reiteration, subordination, or advancement—even if only for rhetorical or stylistic effect. The two clauses are neither two separate thoughts nor two parts of one thought. The density of parallelism in Hebrew poetry thus lends an aesthetic quality that differs from what readers find in the more straightforward language of prose. Hebrew poetry also tends to lack elements that readers come to expect from prose: the narrative tense (*wayyiqtol*), the relative pronoun, the definite direct object marker, and the definite article. Therefore, the absence of something like the definite article in poetry may not be as exegetically significant as it is

18. See James L. Kugel, *The Idea of Biblical Poetry: Parallelism and Its History* (New Haven: Yale University Press, 1981; repr., Baltimore: Johns Hopkins University Press, 1998).

in prose. Hebrew poetry's terseness of expression requires a higher level of engagement from the reader, forcing the reader to slow down and to consider how the parts fit together without the customary guides to the correct understanding of the syntax. This terseness, which normally results in about three stressed syllables per clause, has historically led interpreters to confuse it with meter, which they have expected from their experience with the poetic literature of other languages like Greek and Latin. It is important, however, to allow Hebrew poetry to have its own character. No theory of meter has been proven for Hebrew poetry, and no such theory should be allowed to dictate textual or exegetical decisions.

While it is common to think of biblical poetry in the Writings (e.g., the book of Psalms and the wisdom literature), there are also major poetic units in the Pentateuch (Gen 3:14–19; 49:1–27; Exod 15:1–18; Num 23–24; Deut 32–33) and the Former Prophets (1 Sam 2:1–10; 2 Sam 1:17–27; 22; 23:1–7). The Latter Prophets (Isaiah, Jeremiah, Ezekiel, and Hosea–Malachi) are also known for their heightened style (parallelism and terseness). According to Hosea 12:10b, it is by the agency of the prophets that God makes comparisons. That is, the prophets tend to speak in metaphors,[19] which is exactly what happens in Hosea 12 where an analogy is drawn between Jacob/Israel the man and Israel/Jacob the nation.

The Psalter features many different types of psalms, but the three most common are the petition (or lament), the thanksgiving, and the praise hymn.[20] The petition dominates the first half of the Psalter and features three main components: opening outcry, petition with motive, and final expression of trust or confidence. The opening outcry of a petition psalm is often framed as a question ("How long?" or "Why?") and is typically a brutally honest expression of how the psalmist feels in the moment rather than a valid truth claim about God (see, e.g., Ps 13:1–2). The petition itself is usually accompanied by a motive for God to act in response to the petition. This is normally an appeal to God's concern for his name/reputation or glory. If the psalmist bears God's name or represents him, then his fate reflects upon God himself (see, e.g., 13:3–4). Finally, no matter how bleak the situation appears in the earlier parts of the psalm, the petition psalm

19. See Claus Westermann, *Basic Forms of Prophetic Speech*, trans. Hugh Clayton White (Philadelphia: Westminster, 1967; repr. with new foreword by Gene M. Tucker, Louisville: Westminster John Knox, 1991).
20. See Hermann Gunkel, *An Introduction to the Psalms: The Genres of the Religious Lyric of Israel*, completed by Joachim Begrich, trans. James D. Nogalski (Macon, GA: Mercer University Press, 1998).

almost always concludes with an expression of trust or confidence (see, e.g., 13:5). This is not because the psalmist's question has been answered or his problem resolved. Rather, it is an affirmation of what the psalmist already knows to be true about God from what God has revealed about himself. These psalms are for the most part stripped of their historical moorings so that they can function as model prayers for readers. They teach readers to pray with honesty but also to work through the present situation and to look beyond the current problem to what is known to be trustworthy about God. The appeal to God's concern for his glory reminds readers that God is God-centered and not man-centered. Thus, readers are encouraged not to turn inward in their times of trouble but to look Godward.

It is important to follow the structure of a psalm from beginning to end in order to avoid errors in interpretation. The so-called cry of dereliction in the Gospels (Matt 27:46; Mark 15:34), which cites the opening line of Psalm 22, is often misconstrued theologically as some sort of fracture in the Trinity. Such a misunderstanding is due both to a lack of knowledge about the function of opening outcries in petition psalms and to a failure to follow the progression of the psalm. There were no chapter or verse numbers in antiquity. Citation of an opening line of a psalm was a way to refer to the entirety of a psalm. Thus, the cry from the cross ultimately looks beyond the distress of the moment to the vindication anticipated at the end of the psalm.

Thanksgiving psalms also feature three main components: an opening declaration of deliverance from distress (e.g., Ps 30:1–2), a poetic narrative of the psalmist's deliverance from distress (with an invitation to join in the thanksgiving) (e.g., 30:3–12a), and a concluding vow (e.g., 30:12b). In a noble effort to avoid treating God like a genie or a vending machine, it is often said that God ought to be worshiped for who he is and not for what he does. However, God's character is known primarily from what he has revealed about the things that he has done. Thanksgiving psalms are excellent reminders of this reality.

The three main components of a praise hymn are the call to praise, the cause or reason for the praise, and the conclusion. Psalm 8 is the first example of a praise hymn in the Psalter. In this case, the call to praise (Ps 8:1a) and the conclusion (8:9) are identical. The cause or reason for the praise constitutes the main body of the psalm (8:3–8). Modern English translations tend to translate the conjunction at the beginning of Psalm 8:3 as temporal ("when"), but the form of the psalm strongly suggests that the early versions (LXX, Syr., Tg., Vulg.) were correct to translate this as a causal conjunction ("for"). This causal section of a praise hymn often features a string of participles describing God's praiseworthy activity (see, e.g., Ps 147). In Psalm 8, however, the cause or reason for the praise is a poetic exposition of the narrative in Genesis 1.

The wisdom literature is also predominantly poetic, and this should inform the way the wisdom sayings are received. A proverb is not like a law. It is not absolute.[21] Proverbs 26:4–5 illustrates this well. Verse 4 says, "Do not answer a fool according to his folly, lest you too become like him" (cf. Prov 9:8; 23:9). Verse 5 says, "Answer a fool according to his folly, lest he be wise in his eyes" (cf. Prov 3:7). Which one is it? Should the fool be answered or not? It depends upon the circumstances. The reader who has come to know the kind of fear-of-the-LORD wisdom that the book teaches (1:2, 7; 9:10; see also Job 28:28) will be able to read the situation and make the right decision.

Genealogy

It is tempting for readers of the Bible to skip the genealogies or to regard them as isolated historical records, but genealogies have much to contribute to the contexts in which the biblical authors place them. The very recognizable patterns of genealogies make it easy for readers to spot meaningful breaks in the patterns, and these breaks are often the clues that readers need to understand how the genealogies function in their respective compositions. The first example of a genealogy in the Bible is Genesis 5. It establishes a very clear pattern in which the numbers of the years that a man lived both before and after the birth of his firstborn son are given; then there is an indication that the man had other sons and daughters, and the total number of years that the man lived is provided before the notice of his death (Gen 5:6–8). The death notices, together with the story of the first death (Abel) in chapter 4, serve to highlight the fact that death has entered the world in the wake of the events narrated in chapter 3 (see Gen 2:17; Rom 5:12–21).

There are three very obvious breaks in the pattern of chapter 5. They occur with the first (Adam), seventh (Enoch), and tenth and final (Noah) names in the list. The additional material in Adam's section (Gen 5:1–5)

---

21. See Tremper Longman III, *Proverbs*, BCOTWP (Grand Rapids: Baker Academic, 2006), 31.

makes a connection back to the creation of humankind in the image of God (Gen 1:26–28) and highlights the fatherhood of God (see Exod 4:22; Deut 32:6; Isa 63:16; 64:8; Jer 31:9; Mal 1:6; 2:10). Just as Seth named his son Enosh (man) (Gen 4:26), so God named "them" (male and female) 'adham (human[kind]). Enoch's section includes two expansions (Gen 5:21–24). The first indicates that he did not merely "live" a certain number of years after the birth of his firstborn son. Rather, he "walked with God" during that time (Gen 5:22a)—that is, he lived a life of faith (cf. Gen 6:9; 17:1; Deut 10:12; Mic 6:8). The second builds upon this idea to say that Enoch did not die: "And Enoch walked with God, and he was not, for God took him" (Gen 5:24; cf. 2 Kgs 2:11).

The material added for Noah begins already in the section devoted to his father Lamech: "And he called his name Noah [*nh*], saying, 'This is the one who will comfort [*nhm*] us from our work and from the grief [*'itstsavon*] of our hands because of the ground that the LORD cursed'" (Gen 5:29; see also Gen 3:17–19). This begins an extended play on Noah's name: "And the LORD was sorry [*nhm*] that he made humankind on the earth, and he was grieved [*'tsv*] in his heart" (6:6); "But Noah [*nh*], he found grace [*hn*] in the eyes of the LORD" (6:8). Noah's section of the genealogy begins in Genesis 5:32 but does not resume until 9:28–29, which means that the entire flood narrative is the break in Noah's section. Related to this is the question of whether the unit in Genesis 6:1–4 should be read with what precedes it (5:32) as a description of life in the days of Noah (Matt 24:37–39) or with what follows it (Gen 6:5) as an introduction to the flood story (1 En. 6–11).[22]

The next major genealogy is the Table of Nations from the three sons of Noah in Genesis 10. Once again, it is important to observe how the genealogy relates to its narrative context. The genealogy of Shem is divided into two parts. The first part traces Shem's descendants through the line of Eber's son Joktan (Gen 10:21–32). The second part traces Shem's descendants through Eber's other son Peleg (11:10–26). In the middle of these two parts is the account of the Tower of Babylon in which the people attempt to make a "name" (Hebrew: *shem*) for themselves (11:1–9). The placement of this account not only serves to explain why there are different languages (10:5, 20) but also sets up a contrast between Babylon and the

22. See John H. Sailhamer, *The Pentateuch as Narrative: A Biblical-Theological Commentary* (Grand Rapids: Zondervan, 1992), 120–22.

descendants of Abram, whose name appears at the end of the second part of Shem's genealogy (11:26). For Abram, the LORD is the one who will make his "name" (*shem*) great (12:2). This contrast between Babylon and the descendants of Abram not only anticipates the later historical conflict between Babylon and Judah but also the worldly opposition to God and his people that ultimately manifests itself in the last days (Rev 17–18).

Sometimes an author may employ an abbreviated genealogy in order to serve a particular purpose. The abbreviated genealogy at the end of Ruth (Ruth 4:18–22; cf. 1 Chr 2:9–15) is not intended to provide a full historical record but to highlight the fact that Ruth is the ancestor of David and thus ultimately the ancestor of the Davidic Messiah (Matt 1:1–17). On the other hand, an author may choose to give a very full genealogy or to string together multiple genealogies. First Chronicles 1–9 is the most outstanding example of this in the Bible; this is not merely for the sake of record keeping. The Chronicler seeks to provide a comprehensive account of biblical history from Adam (1 Chr 1:1) in Genesis to the decree of Cyrus (2 Chr 36:22–23) in Ezra-Nehemiah, while focusing in particular on the Davidic monarchy and the hope of the covenant with David in Samuel and Kings. In order to do this, the Chronicler must cover large amounts of material in a relatively short amount of space. The listing of names in 1 Chronicles 1–9 enables him to go from Adam to the death of Saul (1 Chr 10) fairly quickly so that he can move directly into the story of David.

Matthew's genealogy of Jesus (Matt 1:1–17) helps to introduce Jesus as "the son of David, the son of Abraham" (1:1). The genealogy counts fourteen generations from Abraham to David, fourteen generations from David to the Babylonian exile, and fourteen generations from the Babylonian exile to Christ (1:17). According to gematria, fourteen is the numerical value of the name "David" in Hebrew (*dwd*, 4+6+4). Luke's genealogy of Jesus (Luke 1:23–38) differs considerably from Matthew's. Opinions vary on why this is the case. Perhaps one is the lineage of Joseph, while the other is the lineage of Mary. Perhaps one is the legal lineage, while the other is the actual lineage. Exploration of these options, however, is beside the point. Luke's genealogy of Jesus moves in the opposite direction of Matthew's. It begins not with Jesus's ancestor Abraham but with Jesus himself. The genealogy then goes backward not to David or to Abraham but to "Adam, the son of God" (Luke 3:38). Thus, whereas Matthew's genealogy of Jesus presents him as "the son of David, the son of Abraham" (Matt 1:1), Luke's genealogy of Jesus presents him as the second Adam, the Son of God. This is likely something that Luke learned from his traveling companion, the apostle Paul (Acts 16–28). According to Paul, sin and death came through the first Adam, but grace and life came through the second Adam, Jesus Christ (Rom 5:12–21; 1 Cor 15:21–22).

Law

The big question concerning the Mosaic law has to do with its role in the composition of the Pentateuch. This question will be addressed in chapter 3. For now it will suffice to mention two types of law that readers encounter in the various law codes. The first type is apodictic law. Apodictic laws are simple commands or prohibitions that apply absolutely in every circumstance. The best example of apodictic law is the Decalogue in Exodus 20:1–17 (also Deut 5:6–21). The second type of law is case law. Case law only applies if the conditions of the situation stated in the law are met. The divorce law in Deuteronomy 24:1–4 is a good example of this type of law. Only when the conditions of Deuteronomy 24:1–3 are met is the first husband unable to take back the woman to be his wife (24:4; cf. Jer 3:1–5; see also Matt 19:1–12).

Letter

There are many examples of letters in the Bible (e.g., Jer 29; Ezra 4:8–6:18; 7:12–26), but the best known of these are the epistles of the New Testament. The straightforward, expository character of these documents makes them some of the most accessible writings in the entire Bible. The basic structure of a New Testament epistle consists of a salutation, the main body of the letter, and a conclusion. Paul characteristically transforms the typical salutation into a theological one: "Grace to you and peace from God our Father and the Lord Jesus Christ" (Rom 1:7; 1 Cor 1:3; 2 Cor 1:2; Gal 1:3; Eph 1:2; Phil 1:2; 2 Thess 1:2; Phlm 3). Paul also tends to structure the main body of his letters so that the first half is devoted to theology (e.g., Rom 1–11; Eph 1–3), and the second half is devoted to practice (e.g., Rom 12–15; Eph 4–6). Thus, the "application" of the first half is to understand and to believe the theology, which then forms the basis for the practice. It is premature to add practical application to the first half. Such practical application has already been provided by the author in the second half of the letter's body. The readers should focus on what they need to know before turning to what they need to do. The conclusion to a letter may or may not include greetings, depending upon how well the author knows the recipients. Paul's letter to the Ephesians—a church Paul knows very well (Acts 19–20)—does not have many final greetings (Eph 6:21–24). On the other hand, Paul's letter to the Romans—a church Paul has not yet visited—contains more greetings than any of his other letters (Rom 16).

One of the challenges faced by modern readers of the New Testament epistles is the supposedly occasional nature of the letters—otherwise known as the problem of particularity. If the epistles were written to a specific audience for an occasion at a particular time and place in the past, how can they function as applicable Christian Scripture for modern readers? This creates a rather awkward situation in which modern readers feel the need to give the epistles a kind of artificial update in order to appropriate them in some way. There are several indications, however, that the epistles are not intended to be as particular as many have thought. For instance, in Colossians 4:16, Paul gives instructions to have his letter to the Colossians read to the Laodiceans and to have his letter to the Laodiceans, which is no longer extant, read to the Colossians. There is also sufficient evidence to conclude that the epistles to the Colossians and the Ephesians are cognate letters. Likewise, Peter speaks of a scriptural corpus of Paul's letters known to his readers, which suggests that the letters have already been circulating among multiple churches as Scripture. The book of Revelation, which is apocalyptic in genre but epistolary in form, addresses seven different churches (Rev 1:4; 1:9–3:22). Each church is able to read the mail of the other churches, so to speak. The New Testament epistles were not written specifically for an original audience of readers but for Christian readers in general.

Interpretation of biblical literature, like interpretation of any other body of literature, is not an exact science or like solving a simple mathematical problem. This is not to say that there are no rules, nor is it to say that the hermeneutical process is completely subjective. Rather, there is inevitably a subjective element, and interpreters must be careful not to be too dogmatic about their claims as if they were giving incontrovertible proof of something. Interpreters should have good reasons (supported by evidence) for their claims, and they should have warrant for connecting those reasons to their claims, but often interpreters disagree because there may be more than one possible interpretation of a text. It is thus best to think in terms of degrees of probability. Given the available options for interpretation, is there evidence that suggests one of the options is more plausible than the others? Incidentally, this way of thinking also applies to textual criticism, which is the art and science of determining the original text and one of the topics of the next chapter. When textual critics are faced with variant readings in the textual witnesses, it is often difficult to decide which one is more original. An argument can be made for more than one, and the critic must be content to acknowledge this and to weigh the probabilities.

TEXT, TRANSMISSION, AND TRANSLATION | 2

Since the ancient textual witnesses to the Hebrew Bible and the Greek New Testament do not agree with one another in all parts, it is necessary to establish for each document the text that stood at the beginning of the transmission process.[1] The discipline that is devoted to this task is known as textual criticism. While this can be painstaking work, there is good reason to be optimistic about it, and it has the added benefit of bringing the textual critic into the world of the Bible's early history of interpretation. Many of the scribal additions in the manuscript witnesses are exegetical in nature and thus provide insight into the meaning of the biblical text.[2]

THE HEBREW TEXTS

Prior to the discovery of the Dead Sea Scrolls—a collection of ancient biblical and non-biblical scrolls in Hebrew, Aramaic, and Greek from a series of discoveries in the Judean wilderness near the Dead Sea beginning in 1947—the Hebrew Bible was known primarily from the medieval Masoretic Text, which is the traditional, rabbinic text of the Hebrew Bible, and from the Samaritan Pentateuch (SP), which is the Hebrew version of the five books of Moses used by the Samaritan community. While the ancient Greek translations of the Hebrew Bible appeared to some to follow source texts that differed substantially from the Masoretic Text (MT), there was

---

1. See Emanuel Tov, *Textual Criticism of the Hebrew Bible*, 3rd ed. (Minneapolis: Fortress, 2012), 165.

2. See David Andrew Teeter, *Scribal Laws: Exegetical Variation in the Textual Transmission of Biblical Law in the Late Second Temple Period*, FAT 92 (Tübingen: Mohr Siebeck, 2014), 266.

not yet any extant Hebrew manuscript evidence to confirm this. The discovery of the Dead Sea Scrolls altered this landscape dramatically.[3]

Emanuel Tov has classified the biblical Dead Sea Scrolls found in the eleven Qumran caves located near the ancient Qumran settlement in the Judean wilderness in the following manner: MT-like texts, pre-Samaritan texts, texts close to the presumed Hebrew source of the Septuagint (LXX, the ancient Greek translation of the Hebrew Bible), and non-aligned texts (i.e., texts that do not align with any previously known textual grouping).[4] Tov also identifies a group of texts written in what he calls the Qumran Scribal Practice (e.g., 1QIsa[a]),[5] which is known for its very full orthography, but he does not consider this to be a classification according to textual character.[6] All of the Hebrew scrolls found in the Judean desert outside of the Qumran caves are "proto-MT" texts (see below). This situation reveals the coexistence of a plurality of texts from the same time and place and within the same community. It is thus no longer possible to explain the differences among the witnesses according to age or geographical distribution. It is also not possible to divide them into standard and vulgar (i.e., common) texts. The texts must be evaluated according to internal criteria, and their complementary relationship must be taken into consideration.

MT-like texts (e.g., 1QIsa[b]) are similar to the consonantal text of the medieval Masoretic Text but not close enough to be called proto-MT texts. Proto-MT texts, which are known from sites in the Judean desert other than Qumran, have the same Hebrew consonantal framework as the Masoretic Text but without the written vocalization, accentuation, and marginal notes of the Masoretic manuscripts. Proto-MT texts differ from the Masoretic Text only to the same degree that witnesses to the Masoretic Text differ among themselves. Rabbinic Judaism adopted the proto-MT

---

3. For a helpful introduction to the Dead Sea Scrolls, see James VanderKam and Peter Flint, *The Meaning of the Dead Sea Scrolls: Their Significance for Understanding the Bible, Judaism, Jesus, and Christianity* (New York: HarperCollins, 2002). Readers of the English Bible can see all of the biblical Dead Sea Scrolls translated into English in Martin Abegg Jr., Peter Flint, and Eugene Ulrich, *The Dead Sea Scrolls Bible: The Oldest Known Bible Translated into English for the First Time* (New York: HarperCollins, 1999).

4. Tov, *Textual Criticism*, 107–10.

5. The abbreviation 1QIsa[a] stands for manuscript A of the book of Isaiah from Cave 1 near Qumran. It is the only complete or nearly complete copy of a biblical book preserved among the scrolls from the eleven caves.

6. Tov, *Textual Criticism*, 100–105.

as its standard Hebrew text and eventually gave it a written system of vocalization and accentuation (as well as marginal notations), thus creating what is now known as the Masoretic Text. It is evident from all the available textual witnesses that there was more than one way to vocalize the Hebrew consonants in antiquity. The Masoretic Text represents one very ancient and generally reliable way to vocalize the text. The Masoretic Text is the primary source for modern critical editions of the Hebrew Bible (*Biblia Hebraica Stuttgartensia* uses the Leningrad Codex, ca. 1008 CE, the oldest complete Masoretic manuscript of the Hebrew Bible) and for almost all English translations of the "Old Testament."

The MT-like texts from Qumran and the proto-MT texts from other sites in the Judean desert, which date to the period around the first century BCE and the first century CE, show that the consonantal framework of the Masoretic Text is very old. The relatively large number of these texts and the evidence for revision of Old Greek translations of the Hebrew Bible toward the proto-MT during the same period show that the proto-MT was a very well-received text from an early time. While the consonantal framework of the Masoretic Text is a very good text and perhaps the best text overall statistically, its quality varies from book to book and from section to section, and it does not always represent the most original text. The Masoretic Text is also not a "text type." That is, it does not display typological features that occur throughout its version of the books of the Hebrew Bible.

The pre-Samaritan texts from Qumran are essentially texts known from the Samaritan Pentateuch minus the ideological element of the altar on Mount Gerizim (SP Deut 27:4; see John 4:20). According to MT Deuteronomy 27:4, the command is to build the altar on Mount Ebal (see also MT Josh 8:30–35). The Samaritan Pentateuch makes the command to build the altar on Mount Gerizim the tenth commandment in Exodus 20 and Deuteronomy 5. Both Jewish and Samaritan tradition count Exodus 20:3–6 (= Deut 5:7–10) as a single command rather than two. Jewish tradition counts the prologue (Exod 20:2; Deut 5:6) as the first of the ten words. Samaritan tradition begins with the prohibition against idolatry (Exod 20:3–6; Deut 5:7–10) and thus has room for an extra command at the end. Apart from the ideology of the altar on Mount Gerizim, the Samaritan Pentateuch does not have typological characteristics. It is known for its tendency to harmonize, but this is not unique to the Samaritan Pentateuch. The Samaritan community (see 2 Kgs 17:24–41) adopted the pre-Samaritan text and made it its own. There are many places where the Samaritan Pentateuch and the Septuagint agree against the Masoretic Text. For instance, the version of Balaam's prophecy in MT Numbers 24:7b says that the king will be higher than "Agag" (see 1 Sam 15). The Samaritan Pentateuch and the Septuagint, however, say that he will be higher than "Gog" (see Ezek 38–39; Rev 20:8).

There are also places where the Samaritan Pentateuch and the New Testament agree against the Masoretic Text and the Septuagint. For example, according to the Masoretic Text and the Septuagint of Genesis 11:32, Abram's father Terah died in Haran at the age of 205. Terah fathered Abram at the age of seventy (Gen 11:26), and Abram departed Haran when he was seventy-five. Thus, Abram left Haran when Terah was 145. On the other hand, the Samaritan Pentateuch of Genesis 11:32 says that Terah died in Haran at the age of 145, which means that Abram did not leave Haran until his father's death. This is apparently the version that Stephen's speech presupposes in Acts 7:4: "Then he departed the land of the Chaldeans and dwelt in Haran; and from there after the death of his father he moved him to this land in which you now live."

The Hebrew texts close to the presumed source of the Septuagint were a particularly important discovery among the Qumran scrolls because they confirmed the existence of Hebrew texts that differed substantially from the Masoretic Text. The Septuagint is now generally recognized to be the most important witness to Hebrew texts that vary from the Masoretic Text. This is not to say that all differences between the Masoretic Text and the Septuagint are due to the presence of different Hebrew texts behind the Septuagint. There are many differences that are due to the work of the translators themselves. Perhaps the most outstanding example of a Hebrew fragment close to the presumed source of the Septuagint is 4QJer[b]. This fragment of Jeremiah 10 agrees with the Septuagint against the Masoretic Text in shortness and arrangement—the same two characteristics that distinguish the entire edition of the book of Jeremiah represented by the Septuagint from that represented by the Masoretic Text. This distinction will be discussed in more detail later.

Finally, the large group of non-aligned Hebrew texts discovered among the Qumran scrolls consists of texts that do not align with any previously known textual grouping (MT, SP, or LXX), nor do the members of this group align with one another. This group revealed that textual plurality in antiquity was much greater than anyone had ever thought. Perhaps the best known example of a non-aligned Hebrew text is the Great Isaiah Scroll from Qumran Cave 1 (1QIsa[a]). This scroll is the only complete or nearly complete scroll of an entire biblical book preserved among the Qumran scrolls. Its readings often agree with the Masoretic Text or the Septuagint or both, but the scroll also contains a large number of readings that are unique to it.

EARLY TRANSLATIONS OF THE HEBREW BIBLE

The early translations of the Hebrew Bible (Septuagint, Syriac Peshitta, Targums, and Latin Vulgate) are important for at least two reasons. First, they provide evidence of Hebrew readings in their source texts that differ from other known Hebrew witnesses. Second, they give insight into the different ways in which the Hebrew Bible was received and interpreted at a very early period of time. The most important of these early translations is the Septuagint, which bears witness to more variant Hebrew texts than any other early translation. As the ancient Greek translation of the Hebrew Bible, the Septuagint had a major influence on Greek-speaking Jews and Christians. For Greek-speaking Christians, not only was the Hebrew Bible mediated to them in Greek, but also the language of the Greek versions of the Hebrew Bible was incorporated into the documents of the Greek New Testament.[7]

The name "Septuagint" comes from the legend of the Letter of Aristeas about the Greek translation of the Pentateuch (Genesis–Deuteronomy) in Alexandria, Egypt, in the third century BCE. According to this legend, there were seventy-two Jewish translators who worked on this project, and the translation thus became known as the work of the "seventy" (hence "LXX"). This term was subsequently applied to the entire Greek Bible, although many scholars prefer to reserve it for the Greek translation of the Pentateuch, opting for the term "Old Greek" for the other books of the Greek Bible. Nevertheless, the Greek version of the Hebrew Bible, which was in many ways an unprecedented translation project, is by no means a monolithic translation produced by the same group of translators at the same time and place. The translation technique and the quality of the Hebrew source texts differ from book to book and from section to section. In reality, the Greek translation of the Pentateuch was probably made by five different translators.

---

7. See Michael B. Shepherd, "Is the Septuagint the Christian Bible?" *TrinJ* 41 (2020): 149–64.

It is now customary to distinguish between the original Greek or the Old Greek translations of the books of the Hebrew Bible and the revised Greek versions (Aquila, Symmachus, and Theodotion). The revised Greek versions from the second century CE were the heirs of a translation tradition (known as the kaige tradition) that attempted to revise the Old Greek translations in a very literalistic fashion toward what was becoming the standard, received rabbinic text of the Hebrew Bible (the proto-MT). Evidence for this kaige tradition goes back at least as early as the latter half of the first century BCE (see the Greek Minor Prophets Scroll from Naḥal Ḥever).

The major Septuagint codices of the fourth and fifth centuries CE (Vaticanus, Sinaiticus, and Alexandrinus) have a mixture of Old Greek and revised Greek. For example, the A text of Judges (mostly represented by Alexandrinus) is the Old Greek form of the book, while the B text (mostly represented by Vaticanus) is the revised form (see also LXX Megilloth). The early church father Jerome was aware in his time (fourth century CE) of three recensions of the Septuagint that emerged out of the third century CE: Hesychius (Egypt), Origen (Palestine), and Lucian (Antioch). Hesychius's recension is unknown. Origen's recension is known from the fifth column of his Hexapla, which contained the following: the Hebrew text (proto-MT), a Greek transliteration of the Hebrew text, Aquila, Symmachus, the Septuagint, and Theodotion. Lucian's recension features a very early layer that is close to the Old Greek. This proto-Lucian layer is the key to restoring the Old Greek in the revised sections of LXX Samuel-Kings, which is a mixture of Old Greek (1 Sam 1:1–2 Sam 11:1; 1 Kgs 2:12–21:29) and revised Greek (2 Sam 11:2–1 Kgs 2:11; 1 Kgs 22:1–2 Kgs 25:30).

Modern editions of the Septuagint such as Rahlfs's manual edition and especially the volumes of the Göttingen Septuagint series seek to present an eclectic text that comes as close as possible to the Old Greek. Readers of the English Bible can access the Septuagint via the New English Translation of the Septuagint (NETS) published by Oxford University Press. This translation comes with helpful introductions to each of the books.[8] It is available for a very reasonable price in print and for free online.

8. See also Siegfried Kreuzer, ed., *Introduction to the Septuagint*, trans. David A. Brenner and Peter Altmann (Waco, TX: Baylor University Press, 2019); Emanuel Tov, *The Greek and Hebrew Bible: Collected Essays on the Septuagint*, VTSup 72 (Atlanta: Society of Biblical Literature, 2006); Emanuel Tov, *The Text-Critical Use of the Septuagint in Biblical Research*, 3rd ed. (Winona Lake, IN: Eisenbrauns, 2015).

The Syriac Peshitta (Syr.), which is the name for the "simple" or "plain" translation of the Hebrew Bible into the Aramaic dialect of Syriac, was produced during the first or second century CE by Jewish or Jewish-Christian translators, and it became the preferred translation of the Syriac-speaking church. The Peshitta follows a proto-MT Hebrew source text for the most part, but it also has some distinctive agreements with the Septuagint.[9] There are at least two possibilities for this. On the one hand, it is possible that the Peshitta translators had access to the Septuagint and were influenced by it. On the other hand, it is also possible that the translators employed exegetical and translational techniques that were similar to those of the Septuagint translators. It is generally recognized that the techniques of the Peshitta translators resemble those of the Targum translators (more on this below). In fact, the Targum of Proverbs is essentially the Peshitta version of Proverbs. There is unfortunately no readily accessible English translation of the Peshitta available to readers of the English Bible. The Antioch Bible, which is published by Gorgias Press, is a new idiomatic English translation of the Peshitta, but it is a very expensive multivolume set.

The Aramaic Targums are a rich and varied collection of translations of the proto-MT text of the Hebrew Bible.[10] Unlike the other early translations, the Targums were not intended for people who did not understand Hebrew. Rather, they were intended to serve as guides for those who were reading and studying the Hebrew text.[11] Thus, the interpretive element in the Targums is much more pronounced. Among many other things, the Targums help readers to see the messianism of the Hebrew Bible.[12] The official rabbinic Targums for the Pentateuch and the Prophets are Targum Onqelos (Pentateuch) and Targum Jonathan (Prophets). There is also a Palestinian Targum tradition for the Pentateuch represented by Targum Neofiti, the Fragmentary Targum, and Targum Pseudo-Jonathan.

---

9. See Michael B. Shepherd, *Textuality and the Bible* (Eugene, OR: Wipf & Stock, 2016), 61–77.

10. See Paul V. M. Flesher and Bruce Chilton, *The Targums: A Critical Introduction* (Waco, TX: Baylor University Press, 2011).

11. See Chaim Rabin, "Hebrew and Aramaic in the First Century," in *The Jewish People in the First Century*, vol. 2, ed. S. Safrai and M. Stern, CRINT (Philadelphia: Fortress, 1976), 1030–32; Abraham Tal, "Is There a Raison d'Être for an Aramaic Targum in a Hebrew-Speaking Society?" *REJ* 160 (2001): 357–78; Michael B. Shepherd, "Targums as Guides to Hebrew Syntax," *Them* 47.1 (2022): 49–59.

12. See Samson H. Levey, *The Messiah: An Aramaic Interpretation, The Messianic Exegesis of the Targum* (Cincinnati: Hebrew Union College Press, 1974).

The Targums of the Pentateuch and the Prophets, with the exception of Pseudo-Jonathan, reached their final form during the first half of the first millennium CE, but many of the individual renderings and exegetical traditions of the Targums date back to a much earlier time in either oral or written form. Targum Pseudo-Jonathan reached its final form in the early medieval period. While the manuscript evidence for the Targums is generally late, the Targums themselves go back to a time much earlier than their extant copies. For instance, Targum Neofiti is a manuscript from the sixteenth century CE, but it preserves a Targum that dates back to sometime around the second or third century CE. The Targums of the Writings are generally later than those of the Pentateuch and the Prophets. There are two Targums for the book of Esther. There are no Targums for books that have a substantial amount of Aramaic in them (Daniel and Ezra-Nehemiah). English translations of the Targums are available in the Aramaic Bible series published by The Liturgical Press. These translations use italics to distinguish the interpretive expansions from the renderings of the Hebrew text. They also provide a critical apparatus and notes.

The Old Latin translation was produced by Christians during the second and third centuries CE, but it was not a translation of the Hebrew Bible. It was a translation of the Septuagint. It is thus an important witness in many cases to the Old Greek and indirectly to the variant Hebrew texts underlying the Old Greek. Beginning in the latter part of the fourth century CE, the early church father Jerome sought to produce a new Latin translation based on the Hebrew text that was available to him (i.e., the proto-MT). Jerome was one of only a very few in the early church who took the time to learn Hebrew. His translation eventually became known as the Latin Vulgate (Vulg.) and exerted great influence upon the subsequent history of the church and its Bible translations, including modern English translations. The Douay-Rheims English translation of the Latin Vulgate is readily available on a variety of websites.

VARIANT LITERARY EDITIONS

There are many small-scale variants (words, phrases, clauses) in witnesses to the text of the Hebrew Bible whose linear development textual critics are able to trace. In the earliest attested period of textual transmission, scribes saw themselves as active participants in the making of the biblical text, often adding comments or smoothing out difficulties in order to aid the reader's comprehension of the text. There are also many unintended variants in the manuscript witnesses. These are copying errors that arose due to various kinds of common scribal oversight. It was only later that the mindset of the scribes changed to that of a strict copyist who did nothing other than reproduce what was received. The early scribes did not think of their work as tampering with the biblical text. Rather, it was their high regard for the text and their desire to see it understood that led them to do what they did. Thus, while it is often necessary to undo this work in order to restore a more original text, the work still remains valuable to the modern reader who wants to know how the biblical text was interpreted at this early stage of history.

Modern critical scholars sometimes see the textual plurality of antiquity as an occasion to say that there was no such thing as "the Bible." Of course, there was no such thing in antiquity as a bound book called the Bible, but there was such a thing as a collection of authoritative scrolls that had been shaped in light of one another. The canonical status of such scrolls in a given community did not necessarily depend upon the specific textual form that they took. Nevertheless, the interpretive nature of the scribal activity that produced the textual plurality presupposes an authoritative text that was worth reading, studying, and explaining.

In addition to the many small-scale variants, there are also many large-scale textual variations (sections, books) in the extant witnesses to the Hebrew Bible. These are known as variant literary editions.[13] An original version of a section or a book is revised to such an extent that it constitutes a new edition. This new edition then has its own process of transmission apart from that of the original edition. Most of the evidence for this phenomenon comes from a comparison of the Masoretic Text with the Septuagint and its Hebrew source. For example, the account of the construction of the tabernacle in Exodus 35–40 differs considerably between the Masoretic Text and the Septuagint in both length and arrangement. The Septuagint appears to follow a shorter, more original Hebrew text. The Masoretic Text has adopted a revised version designed to align more closely with the instructions for the tabernacle in Exodus 25–31.

Several books of the Hebrew Bible have multiple editions: Joshua, 1 Kings, Jeremiah, Ezekiel, and Proverbs. There are other books suspected to have multiple editions: Psalms, Job, Esther, and 1–2 Chronicles. The

---

13. See Eugene Ulrich, *The Dead Sea Scrolls and the Origins of the Bible* (Grand Rapids: Eerdmans, 1999); Tov, *Textual Criticism*, 283–326.

Psalms scroll known as 11QPs^a features a differently arranged version of books four and five (Pss 90–106 and 107–150) that lacks some of the canonical psalms but includes some non-canonical material. Some consider this scroll to be evidence of a variant edition of the Psalter, while others consider it to be a liturgical document. The book of Job appears on the surface to be extant in two editions (the MT and the LXX), but the Septuagint, which is shorter, likely does not follow a substantially different Hebrew source from what is found in the Masoretic Text. Rather, the major differences between the Masoretic Text and the Septuagint are due to the Greek translator's technique, which is freer and more paraphrastic. The book of Esther may be extant in two editions: the Masoretic Text and the Hebrew source behind the Alpha Text. There are two Greek versions of the book of Esther: the Alpha Text and the Septuagint. When the major Greek additions to the book are removed from these, the proto-Alpha Text appears to follow an earlier, shorter Hebrew text of the book, while the Septuagint essentially follows the proto-MT.[14] Finally, since the Syriac Peshitta generally follows the proto-MT of the Hebrew Bible very closely, the major differences between the Peshitta's version of 1–2 Chronicles and MT 1–2 Chronicles strongly suggests a variant literary edition.[15]

The Septuagint represents the more original edition in some cases (Joshua, Jeremiah, Ezekiel), while the Masoretic Text represents it in others (1 Kings, Proverbs). The Old Greek of Joshua, for example, is a witness to a shorter, more original Hebrew text of the book.[16] Old Greek Joshua does have some pluses when compared to MT Joshua, but the overall length of Old Greek Joshua is about 4 to 5 percent shorter than MT Joshua. Since the translation technique of Old Greek Joshua is fairly literal, it stands to reason to assume that the shortness of its text is not due to the work of the translator but to the shortness of its Hebrew source text. The expanded edition of the book from beginning to end is MT Joshua. On the other hand, the Hebrew text of MT 1 Kings has priority over the

14. See Tov, *Greek and Hebrew Bible*, 535–48; Michael V. Fox, "The Redaction of the Greek Alpha-Text of Esther," in *"Sha'arei Talmon": Studies in the Bible, Qumran, and the Ancient Near East Presented to Shemaryahu Talmon*, ed. Michael Fishbane and Emanuel Tov with the assistance of Weston W. Fields (Winona Lake, IN: Eisenbrauns, 1992), 207–20; Jon D. Levenson, *Esther: A Commentary*, OTL (Louisville: Westminster John Knox, 1997), 27–34.

15. See Shepherd, *Textuality and the Bible*, 61–77.

16. See Kristen de Troyer, *The Ultimate and the Penultimate Text of the Book of Joshua*, CBET 100 (Leuven: Peeters, 2018).

Hebrew source behind Old Greek 1 Kings (also known as 3 Kingdoms). The secondary Hebrew edition of 1 Kings behind the Old Greek is essentially a rewritten version of MT 1 Kings.

Greek Jeremiah is about one-sixth shorter than MT Jeremiah. The longest continuous passages absent from Greek Jeremiah are 33:14–26 and 39:4–13. The presence of a different Hebrew source behind Greek Jeremiah is confirmed by the literal translation technique and also by the Hebrew fragment 4QJer^b, which agrees with LXX Jeremiah 10 in key aspects (shortness and arrangement). In addition to being a witness to a shorter Hebrew text, Greek Jeremiah features a different arrangement of the book from that found in the Masoretic Text. The most obvious difference is its placement of the nations corpus (MT Jer 46–51) directly after 25:13 in the following order: 49:34–39; 46:2–28; 50–51; 47; 49:7–22, 1–5, 28–33, 23–27; 48. The first (49:34–39) and last (48) of these concludes with a prophecy about restoring the fortunes of the foreign nation in the last days (49:39; 48:47). This frames the oracles in such a way that they serve to illustrate things to come, including the incorporation of believing Gentiles into the people of God (see Jer 1:5, 10; 3:17–18; 12:14–17; 16:19). The Greek translator (or the Hebrew scribe responsible for his source text) accidentally omitted 48:45–47 when he skipped from "the prophetic utterance of the LORD" at the end of 48:44 to the same expression at the end of 48:47a. The expression "the prophetic utterance of the LORD" was subsequently dropped altogether. The text of 48:47b ("Up to here is the judgment of Moab") is an editorial addition in the Masoretic Text.

Thus, MT Jeremiah represents a systematic revision of the book, complete with editorial and exegetical additions throughout. The nations corpus has been relocated to the end of the book and rearranged so that the book culminates with the oracles against Babylon (50–51). This is consistent with the MT's overall focus on Nebuchadrezzar/Babylon and its historicization of Jeremiah's prophecies about the enemy from the north and the seventy years of captivity (see MT Jer 25:9, 11). Greek Jeremiah, on the other hand, leaves these prophecies open to an eschatological interpretation (see LXX Jer 25:9, 11; cf. Ezek 38:14–17; Dan 9:24–27).

The Old Greek of Ezekiel also follows a different Hebrew source text and is about 4 to 5 percent shorter than MT Ezekiel. The translation technique of Greek Ezekiel, like that of Greek Jeremiah, is fairly literal. In fact, it has been suggested that the same translator or group of translators worked on Jeremiah, Ezekiel, and the Twelve (Hosea–Malachi). A witness to the Old Greek from the third century CE known as p967 (Chester Beatty papyrus 967) lacks Ezekiel 36:23c–38.[17] In addition, p967 has chapter 37 after chapters 38–39, an arrangement that also appears in the Old Latin Codex Wirceburgensis. The MT of Ezekiel is the result of considerable expansion of the more original Hebrew text behind Greek Ezekiel.[18] Many of these expansions consist of material taken from elsewhere in the book.

The MT of Proverbs preserves an earlier, more original edition of the book than that represented by Greek Proverbs. In particular, Greek Proverbs follows a Hebrew source in which the last third of the book has been rearranged: 24:1–22; 30:1–14; 24:23–34; 30:15–33; 31:1–9; 25–29; 31:10–31. This displaces the words of the Gentiles Agur (30) and Lemuel (31:1–9) to a less prominent position in the book. The names of Agur and Lemuel do not appear in the Greek translation at all. The heading "The words of Agur, the son of Jakeh" (30:1) becomes "My words, O son, fear." The phrase "The words of Lemuel" (31:1) becomes "My words have been spoken by God." While the major differences in Greek Proverbs are due to its secondary Hebrew source, there are also examples of additions composed in Greek.[19]

In addition to variant literary editions of whole books, there are also variant editions of sections of books. For instance, the introduction to the story of Gideon in 4QJudg[a] is missing Judges 6:7–10 (cf. Judg 2:1–5; 10:11–16).[20] This appears not to be an accident or a deliberate omission. Rather, an earlier edition of the story simply lacked the passage. Likewise, witnesses to the book of Samuel (MT, LXX, and 4QSam[a]) attest to three different Hebrew editions of the Song of Hannah (1 Sam 2:1–10; cf. Pss 75:3–5, 7, 10; 113:7–9; see also Jer 9:23–24; Luke 1:46–55), which reveal the unsettled nature of its placement between 1 Samuel 1:28 and 2 Samuel 2:11, and two different Hebrew editions of the story of David and Goliath (1 Sam 17–18)—one short (LXX), which lacks 1 Samuel 17:12–31, 41, 50 and 17:55–18:5, 10–11, 17–19, 30, and one long (MT), whose added material appears to constitute a parallel, summary version of the story.[21]

17. See Tov, *Greek and Hebrew Bible*, 408–10.

18. See Timothy P. Mackie, *Expanding Ezekiel: The Hermeneutics of Scribal Addition in the Ancient Text Witnesses of the Book of Ezekiel*, FRLANT 257 (Göttingen: Vandenhoeck & Ruprecht, 2015).

19. See Michael V. Fox, *Proverbs: An Eclectic Edition with Introduction and Textual Commentary*, The Hebrew Bible: A Critical Edition 1 (Atlanta: Society of Biblical Literature, 2014), 36–61.

20. Cf. 4QCant[a], which lacks Song of Songs 4:7–6:11, and 4QCant[b], which lacks Song of Songs 3:6–8; 4:4–7. Tov considers these to be excerpted texts (*Textual Criticism*, 321).

21. See Tov, *Greek and Hebrew Bible*, 333–62, 433–55; Shepherd, *Textuality and the Bible*, 44–60.

The fragmentary 4QSamᵃ from the Dead Sea Scrolls is a non-aligned Hebrew text of Samuel that sometimes agrees with the LXX against the MT. It also appears to be close to the sources for the book of Samuel used by MT Chronicles and Josephus.

The differences between MT Isaiah and Greek Isaiah may appear on the surface to constitute two different literary editions of the book or sections of the book, but the translation technique of Greek Isaiah is much freer than that of Greek Jeremiah, Ezekiel, or the Twelve (Hosea–Malachi). Many of the differences between MT Isaiah and Greek Isaiah are not due to the presence of a variant Hebrew text behind LXX Isaiah but to the work of the Greek translator himself.[22] Likewise, the differences in the order of the first six books of the Twelve between MT Twelve (Hosea, Joel, Amos, Obadiah, Jonah, Micah) and LXX Twelve (Hosea, Amos, Micah, Joel, Obadiah, Jonah) are not due to the presence of a variant Hebrew text behind LXX Twelve. For the most part, the LXX translates the same text of the Twelve as that found in the MT. There is no evidence that the order of the first six books of the Twelve found in the LXX ever existed in Hebrew.[23] While MT Twelve shows signs of deliberate composition,[24] the arrangement of LXX Twelve appears to be a later editorial decision based on considerations of length and date.[25]

Finally, the book of Daniel shows signs of substantial variation in its textual witnesses to chapters 4–6. The Old Greek appears to expand and reshape chapters 4 and 6 when compared to the Masoretic Text, and the Masoretic Text appears to expand chapter 5 when compared to the Old Greek.[26] The Old Greek of Daniel, which is now represented only by p967 and by medieval witnesses to the fifth column of Origen's Hexapla, was sup-

22. See Isac Leo Seeligmann, *The Septuagint Version of Isaiah and Cognate Studies*, FAT 40 (Tübingen: Mohr Siebeck, 2004).

23. The Greek Minor Prophets Scroll from Naḥal Ḥever (ca. 50 BCE–50 CE) is a revised Greek translation of the Twelve, but the order of the books that it presupposes likely has priority over the LXX in Greek tradition. The scroll contains parts of Jonah, Micah, Nahum, Habakkuk, Zephaniah, and Zechariah.

24. See Michael B. Shepherd, *A Commentary on the Book of the Twelve: The Minor Prophets* (Grand Rapids: Kregel Academic, 2018), 19–36.

25. See Christopher R. Seitz, *Prophecy and Hermeneutics: Toward a New Introduction to the Prophets*, STI (Grand Rapids: Baker Academic, 2007), 204.

26. P967 has chapters 7–8 between chapters 4 and 5, presumably for chronological reasons. The Greek tradition of Daniel also features several additions to the book. The Prayer of Azariah and the Song of the Three Young Men are inserted between 3:23 and 3:24. The stories of Susanna and Bel and the Dragon are appended to the book. These additions are not known from the Hebrew-Aramaic tradition of the book.

planted at an early time by a revision toward the proto-MT. There is ongoing debate about whether the differences in the Old Greek are due to a variant Aramaic source text (the original text of Dan 2:4b–7:28 is in Aramaic). Andrew Daniel has made a compelling case that the differences are due to the work of the translator.[27] That is, the expansions in chapters 4 and 6 are not following an expanded Aramaic text. Rather, the Greek translator himself composed the expansions in Greek. It remains to be determined why the Greek translator did this kind of work only in these chapters.

THE GREEK TEXTS OF THE NEW TESTAMENT

The textual situation for the Greek New Testament is not nearly as complex as it is for the Hebrew Bible.[28] Roughly 94 percent of its content is identical in the extant manuscripts.[29] The two larger-scale variants—namely, the ending of Mark (Mark 16:9–20) and the account of the woman caught in adultery (John 7:53–8:11)—are generally considered to be secondary additions and thus do not pose any special problems for the textual critic. The two standard critical editions of the Greek New Testament—United Bible Society and Nestle-Aland—both print the same critically reconstructed text. In contrast to editions of the Hebrew Bible, which are normally diplomatic (i.e., based on a single manuscript) due to the complexities of reconstructing an eclectic text,[30] editions of the Greek New Testament evince great confidence in modern scholarship's ability to establish the original text.

There are three main text types or families for the Greek New Testament. These are associated historically with three major centers of the Christian church. The Alexandrian text is associated with the church in Alexandria, Egypt. The Byzantine text, also known as the majority text or

27. Andrew Glen Daniel, "The Translator's Tell: Translation Technique, Verbal Syntax, and the Myth of Old Greek Daniel's Alternate Semitic *Vorlage*," *JBL* 140 (2021): 723–49.

28. See Bruce M. Metzger, *The Text of the New Testament: Its Transmission, Corruption, and Restoration*, 4th ed. (Oxford: Oxford University Press, 2005).

29. "Of the remaining 6 percent, 3 percent constitute nonsensical readings that are transparently not original but the result of various scribal errors. Thus only about 3 percent of the text are properly the subject of investigation" (Andreas J. Köstenberger, L. Scott Kellum, and Charles L. Quarles, *The Cradle, the Cross, and the Crown: An Introduction to the New Testament* [Nashville: B&H Academic, 2009], 35).

30. But see Ronald Hendel, *Steps to a New Edition of the Hebrew Bible*, TCSt 10 (Atlanta: Society of Biblical Literature, 2016).

the received text, is associated with the church of Asia Minor. The Western text is associated with the church in Rome. There are also witnesses known as Caesarean texts, which combine features of the Alexandrian and Western texts. Each text has its own distinctive characteristics. The Alexandrian text, known primarily from the fourth- and fifth-century CE codices Vaticanus, Sinaiticus, and Alexandrinus as well as other earlier witnesses, tends to be a more conservative text that preserves shorter, more original readings.[31] The Byzantine text, which is the text of the overall majority of manuscripts but is known primarily from later witnesses, has a tendency to collect variants from other texts, thus producing either expanded or conflated readings.[32] The Western text, primarily known from Codex D or the Bezan Codex (fifth century CE), is very expansive and appears to be designed to provide clarification and explanation of the text.[33]

The relationships among the three main textual families may be illustrated by an example from Mark 9:49. The Alexandrian text says, "For every one with fire will be salted." The meaning of this text is not entirely clear. The reading found in the Western text appears to offer an explanation of the text based on Leviticus 2:13: "For every sacrifice with salt will be salted." The Byzantine text shows an awareness of both readings, but does not choose one over the other. Rather, it keeps both of them and thus produces a conflated reading: "For every one with fire will be salted, and every sacrifice with salt will be salted." A retroversion of this reading to Hebrew reveals a wordplay: "For everyone will be salted with fire [*'esh*], and every sacrifice [*'ishsheh*] will be salted with salt." On the other hand, it is possible that the longer reading of the Byzantine text is more original. According to this view, both the Alexandrian and the Western readings are the result of scribal oversight (homoioteleuton and homoioarchton). For the Alexandrian reading, the scribe accidentally skipped from the end of the first clause ("will be salted") to the end of the second clause ("will be salted") and inadvertently omitted the intervening text (homoioteleuton). For the Western text, the scribe accidentally skipped from "for every" at the beginning of the first clause to "and every" at the beginning of the

31. See Philip Wesley Comfort and David P. Barrett, *The Text of the Earliest New Testament Greek Manuscripts*, 2 vols., 3rd ed. (Grand Rapids: Kregel Academic, 2019).

32. See Maurice A. Robinson and William G. Pierpont, *The New Testament in the Original Greek: Byzantine Textform* (Southborough, MA: Chilton Book Publishing, 2005), v.

33. See Matthew Black, *An Aramaic Approach to the Gospels and Acts*, 3rd ed., with an introduction by Craig A. Evans and an appendix by Geza Vermes (Oxford: Oxford University Press, 1967; repr., Peabody, MA: Hendrickson, 1998), 280.

second clause, thereby omitting the intervening text (homoioarchton). A decision between the two explanations here depends upon whether the critic thinks the textual variation was intentional or accidental. It also depends upon how much the critic thinks the overall character of each of the witnesses ought to be taken into consideration. New Testament textual critics normally weigh both external (age, geographical distribution) and internal evidence (shorter reading, more difficult reading, reading that best explains the origin[s] of the other reading[s]) in their evaluation process, although some prefer to give more weight to one or the other.

Before translation of the New Testament into common languages like German and English, the standard translation in the church was the Latin Vulgate. Since the Old Latin version of the New Testament was based on the Greek text, Jerome essentially reused and revised that translation in his version. The other important translation of the New Testament in antiquity was the Syriac Peshitta. Prior to the latter part of the nineteenth century CE, the Byzantine text was the basis for all English translations of the Greek New Testament. This was due in large part to the influence of the first printed edition of the Greek New Testament in 1516 CE by Erasmus, who based his work on manuscripts from the Byzantine text family. This was not a conscious decision on Erasmus's part to exclude witnesses from other families. Rather, the late medieval Byzantine manuscripts were simply the best ones available to him at the time. The discovery of Codex Sinaiticus in the nineteenth century led to greater appreciation for the Alexandrian text type and for witnesses like Codex Vaticanus and Codex Alexandrinus. The Alexandrian text type has been the primary basis for modern editions of the Greek New Testament and for almost all modern English translations of the New Testament since the end of the nineteenth century. English translations of the Byzantine text are still widely available in the KJV and NKJV. There are no modern English translations based on the Western text.

ENGLISH TRANSLATIONS OF THE BIBLE

The story of the English Bible in many ways both begins and ends with William Tyndale. There were three factors that created the perfect storm for Tyndale's work during the first half of the sixteenth century CE. The first was the emphasis of the Renaissance period on the return to the original languages of the great literary works of the past. These works, including the Bible, had been known primarily in Latin translation. The second factor was the desire of many during the Renaissance period to translate the great literary works of the past from their original languages into the common European languages of the day, such as German and English. This was particularly attractive to leaders of the early Protestant Reformation who wanted to make the Bible accessible to a general populace whose literacy rate was ever increasing. It may seem odd to some today that anyone would have ever wanted to keep the Bible from the public, but the Catholic Church had concerns that ungoverned distribution of the Bible would lead to division and loss of authority. Of course, this is exactly what happened. On the other hand, keeping the Bible from the people could lead to abuse of authority, which is also something that happened. The third factor was the invention of the printing press, which allowed for the dissemination of new translations to the masses.

While English translations of the Bible were produced prior to Tyndale, those translations were made not from the Hebrew Bible and the Greek New Testament but from the Latin Vulgate. Tyndale was the first to produce an English translation of the Bible from the original languages. Newly available to him at the time were the printed edition of Jacob ben Chayyim's Second Rabbinic Bible (1525 CE), which featured the Masoretic Text, and Erasmus's printed edition of the Greek New Testament (1516 CE), which featured the Byzantine text. Jerome's Latin Vulgate and Martin Luther's German translation, both of which were made from Hebrew and Greek texts, served as guides for Tyndale, but Tyndale did his own work from the original languages, and the result was an English translation that set the pattern for all subsequent English translations. The similarity of English translations to one another through the centuries has largely been due to the quality of Tyndale's work and the tendency of English translators to follow the precedent set by earlier translators. Luther's German translation had a similar effect on the history of Bible translation in Germany. Tyndale's English translation (and subsequently the King James version) and Luther's German translation had a massive influence on their respective languages and cultures. Many generations of English speakers and German speakers learned how to read their language from these translations.

After Tyndale, English translations like the Coverdale Bible and the Douay-Rheims Bible continued to be made from the Latin Vulgate, but a steady stream of translations beginning with Matthew's Bible appeared in the tradition established by Tyndale. The so-called Great Bible (1539) was a new edition of Matthew's Bible. The Geneva Bible was a revision of the

English Bible completed in 1560. The Bishops' Bible was a 1568 revision of the Great Bible. This process of revision culminated in the 1611 King James Version, which eventually became the standard English version for the next several centuries. Among the translators of the King James Version were professors of biblical Hebrew and Greek from Oxford and Cambridge, representing some of the very best in biblical scholarship at the time. Like Tyndale's version, the King James Version followed the Masoretic Text for the Hebrew Bible and the Byzantine text for the New Testament, but the translation was not a completely new translation from scratch. The starting point for the translators was the Bishops' Bible, which they revised either on the basis of their knowledge of the original languages or on the basis of current English usage.

Several developments in biblical scholarship in the nineteenth and twentieth centuries led to the boom in new English translations that has continued to the present day. Developments in philology, modern linguistics, and translation theory greatly improved the ability of biblical scholars to work with ancient manuscripts and their languages in such a way that communicated more accurately and more effectively to audiences in the target language. The newly achieved status of Codex Sinaiticus and Codex Vaticanus in the nineteenth century led to the preference of the Alexandrian text instead of the Byzantine text for editions and translations of the Greek New Testament. The discovery of the Dead Sea Scrolls in the twentieth century led to a greater appreciation for witnesses other than the Masoretic Text to the text of the Hebrew Bible.

The Revised Version (1881–1885) featured among other things an English translation of the New Testament based more upon the Alexandrian text type. The basis for the Old Testament was still the Masoretic Text of Jacob ben Chayyim's Second Rabbinic Bible (1525), also known as the Bomberg Bible. Needless to say, this sudden change in the text base for the New Testament from the long-standing English Bible translation tradition was not received very well. It would take time for the church to see the same value in this change that biblical scholars had come to see. Nevertheless, almost all new English translations of the Greek New Testament from this point on would follow suit. The American Standard Version (1901) was an American edition of the Revised Version that became the basis for two later revisions: the Revised Standard Version or RSV (1952) and the New American Standard Bible or NASB (1971).[34] While these new versions in

---

34. The NASB, which is an evangelical translation, is not to be confused with the New

many ways continued to follow the pattern set by Tyndale and the KJV, they were based upon newer editions of the Greek New Testament and the Hebrew Bible. The RSV in particular showed more of a willingness to depart from the Masoretic Text in its translation of the Hebrew Bible and to follow the Septuagint. The New Revised Standard Version or NRSV (1989) extended this effort to incorporate more witnesses to the Hebrew Bible by including readings from the Dead Sea Scrolls, which were not yet available to the RSV translators (see also the New English Bible or NEB [1971], and its 1989 update, the Revised English Bible or REB). The English Standard Version or ESV (2001) is an evangelical update of the RSV. The New King James Version or NKJV (1982) was produced to offset attempts to depart from the textual basis of the KJV. It essentially reproduced the KJV with updated English.

In addition to an increasing interest in translating sources other than the Masoretic Text and the Byzantine text, the twentieth century also saw for the first time in English Bible translation tradition a substantial movement away from a strictly literal or word-for-word translation technique (formal equivalency) to a freer, more thought-for-thought theory of translation (dynamic equivalency) in an effort to make the Bible more accessible to modern English speakers. The New International Version or NIV (1978) was a fairly modest attempt to do this, and the Committee on Bible Translation has continued to tinker with this translation to the present day. More thoroughgoing examples of dynamic equivalency include: the Today's English Version or TEV (1976), also known as the Good News Bible or GNB; Eugene Peterson's The Message (1993); and the New Living Translation or NLT (1996), which replaced the older paraphrase known as the Living Bible (1971).

Apart from the mainstream English translations of the whole Bible, there are many high-quality translations of individual books of the Bible available directly from biblical scholars in critical commentaries. These translations are not merely revisions of older translations. They are produced by scholars who do all the work from reconstructing the original text to exegeting and translating the original text. Their translations are

---

American Bible or NAB (1970), which is a Catholic translation. See also the Jerusalem Bible or JB (1966) and the New Jerusalem Bible or NJB (1985), which are also Catholic translations. Mention should also be made here of the Jewish Publication Society or JPS translation (1917) and the NJPS (1985), which are translations of the MT of the Hebrew Bible according to the threefold shape of the Tanakh: Torah, Nevi'im (Prophets), and Ketuvim (Writings).

text-critically annotated and are accompanied by textual and exegetical explanations of the text. The closest thing to this among translations of the whole Bible is the New English Translation or NET (2005). The NET follows a broad range of textual witnesses and is more of a dynamic equivalency translation. More importantly, it comes with notes that explain the translators' textual and translational decisions. It is thus not like the usual study Bible. It is designed to explain to readers how the translators arrived at the given translation.

Students of the Bible often ask, "Which English translation of the Bible is the best?" The answer is that there is no such thing as the best English translation of the Bible. All translations have their advantages and disadvantages. They all have their benefits and limitations. The quest for the "best" translation assumes that a Bible translation can do more than is linguistically possible for it to do. It expects too much from a translation. It is important to remember that a translation is not a replacement for the original. There is no such thing as a one-to-one correspondence between two languages. Even when an appropriate translation equivalent is provided in the target language, there is no way to reproduce all of the paradigmatic and syntagmatic relationships of the source language. There is no way to reproduce exegetically significant features of the way words look and sound in the source language (e.g., wordplays). A translation is at best a provisional approximation of the original. Thus, even with good translations available, teachers of the Bible still need to be able to work from the original languages in order to explain the text. The value of translations is that they enable students of the Bible to follow along with teaching from the original languages.

For example, the traditional English translation of Genesis 1:1 is an acceptable one: "In the beginning God created the heavens and the earth." There is, however, much from the Hebrew text that this does not communicate to the English reader. The clause in Hebrew is a type of clause that establishes background information for the narrative. It is not a title or a heading. The phrase *bere'shith* ("in the beginning") normally occurs in what is known as a construct relationship with what follows. This has sparked debate about whether the verse should be translated as it is in the TEV: "In the beginning, when God created the universe." The word "beginning" in English can be used for a starting point, the first stage in a series of equal stages, or an initial indefinite duration of time. In Hebrew, however, there are different words for each of these. The Hebrew word translated "God" (*'elohim*) is a grammatically plural form. The Hebrew verb translated "created" (*bara'*) only has God for its subject in the Hebrew Bible. This is not the case for the verb "created" in the English language. The combination "the heavens and the earth" in the Hebrew original is not a reference to the sky on the one hand and the land on the other, nor is it a reference to God's dwelling on the one hand and humanity's dwelling place on the other. It is a merism that refers to the whole world.

A better question to ask is, "What do the various translations each contribute?" In other words, instead of thinking of the translations in competition with each other, it is preferable to consider how the different translations have been made. There are two items to take into consideration for this. The first is the source of the translation. For the Hebrew Bible, does the translation mainly follow the Masoretic Text (labeled MT in the table below; e.g., NASB), or does it show a willingness to follow other witnesses like the Dead Sea Scrolls, the Samaritan Pentateuch, or the Septuagint when they provide evidence of a more original text (labeled MT+; e.g., NRSV, NET)? For the Greek New Testament, does the translation follow the Byzantine text (labeled Byz; KJV, NKJV) or the Alexandrian text (labeled Alex; all others)? The second item to take into consideration is the translation technique. Does the translation adopt a formal equivalency approach (e.g., KJV, NASB, NRSV), or is it a dynamic equivalence translation (e.g., TEV, NIV, NLT)? The following table provides a guide to some of the more common translations:

Table 1: English Translations

	MT	*MT+*	*Byz*	*Alex*	*Formal*	*Dynamic*
(N)KJV	x		x		x	
NASB	x			x	x	
(N)RSV/ESV		x		x	x	
NIV	x			x		x
TEV/GNB	x			x		x
NLT	x			x		x
NET		x		x		x

It is best to have access to more than one kind of translation. For instance, possession of a KJV, an NRSV, a TEV, and a NET would provide access to the different sources and the different translation approaches.

For full access to different sources like the Septuagint, readers will need to consult resources like the NETS (see again the above discussion of the different textual witnesses).

Debates between adherents of formal equivalency and adherents of dynamic equivalency sometimes give the impression that one is better or more accurate than the other. Again, it is not so much a matter of superiority as it is a question of what each kind of translation contributes. Both kinds of translation approaches have important roles to play. When translators do their work, they must take into account both the source language (Hebrew, Aramaic, or Greek) and the target language (English). A formal equivalency translation seeks to bring the English reader as close as possible to the form and structure of the source language, sometimes even to the point of adopting foreign idioms into the target language. This is a very steady, conservative kind of translation, never really terrible or really great. While this type of translation can be very helpful as a starting point for discussion of the meaning of the original language, it can also be potentially misleading for readers who do not have the guidance of a teacher. On the other hand, a dynamic equivalency translation seeks to bring the source language as close as possible to the idiom of the target language. This kind of translation is very accessible and understandable to English readers, but it is a high-risk, high-reward type of translation. What it gains in its ability to elucidate the meaning of the source language is offset by its inconsistency of method, which has the potential to produce really helpful renderings alongside unnecessarily bad ones within the same context. The irony of dynamic equivalency translations is that they are intended for a wide readership, yet they require someone with knowledge of the original languages and translation theory to explain how the translators arrived at their renderings.

There is no such thing as a completely formally-equivalent translation. This applies even to interlinear translations, which, for example, are unable to reproduce features like the Hebrew definite direct object marker. Even the strictest formal equivalency translation allows for a degree of dynamic equivalency in order to accommodate the needs of the target language. For instance, biblical Hebrew has no verb corresponding to the English verb "have." Rather, it has a construction that employs what is known as the *lamedh* of possession in which the preposition *lamedh* means "to." For example, "And to him (were) two wives" is equivalent to "And he had two wives" (1 Sam 1:2). This is a construction that occurs throughout the Hebrew Bible, yet no English translation renders it literally. Likewise, there is no such thing as a completely dynamically-equivalent translation. All dynamic equivalency translations have a degree of formal equivalency simply because it is often the case that nothing more than this is needed to communicate effectively to readers. For example, the translation of Genesis 1:1 in the NLT ("In the beginning God created the heavens and the earth") is exactly the same as what appears in the ESV. It is thus proper to think of the different translation approaches not as black and white or as opposite poles but as points on the same continuum or spectrum.

Lest too much be claimed for either type of translation, this section concludes with a couple illustrations of their shortcomings. The famous quote attributed to Rabbi Judah (second century CE) is appropriate here: "He who translates a biblical verse literally is a liar, but he who elaborates on it is a blasphemer" (t. Meg. 4:41; b. Qidd. 49a). Those who translate literally often claim too much accuracy for themselves, but those who translate dynamically often allow themselves too much freedom. All translations involve interpretation, and all translators should admit this.

In Zechariah 6:1–8 is a vision of different colored horses pulling chariots in four different directions (north, south, east, and west). According to verse 6, the black horses go northward. The ESV and NET then say that the white horses go "after them." This is a very good formal equivalency translation of the Hebrew phrase. The problem is that it communicates to the English reader the exact opposite meaning of the text. An English reader would naturally assume from this translation that the white horses follow after the black horses northward. In Hebrew, however, directions are always given under the assumption that one is facing east. Thus, to go left is to go north, while to go right is to go south; and to go forward is to go east, while to go backward (or after or behind) is to go west. The NIV ("toward the west") and NLT ("west") capture the sense of this idiom beautifully in their dynamically equivalent translations of Zechariah 6:6. The spotted horses then go south, and the red horses presumably go east to complete the four directions.

Dynamic equivalency translators are well known for their tendency to chop up long, complex sentences into shorter, simpler sentences in an effort to make the translation more readable. They are also known for their tendency to rearrange the word or clause order of what they perceive to be cumbersome syntax. These adjustments are sometimes made even when they are not entirely necessary for the sake of clarity. Such changes to the arrangement of the text often have unintended effects that ultimately obscure the meaning of the text. The following two translations of 1 Kings 9:4–5, one formal (ESV) and one dynamic (NET), serve to illustrate this point:

> ESV (formal): And as for you, if you will walk before me, as David your father walked, with integrity of heart and uprightness, doing according to all that I have commanded you, and keeping my statutes and my rules, then I will establish your royal throne over Israel forever, as I promised David your father, saying, "You shall not lack a man on the throne of Israel."

> NET (dynamic): You must serve me with integrity and sincerity, just as your father David did. Do everything I commanded and obey my rules and regulations. Then I will allow your dynasty to rule over Israel permanently, just as I promised your father David, "You will not fail to have a successor on the throne of Israel."

The ESV brings out the Hebrew text's fronting of the personal pronoun at the beginning of verse 4 ("And as for you"). This is not a feature of the NET. The ESV also makes explicit the "if . . . then" (protasis-apodosis) relationship of verses 4 and 5. The NET does not do this. To the credit of the NET, however, it does provide a note with a literal translation of verse 4 and an explanation of its syntactical relationship to verse 5. According to the ESV's version of verse 4, there is a single protasis—"if you will walk before me"—followed by a series of indications of how Solomon is to walk before the LORD: (1) "as David your father walked," (2) "with integrity of heart and uprightness," (3) "doing according to all that I have commanded you," (4) "and keeping my statutes and my rules." This follows the Hebrew syntax very closely and is not too difficult for the English reader to follow. The NET, however, breaks this up: "You must serve me with integrity and sincerity, just as your father David did. Do everything I commanded and obey my rules and regulations." This translation dispenses with the biblical idiom of walking before the LORD ("You must serve me") and rearranges the syntax so that the phrase "with integrity and sincerity" now precedes the comparative clause ("just as your father David did").[35] It also gives the reader the impression that there are three protases ("You must

---

35. It is doubtful that the idiom "to walk before" means "to serve." Rather, it means "to live before." Thus, to walk before the LORD is to live a life of faith (see, e.g., Gen 15:6; 17:1). The idiom for "to serve" is "to stand before" (see, e.g., 1 Kgs 1:2).

serve me," "Do everything I commanded," "and obey my rules and regulations") rather than one protasis with several elucidations.

The present chapter has introduced the history of the Bible's textual transmission and translation. The following two chapters will explore how knowledge of the Bible's compositional techniques, which were introduced in the first chapter, and knowledge of the Bible's transmission and translation inform interpretation of the biblical books. This is where understanding of the making of the Bible meets interpretation of the meaning of the Bible.

THE MEANING OF THE BIBLE IN THE
COMPOSITIONAL STRATEGY OF THE HEBREW BIBLE

The next two chapters (3 and 4) focus on how the understanding of the Bible's making, transmission, and translation informs interpretation of the Bible. The previous two chapters developed this understanding. Chapter 1 showed how the Bible is built to interpret itself at multiple levels. Now it is time to provide a guided tour of the biblical compositions themselves at the macrostructural level in order to see how the biblical authors arrange their major building blocks to communicate their theological messages to their readers. Just as sentences have meaningful arrangements of verbs, subjects, and objects, so larger literary structures interrelate in a strategic and meaningful fashion. Chapter 2 demonstrated the importance of textual criticism not only for the establishment of the original text but also for the insight that it offers into the interpretive nature of textual variants. The following discussion will have occasion to call upon textual criticism for both of these purposes. Likewise, chapter 2 highlighted the interpretive character of translations both ancient and modern. These translations will be indispensable conversation partners in the hermeneutical process.

THE PENTATEUCH

The Pentateuch (five-part book) or Torah (instruction) is a single composition commonly known as the five books Genesis, Exodus, Leviticus, Numbers, and Deuteronomy. This section will examine two literary structures that cut across the whole of the Pentateuch. The first structure features the alternation of large blocks of narrative with major poetic units. Such use of poetic units to interpret narratives is an easily identifiable and regularly occurring literary technique not only in the Pentateuch but also elsewhere in the biblical canon. The second structure features the use of parallel narratives on opposite sides of the account of the giving of the law in order to frame and interpret the giving of the law for the reader. It answers the question, "What is the role of the law in the composition of the Pentateuch?"

The Poems of the Pentateuch

The major credit for insight into the function of the poems in the composition of the Pentateuch goes to John Sailhamer.[1] What follows here builds upon his work. The five major blocks of narrative in the Pentateuch are the Primeval History (Gen 1–11), the Patriarchs (Gen 12–50), the Exodus (Exod 1–19), the Wilderness (Num 11–36), and Deuteronomy. Accompanying these narratives are the major poetic units of the Pentateuch: Genesis 3:14–19; 49:1–27; Exodus 15:1–18; Numbers 23–24; Deuteronomy 32–33. These poems serve to punctuate and interpret the narratives that precede them in order to guide the reader to see the theological message of the Pentateuch as a whole. Each poem features a major character from the preceding narrative as the speaker, an expectation of what will happen in the last days, and a prophecy of a coming messianic figure. Thus, the author does not see the storyline of his book as a mere documentary of past events but as an opportunity to speak of the future work of God. This contributes greatly to the ongoing function of the Pentateuch as a prophetic book for generations to come (see Deut 31:9–13; Neh 8–9). The following table illustrates the relationship of the poems and their key features to the major narrative blocks:

Table 2: The Poems of the Pentateuch

	Primeval history (Gen 1–11) Gen 3:14–19	Patriarchs (Gen 12–50) Gen 49:1–28	Exodus (Exod 1–19) Exod 15:1–18	Wilderness (Num 11–36) Num 23–24	Deuteronomy Deut 32–33
Major character who speaks	God	Jacob	Moses	Balaam	Moses
"In the end of days"	[Gen 3:15]	Gen 49:1	[Exod 15:18]	Num 24:14	Deut 31:29
The Coming King	Gen 3:15	Gen 49:8–12	Exod 15:18	Num 24:7–9, 17	Deut 33:5, 7, 20

1. John H. Sailhamer, *The Pentateuch as Narrative: A Biblical-Theological Commentary* (Grand Rapids: Zondervan, 1992); John H. Sailhamer, *The Meaning of the Pentateuch: Revelation, Composition and Interpretation* (Downers Grove, IL: InterVarsity, 2009).

The poems are distributed across the whole of the Pentateuch in such a way that each major narrative block includes a poem. There is no poem accompanying the laws in Exodus 20–Leviticus 27. The poems not only relate to the narratives that precede them but also interact closely with one another in matters of great detail.

The first poem (Gen 3:14–19) helps the reader to understand what has transpired in the opening chapters of Genesis. God addresses the serpent (3:14–15), the woman (3:16), and the man (3:17–19) in the reverse order of the blame shifting that has just occurred in the previous narrative: the man, and the woman, and the serpent (3:12–13). He announces the curse of the serpent (3:14) and the curse of the ground (3:17; see also 5:29) as consequences for the serpent's role in the previous narrative (3:1–5) and for the failure of the man and the woman to heed the prohibition against taking fruit from the tree of knowledge (2:17; 3:6). The man and the woman are subsequently banished from the land of blessing, the Garden of Eden, and they lose access to the tree of life (3:22–24). Thus, death enters the world (Rom 5:12).

The text of Genesis 3:15 is unique in that it looks well beyond the immediate circumstances of the narrative: "And I will put enmity between you and the woman, and between your seed and her seed; as for him, he will bruise you on the head; as for you, you will bruise him on the heel." The progressive parallelism of the verse moves from opposition between the serpent and the woman to opposition between the serpent's seed and the woman's seed before finally landing on opposition between the woman's seed and the serpent. The woman's seed will deal a fatal blow to the serpent's head, and the serpent will injure the heel of the woman's seed—an injury from which the woman's seed will presumably recover. The theme of the striking of the enemy's head is a common one in biblical poetry (see Num 24:17; Judg 5:26; Hab 3:13; Pss 68:21; 110:1, 5–6).

The cryptic nature of Genesis 3:15 requires the reader to continue reading the book in order to understand its meaning. The most pressing unanswered questions at this point concern the identities of the woman's seed and the serpent and also the manner in which their opposition will play itself out (i.e., the bruising of the serpent's head and the bruising of the heel of the woman's seed). The subsequent narrative of Genesis makes it very easy for the reader to follow the story of the woman's seed or offspring. After the account of the flood, there are only eight members of the human race: Noah and his three sons (Shem, Ham, and Japheth) and their wives. The seventy nations of Genesis 10 come from the three sons of Noah. The narrative then focuses on Abram (from the line of Shem) and his "seed" (12:7; 13:15–16; 15:1–6, 18).

In Genesis 12:3, God says to Abram, "And I will bless those who bless you, and each one who treats you lightly will I curse, and all the families of the earth will be blessed in you." This speaks of the restoration of the blessing that was lost in the opening chapters of Genesis (see 1:26–28). Genesis 12:3a begins a trail of texts that ultimately leads into the other poems of the Pentateuch and guides the reader to see that the seed of the woman in Genesis 3:15 who will defeat the enemy is a coming king from the tribe of Abram's great-grandson Judah (12:3a; 27:29; 37:5–11; 42:6–9; 49:8–12; Num 24:7–9, 17).[2] Of course, both Eve and Abram have many descendants, but these texts serve to identify one particular descendant. The first clue to this is Genesis 27:29: "May peoples serve you, and may nations bow down to you. Be lord to your brothers, and may the sons of your mother bow down to you. May each one who curses you be cursed, and may each one who blesses you be blessed." The last part of this verse clearly takes up the language of Genesis 12:3a. The words are those of Abram's son Isaac, who is unwittingly blessing his son Jacob as if he were his firstborn son Esau. The strangeness of the language of Genesis 27:29a suggests that the words may ultimately apply to someone other than Jacob. When do peoples or nations ever serve or bow down to Jacob? Since Jacob only has one brother (Esau), who are his brothers or the sons of his mother?

The image of brothers bowing down resurfaces in the narrative of Jacob's son Joseph, whose dreams indicate that his brothers will one day bow to him (Gen 37:5–11). These dreams come to fruition in the story of Genesis 42:6–9, but Jacob's final blessing of his twelve sons in the poem of Genesis 49:1–27 reveals that what has happened with Joseph is a prefiguration of what will happen with the coming king from the tribe of Judah (49:8–12). It is to Judah that the brothers or the sons of the father will bow down (49:8). It is to the coming king from the tribe of Judah that the obedience of peoples will belong (49:10). Furthermore, the comparison of Judah to a lion in Genesis 49:9b ("He bows down, he lies down like a

---

2. The text of Genesis 12:3b ("and all the families of the earth will be blessed in you") begins another trail of texts (12:3b; 18:18b; 22:18a; 26:4b; 28:14b; Jer 4:2; 23:5–6; Ps 72:17; Gal 3:8, 16, 28–29). See Benjamin J. Noonan, "Abraham, Blessing, and the Nations," *HS* 51 (2010): 73–93. Both Jer 4:2; 23:5–6 and Ps 72:17 identify the seed of Abraham in whom all the nations will be blessed (Gen 22:18a; 26:4b) as an individual messianic figure. Thus, the apostle Paul can say that the seed of Abraham is Christ (Gal 3:16). He can also say that those who are in Christ by faith are the seed of Abraham (3:28–29; cf. Rom 4:11–12, 16–18).

lion, and like a lioness who will rouse him?") is reiterated in the poetry of Balaam's third oracle (Num 24:9a), where the words of Genesis 12:3a and 27:29b appear once again: "Each one who blesses you is blessed, and each one who curses you is cursed" (Num 24:9b). The coming king of Balaam's third and fourth oracles is the one who will strike the head of the enemy (24:7–8, 17; cf. Gen 3:15).[3]

Discussion of the first poem (Gen 3:14–19) has thus led to the second poem (49:1–27), a poem that serves to interpret the patriarchal narratives (12–50). The speaker for the second poem is Jacob—the last of the three great patriarchs Abraham, Isaac, and Jacob. The poem constitutes Jacob's final blessing of his twelve sons (cf. Deut 33). In the preface to Jacob's words of blessing (Gen 49:1), he summons his sons to gather so that he might declare to them what will happen to them "in the end of days" (*be'aharith hayyamim*). This phrase only occurs four times in the Pentateuch (Gen 49:1; Num 24:14; Deut 4:30; 31:29), three of which appear in direct connection with the poems (Gen 49:1; Num 24:14; Deut 31:29). Outside of the Pentateuch, the phrase occurs very sparingly and strategically in the programmatic passages (Isa 2:2; Hos 3:5) and restoration passages (Jer 30:24; Ezek 38:16; Mic 4:1) of the Latter Prophets (see also Jer 23:19; 48:47; 49:39) and in the framework of the book of Daniel (Dan 2:28; 10:14). It is apparent from the contexts of these uses that the phrase refers not merely to days to come but to the last days of the eschaton.

The poem of Genesis 49:1–27 establishes itself right away as an exegesis of the preceding narratives. Verses 3–7 interpret the previous stories as

---

3. This enemy is a historical enemy (Agag) according to MT Num 24:7b (see 1 Sam 15); but according to the SP and the LXX of Num 24:7b, the enemy is an eschatological one (Gog) (see Ezek 38–39; Rev 20:8). The relationship between the eschatological enemy and the serpent in Gen 3 is worked out over the course of the biblical canon. Isaiah's prophecy of peace in the messianic kingdom (Isa 11:6–9), which includes among other things the image of an infant playing unharmed near snakes (11:8), is predicated upon the defeat of "Leviathan a fleeing serpent and Leviathan a twisted serpent" (27:1). Thus, the repetition of material from Isa 11:6–9 in Isaiah's prophecy of the new creation and the new Jerusalem (65:17–25) replaces the image of the infant near snakes with a reference to Gen 3:14–15: "and a serpent, dust will be his food" (cf. Gen 3:14: "on your belly will you go, and dust will you eat all the days of your life"). The apostle John's vision of the dragon in Rev 12:9 features an identification of the dragon as "the ancient serpent, the one called devil [slanderer] and Satan [the adversary]." The vision incorporates the three figures from Gen 3:15—the serpent, the woman, and the woman's seed—and portrays its drama as unfolding in the eschaton. See Pauline Paris Buisch, "The Rest of Her Offspring: The Relationship between Revelation 12 and the Targumic Expansion of Genesis 3:15," *NovT* 60 (2018): 386–401.

reasons why the kingship will not come from the first three sons born to Jacob. The brief account of the firstborn Reuben lying with his father's concubine Bilhah in Genesis 35:22 provides the basis for Jacob to pass over him (49:3–4; cf. Deut 33:6). Likewise, the efforts of Simeon and Levi to avenge their sister Dinah against their father's will in the story of Genesis 34 give Jacob cause to distance himself from them (Gen 49:5–7; cf. Deut 33:8–11). The two sons who receive by far the most attention in Jacob's blessing are Judah (Gen 49:8–12) and Joseph (49:22–26). Since Joseph is the main character in the immediately preceding narratives, it is no surprise that such attention is devoted to him. On the other hand, the reader may not have noticed the prominence of Judah in the Joseph stories. Judah's willingness to offer himself as a substitute for Benjamin (see his lengthy speech in 44:18–34) not only redeems his earlier failures in Genesis 37 and 38 but also sets him apart from the other brothers and paves the way for Joseph to reveal himself to his brothers in the climax of the story (45).

It has already been noted above how the opening words to Judah in Genesis 49:8 take up the image of the brothers bowing down from Genesis 27:29; 37:5–11; 42:6–9. What has happened to Joseph in the preceding narrative is now given a prefigurative significance. The poem of Genesis 49 infuses the narrative with ongoing relevance for future readers, relieving the modern reader of the need to update the text artificially. The historical account of the brothers bowing down to Joseph does not exist for its own sake but for the purpose of illustrating what will happen to the king from the tribe of Judah in the last days. This king will be comparable to a lion (Gen 49:9; Num 24:9)—an image that becomes closely associated with the messianic king from the tribe of Judah who comes in fulfillment of the covenant with David (see Rev 5:5; see also 2 Sam 7; Isa 11:1–10; cf. Ezek 19:1–9). Indeed, the prophecy of Genesis 49:8–12 provides much of the basis for that covenant.

The text of Genesis 49:10 comes with several possibilities for interpretation. The first issue involves the Hebrew word *'adh*, which can mean either "until" (i.e., either until a point of cessation or until a point of culmination) or "(for)ever," yielding the following four options: (1) "A scepter will not depart from Judah . . . until ['adh]," that is, until a point of cessation (see Ezek 21:27); (2) "A scepter will not depart from Judah . . . until ['adh]," that is, until a point of culmination (see Zech 9:9–10); (3) "A scepter will not depart from Judah . . . forever ['adh]," that is, it will depart but not always (see 1 Kgs 11:39); or (4) "A scepter will not depart from Judah . . . ever ['adh]," that is, the scepter will not ever depart, and the kingdom will last forever (see 2 Sam 7:13, 16; Dan 2:44; 7:14, 27).[4] The second and fourth options have messianic implications.

The second issue in Genesis 49:10 concerns how to understand the Hebrew word that has been variously rendered as "Shiloh" (KJV: "until Shiloh come"; or, "until he/it comes to Shiloh"), "to whom it belongs" (NIV, NET: "until he comes to whom it belongs"; cf. Syr.), and "tribute to him" (ESV: "until tribute comes to him").[5] All Targums of the Pentateuch interpret Genesis 49:10 in an explicitly messianic way (see also 4QComm-Gen A), something that can be said of only one other text in the Pentateuch (Num 24:17). Not only will the brothers bow down to the Messiah, but also the obedience of the nations will belong to him (Gen 27:29; 49:10; Dan 7:14; see LXX, Vulg.: "the expectation of the nations").

The final image of the messianic king in Genesis 49:11–12 may be understood in more than one way. On the one hand, the picture of the king binding his colt to the grapevine and washing his clothing in wine could be a depiction of great agricultural abundance in the messianic kingdom (see Tg. Onq.; see also Amos 9:11–15). On the other hand, it could be a depiction of a victorious warrior with blood-stained garments enjoying the spoils of battle (see Pal. Tgg.; see also Isa 53:12; 63:1–6; Zech 9:9–10). This latter option is adopted in Isaiah 63:1–6 where the one whose garments appear to be those of one who has been treading in a winepress turns out to be a victorious warrior whose garments are stained with the blood of his enemies. Isaiah's prophecy then mediates this interpretation of Genesis 49:11–12 to the book of Revelation where Christ, under the metaphor of one treading in a winepress, is the victorious warrior with blood-stained garments (Rev 14:14–20; 19:11–16).

The third major poem of the Pentateuch is the Song at the Sea in Exodus 15:1–18, which features Moses and offers a poetic rendition of the exodus account. The poem characterizes the Egyptians' pursuit of the Israelites into the sea as if God cast them into the sea (Exod 15:1, 4; cf. Exod 14:27b). It also characterizes the strong east wind of Exodus 14:21–22 as the blast of God's nostrils (15:8). This imagery highlights the theological truth that God was the one who was fighting for the Israelites (14:14; 15:3).

4. See Richard C. Steiner, "Four Inner-Biblical Interpretations of Genesis 49:10: On the Lexical and Syntactic Ambiguities of עַד as Reflected in the Prophecies of Nathan, Ahijah, Ezekiel, and Zechariah," *JBL* 132 (2013): 33–60.

5. See LXX ("until the things stored up for him come") and Vulg. ("until the one who is sent comes").

Much like the other poems, however, the perspective of this song is not limited to the immediate historical circumstances of the preceding narrative. Rather, the previous narrative becomes an opportunity to look to the future. The text of Exodus 15:14–18 looks beyond the deliverance from Egypt to the conquest of the land, the establishment of the temple site, and the everlasting kingship of God. (See 4QFlor, which cites Exod 15:17–18 along with other biblical texts to speak of the eschatological temple and the messianic kingdom.)

The fourth poetic unit of the Pentateuch is a sequence of four prophetic oracles in Numbers 23–24 given through Balaam, a character who figures prominently in the immediately preceding section of the wilderness narratives (Num 22). Moses has led the people of Israel to the eastern side of the Jordan, and Balak the king of Moab has decided to summon Balaam to curse the people of Israel for him, for he knows that whoever Balaam blesses is blessed and whoever he curses is cursed (22:6). This puts to the test God's word to the patriarchs that he would bless those who bless them and curse those who curse them (Gen 12:3; 27:29). Thus, the very first oracle of Balaam in Numbers 23:7–10 addresses this issue. Balaam declares that he is unable to curse a people whom God has blessed (cf. Num 22:10–12, 18, 20, 35, 38; 23:12).

Balaam's second oracle (Num 23:18–24) describes the people of Israel as those who have the shout of a king among them as God brings them out of Egypt (23:21–22). The people are compared to a lion that does not lie down until it has devoured its prey (23:24). This language then becomes the basis for the content of Balaam's third oracle (24:3–9) in which he speaks of a king who will be higher than Agag/Gog and whose kingdom will be exalted (24:7b). The reading "Agag" in the Masoretic Text is most likely a historicized version of the prophecy that refers to the defeat of the Amalekite king (Agag) by Israel's first king (Saul) in the story of 1 Samuel 15. The Samaritan Pentateuch and the Septuagint, however, have the reading "Gog," which refers to an eschatological enemy to be defeated by the messianic king (Ezek 38–39; Rev 20:8). According to Numbers 24:8a, this king is the one whom God brings out of Egypt in a new exodus ("God brings him out of Egypt"; cf. Num 23:22: "God brings them out of Egypt"; see Hos 11:1, 5, 11; Matt 2:13–15).[6] This king is also the one who devours his foes and then

---

6. See John H. Sailhamer, "Hosea 11:1 and Matthew 2:15," *WTJ* 63 (2001): 87–96; Michael B. Shepherd, *The Twelve Prophets in the New Testament*, StBibLit 140 (New York: Lang, 2011), 17–24; Michael B. Shepherd, "The New Exodus in the Composition of the

lies down like a lion (Num 24:8b–9a; cf. Gen 49:9; Num 23:24). Blessed is each one who blesses him, and cursed is each one who curses him (Num 24:9b; cf. Gen 12:3; 27:29; Num 22:6, 12; 23:8).

Balaam prefaces his final, bonus oracle in Numbers 24:15–24 by inviting Balak to come so that he might advise him concerning what this people (Israel) will do to his people (Moab) "in the end of days" (*be'aharith hayyamim*) (Num 24:14)—the same phrase that appears in Genesis 49:1 and Deuteronomy 31:29. Balaam is explicit that his last oracle looks beyond the history of Israel to the last days. Indeed, the text of Numbers 24:24 looks to a time when ships will come from Kittim (Cyprus) (see Dan 11:30). In Numbers 24:17a, Balaam says that he sees "him" but not now, he sees "him" but not near. It becomes apparent from what follows that the referent of the pronoun "him" is the coming king mentioned in Numbers 24:7–9. This king is not one who is currently present, nor is he one who will appear in the near future.

The Masoretic Text for Numbers 24:17b says, "A star treads from Jacob, and a scepter rises from Israel." The Septuagint translates, "A star will rise [*anatelei*] from Jacob, and a man [*anthrōpos*] will rise up from Israel" (cf. LXX Num 24:7a: "a man will go forth from his seed"). This translation connects the text to a significant number of messianic prophecies in the Septuagint in which the coming one is known either as the "rising one" (*anatolē*) (see LXX Jer 23:5; Zech 3:8; 6:12; cf. Luke 1:78) or as a "man" (*anthrōpos*) (see LXX Isa 19:20; cf. 2 Sam 23:1 [LXX, 4QSamᵃ]; Zech 6:12; Dan 7:13; John 19:5; 1 Tim 2:5; see also Mal 3:20; Matt 2:2; 2 Pet 1:19; Rev 22:16). All Targums of the Pentateuch identify the star in Numbers 24:17b as "the king." Targums Onqelos and Pseudo-Jonathan identify the scepter as "the Messiah," while Targum Neofiti and the Fragmentary Targum identify the scepter as "redeemer and ruler." This messianic king will strike the sides of Moab's head and the top of the head of the sons of destruction (Num 24:17b; cf. Gen 3:15; Jer 48:45).

The final poetic section of the Pentateuch features the Song of Moses (Deut 32) and the Blessing of Moses (33) back-to-back. These two poems are preceded by the statement from Moses that harm will befall the people "in the end of days" (*be'aharith hayyamim*) (31:29; cf. Gen 49:1;

Twelve," in *Text and Canon: Essays in Honor of John H. Sailhamer*, ed. Robert L. Cole and Paul J. Kissling (Eugene, OR: Pickwick, 2017), 120–36; Michael B. Shepherd, *A Commentary on the Book of the Twelve: The Minor Prophets* (Grand Rapids: Kregel Academic, 2018), 92–98.

Num 24:14). The design of the Song of Moses is to serve as an ongoing witness against the people (Deut 31:19–22), attesting to the LORD's faithfulness (32:1–14) and the people's infidelity (32:15–43). The Blessing of Moses for the twelve tribes of Israel (33) is comparable to Jacob's blessing of his twelve sons (Gen 49:1–27).

The Blessing of Moses divides into three main sections: prologue (Deut 33:1–5), blessings (33:6–25), and epilogue (33:26–29). The conclusion to the prologue says, "And he was king in Jeshurun" (33:5a). Some English translations supply "the LORD" as the subject (e.g., NET: "The LORD was king over Jeshurun"), even though the divine name does not appear in the Hebrew text. It is more likely, however, that the subject from the previous verse, Moses, carries over to this verse: "And he [Moses] was king in Jeshurun" (see KJV). Moses functioned as a kind of ruler among the people of Israel and thus became a prototype of the messianic king anticipated in the poems of the Pentateuch.[7] Thus, Targum Neofiti (Tg. Neof.) and the Fragmentary Targum of the Pentateuch (Frg. Tg.) interpret Deuteronomy 33:5 to be a prophecy of a king who will rise up from the house of Jacob (cf. Num 24:17).

The material devoted to the tribe of Judah in the Blessing of Moses (Deut 33:7) is much more concise than that found in Jacob's blessing of his son Judah (Gen 49:8–12), but the text of Deuteronomy 33:7 appears to presuppose the reader's knowledge of Jacob's blessing: "Hear, O LORD, the voice of Judah, and to his people may you bring him." Who is the referent for the pronoun "him"? Moses's blessing here seems to be a prayer that the LORD would hear the cry of the people of Judah for their messianic deliverer to come to them (see Gen 49:10; Mic 4:8). Likewise, the blessing of the tribe of Gad (Deut 33:20–21) speaks not so much about Gad as it does about the lion king (Gen 49:8–12) who benefits Gad: "Blessed is the one who enlarges Gad. Like a lioness he dwells, and he tears an arm, also the top of the head" (Deut 33:20; cf. Num 24:17). The coming king restores blessing not only to Judah but also to the other tribes.

The poems of the Pentateuch work in tandem with the major narrative blocks and in close association with one another to develop an eschatological messianism that has exerted a great influence on the Prophets, the Writings, and the New Testament.

---

7. See William Horbury, *Jewish Messianism and the Cult of Christ* (London: SCM, 1998), 31.

Yet although the lengthy development of messianism *from* the Old Testament is obvious, not least when the influence of messianic prototypes is considered, it has also become clear that messianism is important *within* the Old Testament. It flourished especially in the period of the collecting and editing of the books, it deeply influenced the ancient versions, notably the Septuagint and the Targums, but within the corpus of Hebrew scriptures it was integrally linked with the future hopes which form a great theme both of the Pentateuch and of the Prophets, and from the inception of Davidic monarchy and the Israelite capture of Jerusalem it was bound up with the traditions of kingship in Zion.[8]

The macrostructural arrangement of the poems now informs the way lower levels of the text are read. Thus, Jesus can say with full exegetical warrant that Moses wrote about him (John 5:39, 46–47; see also 8:56). Such a statement does not require allegorical interpretation of the Pentateuch. It only requires attention to the details of the poems and their coordinated and strategic role in the composition of the Pentateuch as a whole.

The Role of the Law in the Composition of the Pentateuch

One of the most pressing questions in the history of Christian theology concerns what to do with the laws of the Pentateuch. Readers are generally interested in whether they have to "keep" the Mosaic law, but this is not necessarily the question that the author of the Pentateuch is seeking to answer. The following section will explore the way in which the author has framed the collections of laws with narratives designed to help the reader understand why the laws in their entirety are included in the book. Once this understanding is in place, the reader is in a better position to think about what to do with the individual laws.

Hans-Christoph Schmitt has demonstrated the presence of what he calls a "faith theme" in the composition of the Pentateuch.[9] This faith theme manifests itself with distinctive terminology (*hiphil* of *'mn*) at strategic junctures in the storyline of the Pentateuch where the narrative displays the pattern of a petition psalm (problem, promise, sign, faith). The

8. Horbury, *Jewish Messianism*, 35, emphasis original.
9. Hans-Christoph Schmitt, "Redaktion des Pentateuch im Geiste der Prophetie," *VT* 32 (1982): 170–89.

arrangement of these narratives on opposite sides of the law (Exod 20–Lev 27) sets up a contrast between faith and the works of the law.

Table 3: The Faith Theme

	Gen 15	*Exod 4*	*Exod 14*	*Law*	*Num 14*	*Num 20*
Problem	Child-less (15:2–3)	Doubt (4:1)	Egypt pursues Israel (14:1–12)		Rejection of leadership (14:1–4, 10)	Lack of water (20:1–6)
Promise	Seed (15:4–5)	Faith (4:5, 8, 9)	God will fight for Israel (14:13–14)		The land (14:5–9)	Water (20:8)
Sign	Stars (15:5)	Staff, hand, water (4:3–4, 6–7, 9)	Divine power displayed at the sea (14:31)		All the signs performed by God (14:11)	Water from a rock (20:11)
Faith	Abram believes (15:6)	People believe in Egypt (4:31)	People believe after exodus (14:31)		People lack faith in the wilderness (14:11)	Moses and Aaron lack faith (20:12)

The exposition of Deuteronomy (Deut 1:5) then refers back to this faith theme (1:32; 9:23), and subsequent retellings of the biblical narrative reveal the influence of the faith theme (Pss 78:22, 32; 106:12, 24). Of course, the point of this positioning of the narratives in the Pentateuch is not to say that the people were always faithful and flawless before the giving of the law. It is only to show that the giving of the law itself did not produce the faith and obedience that God desired from his people.

At opposite ends of the faith-theme narratives are the two most prominent characters of the Pentateuch: Abraham and Moses.[10] On the one hand, Abraham is declared righteous by faith (Gen 15:6; cf. Hab 2:4) and is said to have kept the law (Gen 26:5; cf. Deut 11:1) even though he did not have the law and despite the fact that he did not keep the law (e.g., Gen 20:12; Lev 20:17).[11] On the other hand, Moses, the mediator of the

---

10. See Sailhamer, *Pentateuch as Narrative*, 60–78.

11. Genesis 22 is the demonstration of Abraham's faith (see Jas 2:21–24).

law, is disallowed entry into the land of the covenant due to a lack of faith (Num 20:12) and thus dies in the wilderness (Deut 34:5). This is not so much about Abraham and Moses themselves as it is about what they represent. The righteousness embodied by the law is credited to Abraham not by works of law but by faith. He represents justification by faith. Moses lacks faith despite having the works of the law. He represents the hypothetical yet unattainable justification by works (Lev 18:5). It is this contrast between faith and the works of the law that informs the theology of Paul's letters to the Galatians (Gal 3:1–14) and the Romans (Rom 4:1–12).

Proponents of the so-called New Perspective on Paul would do well to pay attention to this feature of the Pentateuch's composition. Such proponents have suggested either that Paul misunderstood first-century Judaism or that Protestant scholarship has misunderstood Paul's view of first-century Judaism, but their preoccupation with a reconstructed first-century Judaism has misdirected them away from the text that Paul actually cites, namely, the Pentateuch. The suggestion that Paul is not concerned with salvation by works (of which the works of the Mosaic law are the prime example) but with the requirement of first-century badges of Jewish identity (such as circumcision, Sabbath keeping, and dietary laws) is motivated at least in part by a desire to "rescue" Judaism from what is considered to be a misperception among Protestant Christians. The thinking is that first-century Judaism did not believe in salvation by works of law. Rather, membership in the covenant was a birthright, and the works of the law were a means of staying in that covenant relationship. It is not clear, however, how this differs materially from salvation by works if the works are still necessary to achieve the desired end. Furthermore, while some modern Jews have welcomed this redefinition of ancient Judaism, others have objected that Judaism is indeed a religion of salvation by works, and frankly they like it that way.[12]

If justification is by faith and not by works of law, then why is the law added at all? This is the question that the apostle Paul is asking and answering in Galatians 3:19. He says that the law was added because of transgression (cf. Jer 7:21–23). On the one hand, this means that transgression led to the addition of law, which was by definition secondary to the covenant relationship. On the other hand, it means that the addition of law led to an

---

12. See James Barr, *The Concept of Biblical Theology: An Old Testament Perspective* (Minneapolis: Fortress, 1999), 272.

increase in transgression (Rom 5:20).[13] That is, the addition of law did not resolve or restrain the sin problem of the people. Rather, it exposed and exacerbated their sin. The good and holy law written on tablets of stone proves to be ineffective and unable to penetrate the hard hearts of the people (see Ezek 20; Rom 7), thus showing the need for a new covenant relationship in which the people's hearts are made soft and receptive to the will of God.

When the people come to Mount Sinai in the narrative of Exodus 19, God says that if they will only obey his voice and keep his covenant, then they will be his treasured or special possession, a kingdom of priests (LXX: royal priesthood; Tg. Onq.: kings, priests), and a holy nation (Exod 19:4–6; cf. Isa 61:6; 66:21; 1 Pet 2:5, 9; Rev 1:6; 5:10; 20:6). This presupposes that a covenant relationship is already in place—the covenant with the patriarchs (Gen 15:18; 17:4, 9; Exod 2:24; 6:4–5). God then instructs Moses to prepare the people to meet with him on the third day on the mountain (Exod 19:10–13; cf. Exod 3:12). This is where English translations tend to obscure what is happening in the Hebrew text. Most English translations render Exodus 19:12–13 in such a way that they give the reader the impression that the people are not to ascend the mountain, but the Hebrew text of Exodus 19:12 should be understood as follows: "Set bounds for the people all around, saying, 'Watch yourselves going up on the mountain and touching its edge. Anyone who touches the mountain will certainly be put to death.'"[14] There is no negation in the Hebrew text forbidding the people to ascend or to touch the mountain. Rather, they are to ascend the mountain on a designated path. If they veer off this path, then they face the death penalty. Thus, according to Exodus 19:13b, when the people hear the ram's horn blast long, they are to go up "on the mountain" (*bahar*). The Hebrew phrase *bahar* does not mean "to the mountain" but "on the mountain." The common English translation "to the mountain" for this phrase in this particular verse is perhaps motivated by thoughts of the logistical problem of getting so many people on the mountain (see Exod 12:37). It must be said, however, that this is not the way that translation decisions should be made. The meaning of a word or phrase has to be established on the basis of usage within the language, not on the basis of how the translator imagines or reconstructs the situation being described in the narrative.

---

13. See Jason C. Meyer, *The End of the Law: Mosaic Covenant in Pauline Theology*, NAC Studies in Bible & Theology 6 (Nashville: B&H Academic, 2009), 166–71.

14. See Sailhamer, *Pentateuch as Narrative*, 51–57.

The above discussion is crucial for understanding what comes next in the narrative. When the third day comes, and the people hear the sound of the horn, they do not follow God's instruction to ascend the mountain to meet with him (Exod 19:16a). Rather, they remain in the camp and tremble with fear (19:16b). It is important to note how this transgression fundamentally changes everything that has been said about the people's relationship with God thus far. Now Moses brings forth the people to meet with God not on the mountain but only at the foot of the mountain (19:17). The people are no longer allowed to ascend the mountain (19:23a). Whereas there were once boundaries set for the people to ascend the mountain, now there are boundaries set for the mountain itself to keep the people away from the mountain (19:23b). The people who were called to be a "kingdom of priests" on the basis of the unconditional patriarchal covenant of simple faith and obedience are now a "kingdom with priests" (19:22). A separate class of priests will now stand between God and the people and mediate the laws now added for the terms of a conditional covenant relationship (24:8).

The transgression of Exodus 19:16 sets off a chain reaction in the composition of the Pentateuch that shows a clear pattern of law added because of transgression and transgression added because of law.[15] After the failure of the people in Exodus 19, the Decalogue and the Covenant Code are added in Exodus 20–24, followed by the Priestly Code in Exodus 25–Leviticus 16. The Priestly Code then divides into several subsections in which the vicious cycle of the pattern continues. The instructions for the tabernacle in Exodus 25–31 are followed by the transgression of the golden calf incident (Exod 32) in which the people violate the first of the commands (20:2–6), requiring another covenant to be made on the same terms (34:10–26). Following the account of the tabernacle's construction in Exodus 35–40 is the addition of the sacrificial laws in Leviticus 1–7. The transgression of Aaron's sons, Nadab and Abihu, in Leviticus 10:1–3 leads to the addition of the purification laws in Leviticus 11–16. The final law code, the Holiness Code (Lev 17–27), is prefaced by a reference to the people's practice of making sacrifices to goat idols (17:7; cf. Exod 32).

It is evident from the above pattern that the addition of law because of transgression only increases the transgression. It is as if the sole purpose of the giving of the law is to show the people's inability to keep it (see Hos 8:12). This is why the conclusion to the Pentateuch looks beyond the giving of the law under the old covenant to the hope of a transformative

---

15. See Sailhamer, *Pentateuch as Narrative*, 47–51.

new covenant relationship. The list of curses for disobedience to the Sinai covenant in Deut 28:15–68 (cf. Lev 26:14–41) already presupposes the breaking of the covenant and anticipates exile from the land of the covenant as the ultimate consequence of the broken covenant relationship (Deut 28:64–68; see also 29:28). The text of Deuteronomy 29:1 then begins a new section (cf. Deut 1:1; 4:44; 12:1) that turns the reader's attention to the words of a covenant "apart from" the covenant that was made at Horeb/Sinai.[16] This is not a renewal of the covenant that was made at Sinai but a new covenant altogether.[17] The new covenant was not made in the land of Moab, but the LORD did entrust to Moses the words of the new covenant there.

Deuteronomy 29 prefaces the words of the new covenant by explaining the way things currently are under the Sinai covenant. The LORD has not yet given the people a heart to know or eyes to see or ears to hear (Deut 29:4). Thus, the current covenant relationship will end in exile (29:28). Once the curses of disobedience to the covenant have come upon the people, the LORD will restore the fortunes of the people and return them to the land of the covenant and circumcise their hearts (30:1–6; cf. Deut 10:16). The spiritual circumcision of the heart in the new covenant relationship is what will enable the people to love the LORD their God with all their heart and with all their being so that they might live (30:6; cf. Deut 6:5; see also Lev 18:5). It is this same message from Deuteronomy 29–30 that appears in the Prophets when they highlight the failure of the people under the old covenant, anticipate exile, and look forward to restoration in a new covenant relationship (see, e.g., Jer 4:4; 9:25–26; 31:31–34; 32:36–41; Ezek 11:19–20; 18:31; 34:25; 36:26–27; 37:26; see also Rom 2:28–29; 2 Cor 3; Col 2:11). The Pentateuch and the Prophets are thus already new covenant documents.

If the presentation of the law in the Pentateuch is designed to point the reader beyond the law to the hope of a new covenant, then why are there so many laws in the Pentateuch for the reader to contemplate? Here it is important to remember that the laws are not given directly to the reader in the book. Rather, the laws are given to ancient Israel at Mount Sinai. For example, the reader does not receive the Decalogue on tablets of stone but as part of the composition of the Pentateuch. Thus, the question is how

16. Horeb is the name that Deut 29:1 uses for Sinai.
17. See J. G. McConville, *Deuteronomy*, ApOTC 5 (Downers Grove, IL: IVP Academic, 2002), 37.

the laws function for readers of the book who have embraced the book's new covenant message. It is also important to remember that "Torah" is not "law" but "instruction." Therefore, even if readers are no longer bound to sin under the terms of the old covenant (Rom 6:14), the laws still have something to teach them, and the grace of the new covenant allows that teaching to be effective.

Theologians have historically attempted to explain the ongoing function of the law for Christians by dividing the laws into three categories: moral, civil, and ceremonial. The moral laws are the absolute, unchanging laws such as those found in the Decalogue. These laws still apply in the new covenant. Believers are not justified by the moral laws, but they are called to obey them, and their obedience to the moral laws demonstrates the authenticity of their faith. The civil laws are the laws intended to govern the theocracy of ancient Israel and as such they no longer apply outside that context. Likewise, the ceremonial laws such as those for the sacrifices and festivals no longer apply because Christ has been offered as the ultimate sacrifice.

The above division of laws is acceptable to a point, but it is important to recognize a couple of potential problems. First, this categorization of the laws is not something that comes from the author of the Pentateuch. It is something that comes from theologians in an effort to answer the question of what laws still need to be kept, but that is not the question that the author of the Pentateuch is necessarily seeking to answer. Second, once readers are told that they do not have to keep the civil laws and the ceremonial laws, they no longer bother to read them or to learn from them. This is a mistake. The fact that readers are not justified by these laws or required to keep them is not a reason to ignore what they have to teach. For example, even if something like disobedience to parents is no longer a capital offense (Exod 21:15, 17), the law still has something to teach readers about the seriousness of the offense.

The collections of law in the Pentateuch are neither comprehensive nor systematic, thus creating the need in later Jewish tradition for the so-called oral law. The representative selection of laws as they appear in the Pentateuch is not intended to function as a legal code of conduct in an actual community or society. Rather, the laws are designed to reveal the justice and wisdom of the lawgiver himself.[18] The exposition of the Torah found in the book of Deuteronomy (Deut 1:5) reveals that the Torah is

---

18. The Babylonian Code of Hammurabi has a similar function. See James B. Pritchard,

now "wisdom" (*hokmah*) for the reader of the Pentateuch (4:6).[19] Some of the laws even appear now as proverbial sayings in the wisdom literature (e.g., Deut 19:14; 27:17; Job 24:2; Prov 22:28; 23:10). Indeed, the purpose given for the regular reading of the Torah among future generations of the people of God is to learn the fear of the LORD (Deut 31:13), which is the very definition of wisdom in the biblical wisdom literature (Job 28:28; Prov 1:7; 9:10). Psalm 19:9 even adopts the phrase "the fear of the LORD" as one of several synonyms for the Torah.

While it is not possible here to show how the above framework informs reading and interpretation of every single law in the Pentateuch, it is possible to provide a few representative examples from the major collections. From the Decalogue and Covenant Code (Exod 20–24), the law that is likely to raise the most questions is the Sabbath law, the sign of the covenant (31:12–17). To begin, it is important to state that the Sabbath (the seventh day of the week) is not the same as the Lord's Day (the first day of the week), which is intended to commemorate the resurrection (Matt 28:1; 1 Cor 16:2; Rev 1:10). There are two different, yet related reasons given for the remembrance or observance of the Sabbath in Exodus 20:8–11 and the parallel text of Deuteronomy 5:12–15. In Exodus 20:8–11, the reason for the Sabbath comes from the creation account in Genesis 1:1–2:3: "For in six days the LORD made the sky and the land and the sea and all that is in them, and he rested on the seventh day. Therefore, the LORD blessed the day of the Sabbath and set it apart" (Exod 20:11). In Deuteronomy 5:12–15, the observance of the Sabbath recalls the exodus account in Exodus 14: "And you will remember that you were a slave in the land of Egypt, and the LORD your God brought you out of there with a mighty hand and an outstretched arm. Therefore, the LORD your God has commanded you to observe the day of the Sabbath" (Deut 5:15).[20]

The accounts of creation, flood, and exodus are all related by virtue of their common theme of the division of water to make dry land (Gen 1:9–10; 8:1–14; Exod 14:21–22). The creation account culminates with the

---

ed., *Ancient Near Eastern Texts Relating to the Old Testament*, 3rd. ed. (Princeton: Princeton University Press, 1969), 163–80.

19. See Kevin Chen, "Wisdom Is Worth a Thousand Laws: Legal Insufficiency and Exception as Intentional Compositional Strategy in the Pentateuch," in *Text and Canon: Essays in Honor of John H. Sailhamer*, ed. Robert L. Cole and Paul J. Kissling (Eugene, OR: Pickwick, 2017), 37–59.

20. See Brevard S. Childs, *The Book of Exodus: A Critical, Theological Commentary*, OTL (Louisville: Westminster John Knox, 1974), 417.

granting of rest to humanity in the land (see Tg. Neof. Gen 2:15: "And he gave him rest in the Garden of Eden to worship in the Torah and to keep its statutes"). Likewise, the ultimate goal of the exodus is to give the people rest in the land (Deut 3:20). The narrative of the conquest in the book of Joshua, however, is clear that Joshua was unable to grant that rest to the people (Josh 13:1; see also Judg 1:27–33; Heb 4:8), even though he was faithful to bring the people into the land (Josh 11:22–23; 21:43–45). Therefore, while acknowledging the spiritual rest that believers now have in Christ (Heb 4:3), the writer to the Hebrews says that a future rest still remains for the people of God (4:9)—a rest to be enjoyed in the messianic kingdom and the new creation. The reading of the instruction for the Sabbath thus continues to teach the new covenant believer by reminding him or her of the rest that was lost in the beginning and the rest that will be restored in the end. This connects the reader to a larger biblical-theological message of rest that is of much greater importance than a mere break from work on the seventh day of each week. Indeed, observance of the Sabbath is meaningless apart from an understanding of the theological significance attached to it by the biblical text. The "keeping" of the Sabbath now takes the form of reading about the Sabbath. It is not wrong to set aside the seventh day as a day of rest from work. It would only be wrong to assume the terms of the old covenant and to observe the Sabbath as a means of obtaining blessing.

Much like the Sabbath law, the instructions for the tabernacle in Exodus 25–31 now serve to point the reader both backward and forward. The continued existence of these instructions beyond the original construction of the tabernacle (Exod 35–40) naturally raises the question of their ongoing function within the composition of the Pentateuch. It is obviously not the role of the instructions to have readers construct a new tabernacle each time they read them. Rather, the instructions for the tabernacle deliberately follow the model of the creation account in Genesis 1:1–2:3 to show that the tabernacle is a temporary, movable sanctuary designed to remind readers of the original sanctuary in the Garden of Eden that was lost and is now in need of restoration (see Gen 3:22–24; Isa 51:3; Ezek 36:35). The instructions are given in the form of the LORD speaking seven times (Exod 25:1; 30:11, 17, 22, 34; 31:1, 12), culminating with the designation of the Sabbath as the sign of the covenant (31:12–17). This imitates the divine speech in the account of the preparation of the land of blessing in six days (Gen 1:3–31; cf. Ps 33:6) followed by the setting apart of the seventh day (Gen 2:1–3). Solomon's temple (1 Kgs 6–8) is a fixed, immovable structure that replaces the tabernacle and establishes the centralization of worship anticipated in Deuteronomy 12:5, yet it too is a temporary sanctuary (2 Kgs 25; Jer 52).

The so-called Second Temple does not measure up to the standard of Solomon's temple (Hag 2:3; Zech 4:10; Ezra 3:12). The glory of the LORD never appears in the Second Temple as it does in the tabernacle (Exod 40:34–35) and in Solomon's temple (1 Kgs 8:10–11; see also Isa 6:3–4; 11:9; Hab 2:14). This glory will return in the future "temple" (Ezek 43:4–5; Hag 2:9; Rev 21:22–23). Ezekiel's vision of a new temple (Ezek 40–48) is not a prediction of a new, separable structure but a priest's way of envisioning future and final restoration for the people of God (see Ezek 1:3). The new "temple" is not another temporary sanctuary but a return to the unbroken fellowship with God enjoyed in the Garden of Eden where the "sanctuary" was all that there was (Isa 51:3; Ezek 36:35): "And a temple I did not see in it, for the Lord God Almighty is its temple, and the Lamb" (Rev 21:22; cf. Isa 66:1–2; Acts 7:44–50). The most important feature of this future sanctuary is the presence of God with his people (Ezek 48:35b; Rev 21:3; cf. Exod 29:45–46). The apostle Paul also speaks of the spiritual temple of the individual believer's body (1 Cor 6:19; cf. John 2:19) and the spiritual temple of the church (1 Cor 3:16; 2 Cor 6:16; Eph 2:21).

The absence of a legitimate tabernacle or temple presses the reader to consider the ongoing function of the instructions for sacrifices in the Priestly Code (Lev 1–7). According to the Babylonian Talmud (b. Menaḥ. 110a), whoever is busy or occupied with the Torah does not need to bring a burnt offering, sin offering, grain offering, or guilt offering. That is, the reading and study of the instructions themselves in the text of the Torah takes the place of offering the sacrifices. In Christian tradition, Christ has made the final sacrifice once and for all (Heb 10:11–14), yet the instructions in Leviticus 1–7 still have something to teach the Christian reader. For example, the substitutionary sacrifice of the messianic servant of the LORD in Isaiah's prophecy (Isa 53:10) draws from the language of Leviticus 5 to describe the servant's offering of himself as a "guilt offering." Without the conceptual framework provided by the sacrificial laws, the sacrifice of Christ would make little sense. It is easy to take the meaning of Christ's sacrifice for granted now, but it is important to recognize that this meaning is not self-evident apart from the preparation provided by the sacrificial system. For instance, when the gospel is taken to a place where the people have never read the Bible, it is not immediately intelligible to them that God would send his Son to die for their sins.

The instruction for the individual sin offering in Leviticus 4:27–31 illustrates well how this section of the law continues to inform the Christian reader. According to this instruction, when someone commits a sin unwittingly and then becomes aware of it, that person must bring an unblemished female goat as a sin offering (4:27–28). The worshiper then identifies with the animal as his substitute by placing his hand on its head before slaughtering it (4:29). Once the priest has put some of the animal's blood on the horns of the altar and poured out the rest at the base of the altar (4:30), he removes the fat and makes the offering go up in smoke on the altar as a "soothing aroma" to the LORD (4:31a). This indicates that the offering satisfies the LORD by appeasing his wrath on behalf of the worshiper. Thus, the priest "covers" the worshiper, and the worshiper receives forgiveness for his sin (4:31b). This entire process may be characterized as atonement or reconciliation. The apostle Paul adopts the language of Leviticus 4 to describe Christ's sacrifice: "He made him who did not know sin a sin offering for us that we might be the righteousness of God in him" (2 Cor 5:21). This verse is often translated to say that Christ was made sin for us, which makes very little sense. The Greek term *hamartia*, which can mean "sin" or "sin offering," is the same word used to translate *hatta'th* (sin offering) in LXX Leviticus 4 (see, e.g., LXX Lev 4:3). The righteousness that God requires is credited to believers by faith in the finished work of Christ on their behalf. Of course, there are also important differences between Christ's sacrifice and the sacrifices of the old covenant. Christ's sacrifice established a new covenant and paid for all sins. The sacrifices of the old covenant presupposed that a covenant relationship was already in place and only appeased God for individual sins.

The food laws in Leviticus 11 (see also Deut 14:3–21) constitute another set of instructions in the Priestly Code that prove to be problematic for readers. Some interpreters believe that the continuing validity of these laws lies in the general healthiness of the prescribed diet, but it is evident from the fine detail of the instructions and from the explanation provided at the conclusion of Leviticus 11 that the food laws transcend concern about healthy eating habits. The purification laws in general show that God's involvement in the life of the community of his people extends to every area. The LORD explains, "For I am the LORD who brought you up out of the land of Egypt to be your God; and you will be holy, for I am holy [*ki qadosh 'ani*]" (Lev 11:45; cf. Lev 11:44; 19:2; 20:7). That is, the LORD set himself apart from the gods of the nations when he delivered his people in the exodus from Egypt (Exod 12:12; Num 33:4). Therefore, his people are to be set apart from the peoples of the nations in every way. Likewise, God has set apart a people to himself through Christ in the new exodus (Num 23:22; 24:8; Hos 11:1, 5, 11; Matt 2:13–15). Consider 1 Peter 1:15–16: "But, like the Holy One who called you, be holy yourselves in all of your conduct, for it is written, 'You will be holy, for I am holy.'" Here Peter plays with two similar Hebrew expressions: (1) "like the Holy One [*kaqqadosh*] who called you"; and (2) "You will be holy, for I am holy [*ki qadosh 'ani*]."

The last major collection of laws (not counting Deut 12–26) is the Holiness Code in Leviticus 17–27. For the purposes of the present discussion, two sets of instructions have been chosen from this section to illustrate how the laws continue to teach readers who are no longer under the terms of the old covenant. The prohibitions against various types of sexual immorality in Leviticus 18 are not included in the following discussion, but a brief note about these is in order here. Modern readers who feel driven by the trends of contemporary culture are tempted to say that such prohibitions no longer apply to those who are new covenant believers, but it is important to remember that the prohibitions are rooted in the created order (Gen 1–2) and thus transcend the confines of any temporal covenant (see also Song of Songs).

The first set of instructions from the Holiness Code to be discussed here is that given for the three major festivals in Leviticus 23: Passover, the Feast of Weeks (or Pentecost), and the Feast of Tabernacles (see also Exod 23:14–19; 34:18–26; Deut 16). Each of these festivals has an agricultural significance (Passover: firstfruits; Pentecost: spring harvest; Tabernacles: fall harvest) and also a religious significance (Passover: exodus; Pentecost: the giving of the law; Tabernacles: the provision in the wilderness). The theological significance of these festivals continues to resonate with those who read about them or observe them. There is certainly nothing wrong with celebrating these festivals as long as their meaning is understood and as long as they are not viewed as requirements for justification or blessing. They can be occasions to remember the work of God and to worship him. This is somewhat comparable to Christian celebrations of Christmas and Easter, neither of which are commanded in Scripture as holidays to be observed. Nevertheless, the Christian tradition has made these occasions into opportunities to remember the work of God and to worship him.

The biblical authors have already taken the opportunity to assign ongoing significance to the major festivals. For instance, Christ is now the Passover lamb (John 1:29, 36; 1 Cor 5:7; 1 Pet 1:19; Rev 5:6; see also Gen 22:8, 13; 44:33; 49:8–12; Exod 12:3, 46; Isa 53:4–7, 10–12; Ps 22:17; John 19:24, 37), and the Feast of Tabernacles has an important role to play in the eschaton (Zech 14:16–19; see also Neh 8–9; John 7). Perhaps the most outstanding example is the exchange of the giving of the law for the giving of the Spirit at Pentecost. This exchange is already set up within the composition of the Pentateuch itself. The narrative of the provision of manna and quail in Exodus 16 prior to the account of the people's arrival at Sinai finds a close parallel in Numbers 11 after their departure from Sinai. Whereas the story in Exodus 16 anticipates the Sabbath law (16:25–30), which, as the sign of the old covenant (31:12–17), represents the giving of the law in general, the story in Numbers 11 highlights the gift of the Spirit to help Moses with his leadership responsibilities (11:17, 29). Ezra's exposition of the Torah in Nehemiah 8–9 shows a keen awareness of the relationship between these two accounts:

Table 4: Ezra's Exposition of the Torah

Pillars of cloud and fire (Neh 9:12)	Pillars of cloud and fire (Neh 9:19)
Gift of the Law (Neh 9:13–14)	*Gift of the Spirit (Neh 9:20a)*
Bread and water (Neh 9:15a)	Bread and water (Neh 9:20b–23)
Land possession (Neh 9:15b)	Land possession (Neh 9:24–25)
Rebellion (Neh 9:16–18)	Rebellion (Neh 9:26–31)

This exposition features two parallel sequences (Neh 9:12–18 and 9:19–31) in which the only substantial difference is the exchange of the gift of the law for the gift of the Spirit. This exchange has also not gone unnoticed by the New Testament authors. The account of the giving of Spirit in Acts 2 is set during the Pentecost festival, which is the traditional date for the giving of the law at Sinai (Exod 19).[21]

---

21. See James C. VanderKam, "The Festival of Weeks and the Story of Pentecost in Acts 2," in *From Prophecy to Testament: The Function of the Old Testament in the New*, ed. Craig A. Evans (Peabody, MA: Hendrickson, 2004), 185–205. See also John 6:31–33, 63; Rom 7:6; 8:4; 2 Cor 3:6.

The second set of instructions from the Holiness Code to be discussed here, and the final example overall from the law, is the instruction for tithing in Leviticus 27:30–34 (see also Deut 14:22–29). There is often an appeal to this instruction in the context of the local church for a general guiding principle of giving 10 percent of personal income to the ministry of the church. Despite the practical value of this principle, it must be admitted that it has very little to do with the actual instruction for tithing provided in the Pentateuch, which is not about monetary contributions for paid staff or other budget needs but about the giving of produce and livestock to support the priestly tribe of Levi and others in need. Furthermore, the principle runs the risk of becoming perceived as a biblical mandate that must be kept in order to obtain blessing from God. Indeed, it is not uncommon for pastors to appeal to the text of Malachi 3:6–12 to make such a requirement explicit, but this is an unwarranted use of the biblical text that disregards the context of the passage.

> It is a blatant misuse of Malachi 3:6–12 to demand a tenth of monetary income from members of the new covenant community to support the ministry of the local church. The pattern of disobedience-curse and obedience-blessing clearly presupposes the context of the old covenant (Lev. 26; Deut. 28). The disputations of the book of Malachi are designed to highlight the continued failure of the postexilic community under the terms of the old covenant. This ultimately points beyond that covenant to the need for a new covenant relationship. The standard for giving in the new covenant is not the tithing of produce for Levites. The standard for giving in the new covenant is the sacrificial death of Jesus Christ on the cross (2 Cor. 8:1–15). In other words, the standard for giving under the old covenant is too low for the new covenant. The new covenant believer must lay down his or her entire life for the sake of the gospel. This includes not only possessions but also time, talents, abilities, spiritual gifts, etc. Such giving is voluntary giving under the guidance of the Holy Spirit (see, e.g., Exod. 35:4–36:7). Thus, pastors would do well to focus more on regenerate church membership than on specific requirements for giving. The result will be an overabundance of gospel ministry rather than a mere balanced budget.[22]

22. Michael B. Shepherd, *A Commentary on the Book of the Twelve: The Minor Prophets*, KEL (Grand Rapids: Kregel Academic, 2018), 502.

There is much more to be said about the composition of the Pentateuch, but the above discussion suffices to provide a general framework for interpreting the macrostructure. The relationship between the narrative blocks and the poetic units helps readers to see the messianic and eschatological message of the book, while the relationship between the narratives and laws helps them to see how the laws continue to teach new covenant believers. Now we turn to the composition of the Former Prophets.

THE FORMER PROPHETS

The Former Prophets—Joshua, Judges, Samuel (1–2 Samuel), and Kings (1–2 Kings)—are known in English translation tradition as the historical books, but in the Hebrew Bible they are prophetic books. In Greek translation tradition, the books of Samuel and Kings are known as a single four-part work called 1–4 Kingdoms. The books of the Former Prophets are prophetic books in part because the narratives of these books feature prophets such as Samuel, Elijah, and Elisha, but also because these books depend heavily upon the book of Moses the prophet (i.e., the Pentateuch) and thus have a prophetic message for their readers. The relationship between the Former Prophets and the Pentateuch has been variously understood in the era of modern biblical scholarship. During the latter part of the nineteenth century and the first part of the twentieth century, the prevailing opinion was that the supposed hypothetical sources of the Pentateuch determined by historical-critical scholars continued into the book of Joshua, thus forming a Hexateuch or six-part book (see, e.g., the works of Julius Wellhausen and Gerhard von Rad). This view eventually developed into a conception of the Pentateuch and the Former Prophets as a single, nine-part book (the Enneateuch). The fundamental problem with these combinations, however, is that the macrolevel compositional structures in the Pentateuch (such as the use of large poetic units to interpret the narratives that precede them) do not continue into the book of Joshua. The seam that connects the end of the Pentateuch to the beginning of the Prophets (Deut 34:5–Josh 1:9) is not book-level composition but canon-level composition. It corresponds to the seam that connects the end of the Prophets to the beginning of the Writings (Mal 3:22–24; Pss 1–2). Furthermore, the Former Prophets have their own structural integrity.

Martin Noth's seminal work, *The Deuteronomistic History*, which was originally published in German in 1943, marked a seismic shift in the study of the Former Prophets. Noth dispensed with the idea of a Hexateuch and argued instead for a Tetrateuch (Genesis–Numbers). According to Noth, the book of Deuteronomy was the beginning of a new literary complex that included both Deuteronomy and the Former Prophets. For Noth, this explained why the distinctive language and theology of Deuteronomy recurred throughout the Former Prophets. Noth's most important contribution was his idea that a single composer was ultimately responsible for this Deuteronomistic History: "In particular, at all the important points in the course of the history, Dtr. [the Deuteronomist] brings forward the leading personages with a speech, long or short which looks forward and backward in an attempt to interpret the course of events, and draws the relevant practical conclusions about what people should do."[23] These speeches follow the model set forth by Moses in Deuteronomy 31 and include those of Joshua (Josh 23–24), Samuel (1 Sam 12), and Solomon (1 Kgs 8).

The critical error in Noth's theory was the separation of Deuteronomy from Genesis–Numbers, which was unprecedented in the history of interpretation. There are, in fact, other ways to explain why Deuteronomy has been so influential for the Former Prophets and for other books like the book of Jeremiah. The introduction to Deuteronomy presents the book as Moses's exposition of the Torah (Deut 1:5). It is the author's own commentary on the preceding narratives and laws of Genesis–Numbers. This commentary forms an integral part of the Pentateuch and provides an interpretive lens through which the entire composition is designed to be read. Thus, any subsequent literary work based upon the message of the Pentateuch is naturally influenced by the language and theology of Deuteronomy.

Nevertheless, Noth's observations about the unity of the Deuteronomistic History are still valid for the Former Prophets. Much the same way that the books of Genesis–Deuteronomy form a single composition, so the books of Joshua, Judges, 1–2 Samuel, and 1–2 Kings constitute a unified literary work. These books draw from a wide variety of sources from different times and places (e.g., Josh 10:13; 2 Sam 1:18; 1 Kgs 11:41; 14:19, 29),[24]

---

23. Martin Noth, *The Deuteronomistic History* (Sheffield: JSOT, 1981), 5.

24. The Chronicler, who follows Samuel-Kings very closely, attributes his sources to the prophets (e.g., 1 Chr 29:29; 2 Chr 9:29; 12:15; 13:22; et al.).

yet the composer has brought this material together to communicate a coherent theological message.[25] He has successfully done this by inserting speeches from his major characters (Josh 24; 1 Sam 12; 1 Kgs 8) and reflections from his narrator (Judg 2; 2 Kgs 17) at strategic junctures in the composition in order to guide the reader to a proper understanding of the stories. These speeches and reflections function in a manner very similar to way the poems of the Pentateuch serve to punctuate and interpret the narratives that precede them. The composer has also inserted texts along the seams of the books in order to connect them to one another.

Table 5: The Composition of the Former Prophets

	Joshua	*Judges*	*Samuel*	*Kings*
Speeches and reflections	Josh 24:1–15 (Conquest)	Judg 2:11–23 (Rebellion)	1 Sam 12 (Monarchy)	1 Kgs 8 (Temple); 2 Kgs 17 (Exile)
Seams	Josh 24:28–33 (LXX); Judg 1:1, 27–33; 2:6–10	Judg 17:1, 6; 18:1; 19:1; 21:25; 1 Sam 1:1; 2:10	2 Sam 9–20; 1 Kgs 1:1–2:11	

These compositional features work together to highlight the faithfulness of God and the infidelity of the people and to point the reader beyond the failure of the people under the old covenant to the hope of one who will come in fulfillment of the covenant with David (2 Sam 7) and in fulfillment of the messianic prophecies found in the poems of the Pentateuch.

Joshua 1 sets the stage not only for the book of Joshua but also for the Former Prophets. The LORD instructs Joshua to "murmur" in the book of the Torah (i.e., the Pentateuch) day and night (Josh 1:8). Joshua's speech in Joshua 24:1–15 and the speeches of Samuel (1 Sam 12) and Solomon (1 Kgs 8) are the products of such reading and study in Moses's book. In Joshua 1:17, the people identify Joshua as a new Moses (see Num 27:20; Deut 34:9). This same identification is later made by the LORD (Josh 3:7) and by the narrator (Josh 4:14). The comparison of Joshua to Moses drives

---

25. This composer lived or was still alive at a time well after the Babylonian invasion of Jerusalem (see 2 Kgs 25:27–30). Jewish tradition attributed the book of Kings, the final part of the Former Prophets, to the prophet Jeremiah (b. B. Bat. 15a; see 2 Kgs 25 and Jer 52).

much of the book's narrative content wherein Joshua essentially relives the stories about Moses in the Pentateuch.

Table 6: Joshua, the New Moses

	Moses	*Joshua*
Presence of God	Exod 3:12	Deut 31:23; Josh 1:9
Sending of spies	Num 13	Josh 2
Exodus	Exod 14	Josh 3
Circumcision and Passover	Exod 4:24–26; 12	Josh 5:1–12
Angel encounter	Exod 3:1–5	Josh 5:13–15
Staff/javelin in battle	Exod 17:8–13	Josh 8:18
Conquest	Num 21; Josh 13	Josh 14
Daughters of Zelophehad	Num 27; 36	Josh 17
Cities of refuge, Levites	Num 35; Deut 19:1–13	Josh 20–21
Reuben, Gad, Manasseh	Num 32	Josh 22
Doubt the people	Deut 31:16, 29	Josh 24:19–20
Servant of the LORD	Deut 34:5; Josh 1:1	Josh 24:29

The two halves of the book of Joshua, which is basically a sequel to the book of Moses, focus on the conquest and possession of the land (Josh 1–12) and on the distribution of the land to the tribes (13–22). The incomplete nature of the conquest is highlighted by Joshua 11:22b; 13:1; 16:10; 17:13 (see also Judg 1:27–33; Heb 4:8–9), although it is stressed that God was faithful to bring the people into the land (Josh 11:23; 21:43–45; 23:14). The speeches of Joshua in chapters 23–24 call for fidelity to the LORD (Josh 23:6–8, 16; cf. Deut 13) and point to his enduring faithfulness to the people (Josh 24). Joshua 24:1–15 essentially rehearses the narrative of the Pentateuch (cf. Deut 6:20–25; 26:5–9; 31:9–13; 32) and thus sets the conquest firmly within the framework of the textual world established by Moses's book. It is within this context that Joshua applies the text and invites the people to fear the LORD (Josh 24:14–15; cf. Deut 31:13), yet he knows that the LORD has not yet given the people a heart to do so (Josh 24:19–20; see Deut 29:4; 31:16, 29).

The seam that connects Joshua to Judges appears to be based in part on the way the end of Genesis connects to the beginning of Exodus:

Genesis-Exodus

And he acquired the portion of the field where he pitched his tent from the sons of Hamor, the father of Shechem, for one hundred units (Gen 33:19). "And I, I have given to you one portion [*shekhem*] above your brothers, which I took from the Amorites with my sword and with my bow" (Gen 48:22). And Joseph said to his brothers, "I am dying. And as for God, he will surely visit you and bring you up from this land to the land that he swore to Abraham, Isaac, and Jacob." And Joseph made the sons of Israel swear, "God will surely visit you, and you will bring up my bones from here." And Joseph died at the age of 110 (Gen 50:24–26a).	*And a new king arose over Egypt who did not know Joseph* (Exod 1:8). And Moses took the bones of Joseph with him, for he had indeed made the sons of Israel swear, "God will surely visit you, and you will bring up my bones from here with you" (Exod 13:19).

Joshua-Judges

And Joshua sent the people each to his inheritance. After these things, Joshua the son of Nun, the servant of the Lord, died at the age of 110. And they buried him in the border of his inheritance, in Timnath Serah, which was in the hill country of Ephraim, north of Mt. Gaash. And Israel served the Lord all the days of Joshua and all the days of the elders who prolonged days after Joshua and who knew all the work of the Lord that he did for Israel. And as for the bones of Joseph that the sons of Israel brought up out of Egypt, they buried them in Shechem in the portion of the field that Jacob acquired from the sons of Hamor, the father of Shechem, for one hundred units (Josh 24:28–32a).	And Joshua sent the people away, and the sons of Israel went each to his inheritance to possess. And the people served the Lord all the days of Joshua and all the days of the elders who prolonged days after Joshua, those who saw all the great work of the Lord that he did for Israel. And Joshua the son of Nun, the servant of the Lord, died at the age of 110. And they buried him in the border of his inheritance, in Timnath Serah, in the hill country of Ephraim, north of Mt. Gaash. And all that generation was gathered to its fathers, too. *And another generation arose after them who did not know the Lord or the work that he did for Israel* (Judg 2:6–10).

There is also a longer version of Joshua 24:33 preserved in the Old Greek of Joshua that shows how the ending of the book once connected directly to the story about Ehud in Judges 3:12–30:

> And it happened after these things that Eleazar son of Aaron, the high priest, died and was buried in Gabaath of Phinees his son, which he gave him in Mount Ephraim. On that day the sons of Israel took the ark of God and carried it around in their midst. And Phinees served as priest in the place of Eleazar his father until he died, and he was interred in Gabaath, which was his own. And the sons of Israel departed each to their place and to their own city. And the sons of Israel worshiped Astarte and Astaroth and the gods of the nations round about them. And the Lord delivered them into the hands of Eglom, the king of Moab, and he dominated them eighteen years. (NETS)

This witness reflects a Hebrew source that was subsequently deleted after the addition of Judges 1:1–3:11 between Joshua 24:33 and Judges 3:12.[26] The added material in Judges 1:1–3:11 deliberately refers the reader back to the account of Joshua's death in Joshua 24:28–32 (see Judg 1:1; 2:6–10) and to the theme of the incomplete conquest in Joshua 11:22b; 13:1; 16:10; 17:13 (see Judg 1:27–33).[27] Thus, the original connection between Joshua and Judges attested by Joshua 24:33 (LXX) and Judges 3:12–30 has been replaced by other connections that link the two books together.

The added material in Judges 1:1–3:11 also features a brief rehearsal of the biblical narrative (Judg 2:1–5; cf. Josh 24:1–15; Judg 6:7–10; 10:11–16) and a reflection from the narrator in Judges 2:11–23 that proves that Joshua's doubts about the people were justified (see Josh 24:19–20) and lays out the pattern of the cycle of rebellion that will characterize each of the narratives about the six major judges in Judges 3:7–16:31 (Othniel, Ehud, Deborah, Gideon, Jephthah, and Samson): (1) evil (idolatry), (2) divine punishment (foreign oppression), (3) outcry of the people, (4) deliverance via a judge empowered by God's Spirit, (5) rest, and (6) repeat.[28] Thus, Judges 2:11–23 sets the trajectory for the main body of the book of Judges and maintains the contrast between God's faithfulness and the people's infidelity.

---

26. See Emanuel Tov, *Textual Criticism of the Hebrew Bible*, 3rd ed. (Minneapolis: Fortress, 2012), 298; A. Rofé, "The End of the Book of Joshua according to the Septuagint," *Hen* 4 (1982): 17–36.

27. According to Josh 1:1–2, leadership of the people is now no longer entrusted to an individual like Moses or Joshua but to a tribe—the tribe of Judah. This decision passes over the other major contender for leadership—the tribe of Ephraim—and creates a tension that surfaces in the later narratives (see Judg 8:1–3; 12:1–7). It also anticipates the later division of the kingdom into north (Ephraim) and south (Judah).

28. The six minor judges who are mentioned only briefly are Shamgar, Tola, Jair, Ibzan, Elon, and Abdon.

The conclusion to the book of Judges breaks away from the pattern of Judges 3:7–16:31 to show the culmination of Israel's cycle of rebellion, even though the material in this section is not necessarily in chronological order (see the reference to Eleazar's son Phineas in Judg 20:28; cf. LXX Josh 24:33). Israel has become the new Sodom and Gomorrah—the gold standard of wickedness (see the stories in Gen 19 and Judg 19). The refrain in Judges 17:6; 18:1; 19:1; 21:25 sums up both the problem and the solution and ultimately anticipates the central theme of Samuel-Kings, which is the coming of the ideal king (1 Sam 2:10): "In those days, there was no king in Israel. Each person did what was right in his own eyes" (cf. Deut 12:8).[29] This reflects the perspective of the later composer of the Former Prophets who knows about the establishment of the monarchy in Israel, but it becomes apparent from Samuel-Kings that he does not see the solution to Israel's problem in the mere establishment of a monarchy. Rather, his hope lies in the one coming in fulfillment of the Pentateuch's prophecies (Gen 49:8–12; Num 24:7–9, 17) and in fulfillment of the covenant with David (2 Sam 7).

The narratives of the book of Samuel hang upon a carefully crafted framework of poetic units that serve to direct the reader to the hope of the coming king (1 Sam 2:1–10; 2 Sam 1:17–27; 22:1–23:7). Hannah's prayer in 1 Samuel 2:1–10 looks beyond her immediate circumstances (see 1 Sam 1) to a time when the LORD will give strength to his king and exalt the horn of his anointed one (2:10b).[30] The poem's dependence upon the poetry of the Pentateuch (see, e.g., 1 Sam 2:2, 6 [Deut 32:39] and 1 Sam 2:10b [Num 24:7b]) positions Hannah as one who expects not a king like the other nations have but the messianic king revealed in her Bible. Thus, when the reader sees the people's request for an ordinary king in 1 Samuel 8:5, 20 (cf. Deut 17:14–20), it is understandable that such a request is not good in the view of Samuel and the LORD (1 Sam 8:6–8). Samuel's speech in 1 Samuel 12 goes back through the narrative of the Pentateuch (cf. Josh 24:1–15) and orients the recent establishment of the monarchy to it. He expresses grave doubts about the sustainability of the current arrangement (1 Sam 12:13–15, 25; cf. Josh 24:19–20). God has given the

29. There is also a surface-level connection in the series of narratives about a man from Ephraim (Judg 17:1; 19:1; 1 Sam 1:1).

30. See S. R. Driver, *Notes on the Hebrew Text and the Topography of the Books of Samuel*, 2nd ed. (Oxford: Oxford University Press, 1912), 28; Emanuel Tov, *The Greek and Hebrew Bible: Collected Essays on the Septuagint*, VTSup 72 (Atlanta: Society of Biblical Literature, 2006), 433–55.

people what they want as a kind of judgment, and the subsequent failures of Saul in 1 Samuel 13 and 15 show that there must be a better way.

When the reader finally meets David in 1 Samuel 16, the initial impression is that this must be the long-awaited king from the tribe of Judah prophesied in Genesis 49:8–12. This would seem to be confirmed by the story of David and Goliath (1 Sam 17), which puts on full display the kind of heart that David has.[31] Furthermore, despite having to flee from Saul, David's lament for Saul and Jonathan in the poem of 2 Samuel 1:17–27 shows his deep and abiding respect for the office of the LORD's anointed king (see 1 Sam 24:7; 26:9, 11). Nevertheless, the covenant with David in 2 Samuel 7 reveals that the responsibility of building the temple and reigning over an everlasting kingdom will fall not to David but to a descendant of David (2 Sam 7:12–16). While the book of Kings presents a number of candidates for this role, especially Solomon (1 Kgs 1–11), it becomes clear by the end of the account of the monarchy that the one of whom the covenant with David speaks is still to come (see Zech 6:12–13).

The failure of David and its consequences in 2 Samuel 11–18 naturally raise some questions for the reader. Is the covenant with David still intact? Is there still hope in an ideal son of David? The appendix in 2 Samuel 21–24 is designed to reassure the reader that David's failure has not altered the covenant relationship. The poems of 2 Samuel 22 and 23:1–7 hearken back to Hannah's prayer (2 Sam 22:3, 14, 28, 32; cf. 1 Sam 2:1–2, 7–8, 10) and to the terms of the covenant with David (2 Sam 22:51; 23:1–5; cf. 2 Sam 7:12–16). Moreover, in the final story of 2 Samuel 24, David's insistence upon not taking what does not belong to him amounts to a reversal of his earlier failure when he took Uriah's wife, Bathsheba, who did not belong to him (24:24; cf. 2 Sam 23:17).

The so-called Succession Narrative of 2 Samuel 9–20 continues directly into the account of David's last days and the transferal of power to his son Solomon (1 Kgs 1:1–2:11). When Solomon builds the temple and reigns over a peaceful and prosperous kingdom, he appears on the surface to be the fulfillment of the covenant with David (2 Sam 7:12–16), but it soon

---

31. The story of 1 Sam 17, which shows the uniqueness of David's heart (1 Sam 13:14; 16:7) is comparable to Gen 22, which demonstrates Abraham's faith (Gen 15:6; see Jas 2:21–24), and 1 Kgs 3:16–28, which demonstrates Solomon's wisdom (1 Kgs 3:12). These stories highlight the primary qualities for which the major characters in the narratives are known. For a discussion of the two editions of 1 Sam 17 found in the MT and the LXX, see Michael B. Shepherd, *Textuality and the Bible* (Eugene, OR: Wipf & Stock, 2016), 44–60.

becomes apparent that he is only a foil for one who is yet to come. His kingdom does not last (1 Kgs 11–12). Indeed, Solomon's own temple dedication speech in 1 Kings 8:46–50 anticipates the prospect of exile. This not only forecasts the way that the book of Kings ends (2 Kgs 25) but also echoes the very sentiment expressed in Moses's book (Deut 28:64–68; 29:28). When the narrator looks back over the history of the divided kingdom (Israel and Judah), he provides a theological interpretation for the downfall of the northern kingdom at the hands of the Assyrians (2 Kgs 17:7–23) and expects the southern kingdom eventually to fall for much the same reason (17:19; 18–25). The people have rejected the Torah sent to them via the prophets and have lacked faith in the LORD their God. They have chosen instead to worship other gods and must now face the consequences of breaking the covenant (17:13–16).

After the account of the Babylonian invasion of Judah and Jerusalem in 2 Kings 25, including the destruction of the temple and the exile of the people, there is a brief narrative about King Jehoiachin still alive in Babylon years later (25:27–30). This is the way the book of Kings and the Former Prophets conclude. On the one hand, it shows the end result of the people's inability to live under the terms of the Sinai covenant and paints a pitiful picture of the surviving remnant of the Davidic monarchy sitting in exile. On the other hand, there is now the prospect of a new covenant relationship and the realization that the one of whom the covenant with David speaks has yet to appear on the scene. This is precisely the perspective that dominates the pages of the Latter Prophets. The book of Jeremiah, for example, concludes with a parallel version of 2 Kings 25 in Jeremiah 52. Much the same way that 2 Kings 25:27–30 depends upon the reader's knowledge of the covenant with David (2 Sam 7:12–16), so Jeremiah 52:31–34 depends upon the reader's knowledge of the messianic prophecy in Jeremiah 23:5–6, which is based upon the covenant with David.

THE LATTER PROPHETS

The books of the Latter Prophets—Isaiah, Jeremiah, Ezekiel, and the Twelve (Hosea–Malachi)—present unique challenges to readers of the Bible. While the book of Kings provides a kind of narrative context for these prophets and their prophecies, the books themselves do not have an overarching storyline nor do they maintain a consistent chronology of events in their presentation. This has suggested to many modern readers that these books are little more than collections of the prophets' messages. According to this view, each book is merely a deposit of transcripts of messages once delivered orally to an audience in the past. The written record of these messages serves as a window into the life and times of the prophet in his historical context. More recent scholarship, however, has come to appreciate the books of the Latter Prophets as literary works in their own right.[32] The books do more than simply document the past. Rather, they have a compositional strategy that makes the past speak to the present and the future.[33]

Recognition of the books of the Latter Prophets as literary phenomena requires an ability to identify and understand the compositional techniques employed therein. There are five techniques that readers will need to know in order to navigate the macrostructures of these texts: (1) use of programmatic passages, (2) framing, (3) parallel structuring, (4) repetition, and (5) seam work. These techniques are not unique to the Latter Prophets, but knowledge of them is indispensable for readers encountering the otherwise seemingly strange arrangement of the prophetic literature. The following discussion introduces the different techniques and provides examples of them in the Latter Prophets. A better grasp of these techniques will equip readers to be more competent interpreters of these texts.

Programmatic Passages

Each of the books of the Latter Prophets has what may be called a programmatic passage. A programmatic passage is a text that stands at or near the beginning of a book and sets the agenda for the book as a whole. It is the literary equivalent of a musical overture. The readers' task is to keep this passage in mind as they read the book and to relate each of the parts

---

32. See Michael H. Floyd, "New Form Criticism and Beyond: The Historicity of Prophetic Literature Revisited," in *The Book of the Twelve and the New Form Criticism*, ed. Mark J. Boda, Michael H. Floyd, and Colin M. Toffelmire, ANEM 10 (Atlanta: Society of Biblical Literature, 2015), 24, 30.

33. See Joseph Blenkinsopp, *Prophecy and Canon: A Contribution to the Study of Jewish Origins* (Notre Dame: University of Notre Dame Press, 1977), 129; William M. Schniedewind, *The Word of God in Transition: From Prophet to Exegete in the Second Temple Period*, JSOTSup 197 (Sheffield: Sheffield Academic, 1995), 11; Karel van der Toorn, *Scribal Culture and the Making of the Hebrew Bible* (Cambridge: Harvard University Press, 2007), 107; Christopher Nihan, "The 'Prophets' as Scriptural Collection and Scriptural Prophecy during the Second Temple Period," in *Writing the Bible: Scribes, Scribalism and Script*, ed. Philip R. Davies and Thomas Römer (Durham: Acumen, 2013), 67–85.

of the book to the program set forth at the beginning. If any part of the book is interpreted in a way that is at odds with the programmatic passage, then the readers know that they must go back to the drawing board. In this manner programmatic passages help to keep readers on course to achieve the ultimate goal of understanding the theological message that the author is trying to communicate. Programmatic passages are similar in this regard to purpose statements, which may appear either at the beginning (e.g., Luke 1:1–4) or at the end (e.g., Deut 31:13; John 20:30–31; 1 John 5:13) of a book.

The programmatic passage for the book of Isaiah is Isaiah 2:1–5 (cf. Mic 4:1–5). This passage immediately follows the introduction to the book in chapter 1, which indicates that the content of the book is the prophetic vision of Isaiah (Isa 1:1) and establishes the two great overarching themes of the prophetic literature—judgment (1:2–17) and restoration (1:18–31). Isaiah 2:1–5 features the first subheading of the book (2:1; cf. Isa 13:1) and then proceeds to lay out the three core elements of the book's message.

First, the book is not primarily about the past but about what will happen "in the end of days" (*be'aharith hayyamim*) (2:2). This is the same phrase from the poems of the Pentateuch (Gen 49:1; Num 24:14; Deut 31:29), and it signals to the readers that they should expect to find in the text of this book a message about the same Messiah and messianic kingdom revealed in those poems (see Gen 49:8–12; Num 24:7–9, 17). This occurs, for instance, in Isaiah 11:1–10 and in numerous other passages throughout the book. The prophecy of Isaiah 11:1–10 takes up not only the prophecy of the king from the tribe of Judah in Genesis 49:8–12 but also that of the words of the covenant with David spoken through the prophet Nathan (2 Sam 7:12–16).

Second, the image of all the nations coming to the all-important Mount Zion in the last days to learn the Torah and the prophetic word of the LORD from God himself indicates that the book is not only for Israel but also for the Gentiles (Isa 2:2–3; cf. Isa 1:10; 8:16, 20). This is a very pervasive feature of the book that extends from the nations corpus in Isaiah 13–23, wherein the reader finds not only words of judgment for the nations but also words of salvation (e.g., 19:16–25), to the image of all the nations coming to the great feast on Mount Zion, where there will be no more death and no more tears (25:6–9; cf. Rev 21:4), and finally to the concluding passage of the book of Isaiah (Isa 66:18–24), which gives a picture of all the nations and Israel coming to the new Jerusalem to enjoy the new creation together (see 65:17–25). According to Isaiah 11:10, the nations will seek the Messiah (cf.

Isa 66:19; Hos 3:5; Amos 9:12; Acts 15:17). The messianic servant of the LORD will be a light to the nations (Isa 42:6; 49:6).

Third, there will be justice and peace in the last days (Isa 2:4; cf. Joel 3:10).[34] These are the hallmarks of the Messiah and his kingdom not only in the book of Isaiah (e.g., Isa 9:6–7; 11:1–10; 42:1–4) but also in the Latter Prophets generally (e.g., Jer 23:5–6; Mic 5:5a; Zech 9:9–10; see also Ps 72).[35] Thus, the house of Jacob is called to walk in the light of the Torah of the LORD and its message of wisdom and salvation in Christ (Isa 2:5; cf. Ps 119:105; Prov 6:23; 2 Tim 3:15).

The programmatic passage for the book of Jeremiah is chapter 1. After the superscription to the book in Jeremiah 1:1–3, the text of Jeremiah 1:4–9 introduces the prophet Jeremiah as an authentic prophet like Moses (cf. Exod 4:10–12; Deut 18:15, 18). The remainder of the book maintains this comparison in a wide variety of interesting ways (e.g., Jer 15:1; cf. Jer 7:16; 11:14; 14:11).[36] Jeremiah 1:10 then provides a very concise statement of the overall message of the book: "See, I have appointed you this day over the nations and over the kingdoms to pluck up and to tear down and to destroy [MT adds: "and to throw down"], and ["and" is lacking in the MT] to build and to plant." The language of this verse is distributed throughout the book both in contexts that speak of historical judgment and restoration and in contexts that speak of eschatological judgment and restoration (12:14–17; 18:7–10; 24:6; 31:27–28, 40; 42:10; 45:4). Jeremiah is a prophet not only to Judah and Jerusalem but also to the nations (1:5b; 46–51), and he has a message of not only judgment but also restoration for both (see 3:17–18; 16:19; 30:3; 46:26 [MT]; 48:47 [MT]; 49:6 [MT], 39). The remainder of Jeremiah 1 introduces a series of subthemes to be developed over the course of the book: divine oversight of the prophetic word (1:11–12; see 31:28), the enemy from the north (1:13–15; see 4:5–6:30; 25:1–13),[37] idolatry

34. The version of this text in Joel 3:10 indicates that the agricultural tools must be made into weapons of warfare for a final battle before the weapons of warfare are made into agricultural tools for peacetime.

35. The parallel text in Mic 4:3–4 adds the image of each person living under his grapevine and under his fig tree, which is borrowed from the description of peace and prosperity in Solomon's kingdom in 1 Kgs 4:25. See also Zech 3:10.

36. See Christopher R. Seitz, "The Prophet Moses and the Canonical Shape of Jeremiah," *ZAW* 101 (1989): 3–27.

37. The identity of this enemy largely depends upon which edition of the book the reader is following. MT Jer 25:9 identifies the enemy as Nebuchadrezzar and Babylon, an identification that seems to be at odds with Jer 50:3. The Hebrew text behind LXX Jer 25:9 does not identify the enemy as a historical foe, leaving the text open to an eschatological

(1:16; see 3:1–4:4 and passim), opposition to true prophecy (1:17–18; see 11–20; 23:9–40; 26–29; 34–44), and divine presence (1:8, 19; see 15:20–21; 30:10–11 [MT]; 46:27–28).[38] Jeremiah 1 thus sets the trajectory for the book as a whole and gives a sense of order and meaning to the various parts of the book's composition. Jeremiah 2:1–13 then orients the prophet's message to the larger context of the biblical narrative (cf. Isa 63:7–14; Ezek 20; Amos 2:6–16; Mic 6:1–8).

Ezekiel's programmatic text in Ezekiel 1 is the first of four visions distributed throughout the book (Ezek 1; 8–11; 37; 40–48). The opening verses of this chapter establish the point of reference for the book's date formulae, which serve to subdivide the book into its various sections (1:2; 8:1; 20:1; 24:1; 26:1; 29:1, 17; 30:20; 31:1; 32:1, 17; 33:21; 40:1), and they introduce the reader to the prophet Ezekiel as a priest (Ezek 1:3; cf. Jer 1:1; Zech 1:1; Neh 12:16), a detail that proves to be important for the reader's understanding of Ezekiel's dependence upon the Holiness Code (Lev 17–27) and his vision of the temple (Ezek 40–48).[39] The apocalyptic vision of otherworldly creatures in Ezekiel 1:4–25 sets up the appearance of one who sits like a man on a throne in Ezekiel 1:26–28 (cf. Dan 7:1–14; Rev 4; see the cherubim in Ezek 10). The bright light around this man is "the appearance of the likeness of the glory of the LORD" (Ezek 1:28a). Ezekiel's second vision (8–11), in which the prophet is transported to the temple in Jerusalem to witness the persistence of the people's idolatry, concludes with the departure of the glory of the LORD (11:23), thus clearing the way for the coming judgment, but not before a brief message of restoration to be echoed later in the book (11:17–20; see 36:24–27). The third vision of the book, which is the vision of the valley of dry bones in Ezekiel 37:1–14, anticipates that just as the dry bones receive "breath" (*ruah*) so will the people receive the LORD's "Spirit" (*ruah*). This vision is accompanied by a sign act (the joining of the sticks) that symbolizes the reunification of Judah and Israel under the rule of the Davidic Messiah (37:15–28; cf. Jer 3:14–18; Ezek 34:23–24). The latter part of the passage looks forward not only to the making of a new covenant (cf. Ezek 34:25) but also to the return of the LORD's sanctuary (37:26–28) and thus the return of his glory. The final vision of the new

---

interpretation (see Ezek 38:14–17). See Michael B. Shepherd, *A Commentary on Jeremiah*, KEL (Grand Rapids: Kregel Academic, 2023).

38. The words spoken to the prophet in Jer 1:8, 19 and 15:20–21 are reapplied to the people of God in Jer 30:10–11 (MT) and 46:27–28, establishing Jeremiah as a representative figure.

39. See Michael A. Lyons, *From Law to Prophecy: Ezekiel's Use of the Holiness Code*, LHBOTS 507 (London: T&T Clark, 2009).

temple in Ezekiel 40–48 completes the sequence and features the return of the glory of the LORD (43:4–5; cf. Exod 40:34; 1 Kgs 8:11).[40] It is a priest's way of depicting future and final restoration—a return to the original ideal of the Garden of Eden where the sanctuary is not a separate structure but is all in all (cf. Rev 21:22–23).

The programmatic text for the Book of the Twelve (Hosea–Malachi) is Hosea 3:4–5: "Because for many days the children of Israel will live without a king and without a prince and without sacrifice and without a pillar and without ephod and teraphim. Afterward, the children of Israel will return and seek the LORD their God and David their king and fear to the LORD and to his goodness in the end of days."[41] This text breaks away from Hosea's story in Hosea 3:1–3 to explain the analogy in terms that extend well beyond the historical situation of the prophet and the northern kingdom of Israel. These words establish the three criteria for identifying the work of the prophetic composer of the Twelve. The first criterion is the distinctiveness of the material that the composer uses to connect each of the parts of the Twelve. Just like Hosea 3:4–5, the texts that lie along the seams of the books of the Twelve stand apart from the surrounding material. The second criterion is development of the program of coming judgment followed by messianic salvation in the last days. Much like the programmatic text of Isaiah 2:1–5, the program of the Twelve set forth in Hosea 3:4–5, which is then developed in the seams of the Twelve, concerns the messianic future "in the end of days" (*be'aharith hayyamim*). The third criterion is citation from the book of Jeremiah. The composer of the Twelve was a careful student of the book of Jeremiah, and his study of Jeremiah has deeply influenced the way that he has shaped the Book of the Twelve. The cited text in Hosea 3:5 is Jeremiah 30:9. Each of the seams of the Twelve feature this calling card. The section below on seam work as a compositional technique in the Latter Prophets will use the composition of the Twelve as a primary example. It is evident that the continuing relevance of the individual books of the Twelve to future generations of readers is largely due to the work of the composer of the Twelve in bringing the texts together in such a way that their message is not limited to the past.

---

40. The "prince/king" who appears in Ezek 44–46 is likely to be identified with the one in Ezek 34:23–24 (see 2 Sam 7:13; Zech 6:12–13).

41. For the historical evidence for the unity of the Twelve and for the internal evidence for the composition of the Twelve, see Michael B. Shepherd, *A Commentary on the Book of the Twelve: The Minor Prophets*, KEL (Grand Rapids: Kregel Academic, 2018), 21–36.

Framing

The compositional technique of framing, otherwise known as inclusio, can be employed at the highest level of a text (i.e., the book level) or at lower levels such as large sections of a book or short passages. This is where an author deliberately coordinates the way a portion of text begins and ends in order to "frame" the intervening material. The resulting framework provides an interpretive context that informs the way the text within its boundaries is read. A visual analogy for this technique would be a series of three consecutive images in a comic strip or on a reel of film in which the middle image is that of a cheerleader. If the first and third images are pictures from a football game, then the viewer assumes that the cheerleader is at a football game; but if the same image is framed by pictures from a basketball game, then the viewer assumes a different context.[42] The same phenomenon occurs in literature when surrounding text influences the reading of what comes in between.

The book of Isaiah features framing at multiple levels of the text. The book as a whole is framed by the shared language in 1:1–2:5 and 65–66.[43] In particular, the image of all the nations coming to Zion/Jerusalem in the last days is prominent both at the beginning (2:1–5) and at the end of the book (66:18–24). This informs the way sections like the nations corpus in Isaiah 13–23 are received. The words of judgment for the nations are balanced by a message of salvation for Gentiles who believe (see 7:9b; 11:10; 19:24–25; 28:16; 42:6; 49:6). At a much lower level of the text is the framing of a section like Isaiah 40–55. Here the words of Isaiah 40:8b—"the word of our God stands forever"—are echoed in Isaiah 55:10–11: "For just as the rain comes down, and the snow, from the sky and thither does not return unless it saturates the land and causes it to bring forth and sprout and provides seed for the sower and bread for the eater, so is my word that goes forth from my mouth; it does not return to me empty but accomplishes that which I desire and prospers in that for which I send it." The contrast between the faithfulness of God (and his word) and the infidelity of the people dominates the content of Isaiah 40–55. Whereas the people are tempted to question God's faithfulness and to turn to the so-called

42. See Sergei M. Eisenstein, *The Film Sense*, trans. and ed. Jay Leyda (San Diego: Harcourt Brace & Company, 1942), 4.

43. See Brevard S. Childs, *Isaiah: A Commentary*, OTL (Louisville: Westminster John Knox, 2000), 542–45.

gods of the nations (40:27), the LORD remains the faithful creator God to whom the manmade idols of the world cannot compare (40:12–26). He is the one who declared the former things before they happened, and he is the one who declares the new things before they happen (41:21–24; 42:8–9; 43:16–21; 46:9–10; 48:1–8). No idol can make such a claim.

The framing of the book of Jeremiah depends upon which edition of the book is being read. Whereas the Hebrew text behind Old Greek Jeremiah begins, "The word of God that came to Jeremiah" (LXX Jer 1:1a), the Masoretic Text of Jeremiah begins with the phrase "The words of Jeremiah" (MT Jer 1:1a) and concludes with an editorial note, "up to here are the words of Jeremiah" (51:64b), which does not appear in the Hebrew source behind Old Greek Jeremiah. The Septuagint characterizes the book as the revelatory Word of God, while the Masoretic Text characterizes it as a collection of the prophet's words. Both editions of the book have the account of the Babylonian invasion in the appendix of chapter 52 (cf. 2 Kgs 25), which, according to the book's superscription (Jer 1:1–3), marks the culmination of Jeremiah's prophetic ministry. The first edition of the book that lies behind Old Greek Jeremiah does not conclude with the nations corpus in Jeremiah 46–51. Rather, these chapters appear after 25:13 in a different arrangement. This leaves the scribal colophon in Jeremiah 45 to end the book (see the dates in 25:1; 36:1; 45:1; see also the colophon in MT Jer 51:59–64).[44] It is worth noting then that this short chapter echoes the language of the programmatic text in chapter 1: "Look, that which I have built I am throwing down, and that which I have planted I am plucking up" (Jer 45:4; cf. Jer 1:10). The LORD tells Baruch that his life will be given to him as plunder in every place where he goes (45:5b; cf. Jer 21:9; 38:2; 39:18), echoing the words of the call of Jeremiah to go to every person or place he is sent (1:7) where he will find that the LORD is with him (1:8, 19; 15:20–21; cf. MT Jer 30:10–11; 46:27–28; see also Exod 3:12; 4:12).

The books of Ezekiel and the Twelve also feature framing. It was noted above in the discussion of Ezekiel's programmatic passage that the book begins with a vision of the glory of the LORD (Ezek 1:26–28) and ends with a vision of the return of the glory of the LORD (43:4–5). The two visions that come in the middle highlight the departure of the glory of the LORD (11:23) and its anticipated return (37:26–28). The messianic hope introduced in the programmatic text of the Book of the Twelve (Hos 3:4–5) is reiterated not

44. See J. R. Lundbom, "Baruch, Seraiah, and Expanded Colophons in the Book of Jeremiah," *JSOT* 36 (1986): 89–114.

only throughout the book but also in the book's conclusion: "Look, I am about to send my messenger, and he will prepare a path before me. And suddenly he will come his temple, the Lord whom you seek" (Mal 3:1). This text anticipates a prophetic messenger who will prepare the way of the Lord (cf. Exod 23:20; Isa 40:3; Mark 1:2; see also Mal 4:5), the very one whom the people will seek in the last days according to Hosea 3:5. An example of framing at a much lower level of the composition of the Twelve is the framing of Nahum and Habakkuk by means of the two theophanies in Nahum 1:2–8 and Habakkuk 3:3–15. These two texts frame the historical prophecies in such a way that they now serve to illustrate eschatological realities.

Parallel Structuring

Parallel structuring at the macrolevel of a book's composition involves at least two substantial sections of text in which the sequencing of identical or near identical content is essentially the same. Identification of this kind of structuring must be based on more than a series of loose associations. The parallels must be grounded in the specific wording of the texts. Parallel structuring encourages readers to interpret the texts in light of one another in order to obtain clues to the proper understanding of their meaning. The book of Isaiah provides what is arguably the best example of parallel structuring among the Latter Prophets in the parallels between Isaiah 2–12 and 24–35, two sections separated only by the nations corpus in 13–23. The parallels between these two sections may be illustrated as follows:

Table 7: Parallel Structuring in Isaiah

Isaiah 2–12	Isaiah 24–35
Future work of God (2:1–4:6)	Future work of God (24:1–27:1)
Vineyard (5:1–7)	Vineyard (27:2–13)
Woes (5:8–30)	Woes (28–31)
King (6:1–9:7)	King (32)
Woes (9:8–10:19)	Woe (33)
Future work of God (10:20–12:6)	Future work of God (34–35)

With the exception of the vineyard parallels, the structuring of these two sections might be labeled "chiastic," highlighting the future work of God in the outer parts and the coming king in the center.

The two salvation oracles in Isaiah 2:1–5 and 4:2–6 frame the judgment oracles in 2:6–22; 3:1–15; 3:16–4:1 and anticipate among other things the coming of the nations to Mount Zion in the last days (see 2:1–5 and 25:6–9) and the deliverance of the people of God from the coming "flood" of judgment (see 4:2–6 and 24:18; 25:4–5; 26:20) in Isaiah 24:1–27:1. Immediately following Isaiah 2:1–4:6 is the vineyard song and its interpretation in Isaiah 5:1–7. Despite the best efforts of the vineyard keeper (the LORD) to have a fruitful vineyard (grapes = justice and righteousness), the vineyard (Israel and Judah) only produces bad or sour grapes (bloodshed and outcry) (see also Ezek 15; 19:10–14; Ps 80:8–13; Matt 21:33–46). Thus, there is nothing left to do but to leave the vineyard to be trampled. This illustrates well the relationship between God and the people of Israel and Judah under the old covenant in which God has remained faithful to an unfaithful people. Now, in accordance with the terms of the covenant, the people must face the consequences of their actions. This is not, however, the end of the story. The parallel text in Isaiah 27:2–6 reveals that the LORD will in the last days make his vineyard fruitful in a new covenant relationship. The larger context of the book of Isaiah shows that the righteousness that the LORD expected the people to produce (5:7) will come through the messianic servant of the LORD (53:11; 56:1; 60:21; 61:3, 8). Thus, the imagery of the vine and the branches in John 15:1–17 is not intended to put Jesus forward as the "new Israel," as is often supposed. Rather, Jesus is the one who makes the branches of the vineyard fruitful.

Isaiah 5:8–10:19 features a series of six woes (5:8, 11, 18, 20, 21, 22) and a refrain (5:25b) on the front end and several recurrences of the refrain (9:12b, 17b, 21b; 10:4b) and two woes (10:1, 5) on the back end. In the middle is a unit (6:1–9:7) that highlights the remnant theme (6:13; 7:3; 8:18; see 10:21) and the hope of a messianic king who is to come in fulfillment of the Immanuel prophecy (7:14; 9:6–7; cf. Isa 11:1–10). The child (born of a maiden/virgin) whose "name" will be "God with us" (cf. Jer 23:5–6; Matt 1:21–23) will come of age (i.e., know to reject evil and to choose good) at some undefined time (the time of eating "curds and honey") after the Assyrian invasion of the north (Isa 7:15–17, 20–22). He will not be a flawed king like Hezekiah (36–39) but an ideal king (9:6–7; 11:1–10). While the prophecy of this child is a "sign" designed to encourage faith in the midst of a crisis, God also provides the visible sign of Isaiah's own son Maher-shalal-hash-baz (born of his prophetess wife), before whose coming of age (i.e., calling to his parents) the threat from the north will be removed (8:1–3). The composition of this section finds a close parallel in Isaiah 28–33, where the woes of Isaiah 28:1; 29:1, 15; 30:1; 31:1, and 33:1 frame the prophecy of the messianic king in Isaiah 32:1 (cf. Isa 28:16–17). In both Isaiah 5:8–10:19 and 28–33 the design of the arrangement of the text is to direct the reader's attention to this king.

The last set of parallels in Isaiah 10:20–12:6 and 34–35 once again looks forward to the future work of God (cf. Isa 2:1–4:6 and 24:1–27:1). For Isaiah 10:20–12:6, this future work of God is primarily about the coming of the Davidic Messiah (11:1–10), the new exodus (11:11–16; cf. Exod 14), and the celebration thereof (12; cf. Exod 15:1–18; see especially Exod 15:2; Isa 12:2; Ps 118:14). In Isaiah 34–35, the anticipated redemption of Isaiah 35 is preceded by the depiction of worldwide judgment of "humankind" ('ad-ham) in Isaiah 34:1–4, which is illustrated by the judgment of "Edom" in Isaiah 34:5–17 (cf. Jer 46:10; Ezek 39:18; Rev 19:17–18). Both Isaiah 10:20–12:6 and 34–35 anticipate the second half of the book of Isaiah. The prophecy of the Davidic Messiah in Isaiah 11:1–10 as one on whom the Spirit of the LORD rests and who brings justice, righteousness, and peace to the world finds close parallels in the servant songs (see, e.g., Isa 42:1–4; 53:5, 11; 61:1, 3). The theme of the new exodus in Isaiah 11:11–16 recurs in 43:16–21 (et al.), and the comfort of the new exodus celebrated in Isaiah 12:1 manifests itself in the opening line of Isaiah 40:1: "Comfort, comfort my people, says your God." Furthermore, virtually every line of Isaiah 35 finds a verbal parallel in Isaiah 40–66.

Repetition

Readers of the Bible are generally familiar with the importance of repetition within short passages, but the focus here is on the use of repetition over large stretches of text and whole books. This can be a very effective means of keeping a message or theme before the eyes of readers so that they do not lose sight of it in the details over the course of a large literary work. Among the Latter Prophets, the books of Jeremiah and Ezekiel provide some of the best examples of this kind of repetition.

The book of Jeremiah contains a large number of doublets and recurring phrases, but the number and the location of these differ depending on what edition of the book the reader is following.[45] For example, the doublet in MT Jeremiah 6:12–15 and 8:10–12 does not occur in LXX Jeremiah because of the absence of the parallel in 8:10–12 (cf. Jer 15:13–14 and 17:3–4 [lacking in the LXX]; 30:10–11 [lacking in the LXX] and 46:27–28), but the dou-

---

45. See Geoffrey H. Parke-Taylor, *The Formation of the Book of Jeremiah: Doublets and Recurring Phrases*, SBLMS 51 (Atlanta: Society of Biblical Literature, 2000).

blet in Jeremiah 6:22–24 and 50:41–43 (LXX Jer 27:41–43) occurs in both editions, although the parallel in 50:41–43 occurs near the end of the book in the Masoretic Text but in the middle of the book in the Septuagint (see also 49:19–21 and 50:44–46).

These are not, however, mere repetitions. Each occurrence makes its own contribution to its respective context. For instance, the text of Jeremiah 10:12–16 is part of a message to the house of Israel (10:1) designed to discourage the worship of idols, but the parallel version in Jeremiah 51:15–19 is part of a message to Babylon (50:1) that announces coming judgment for their worship of such idols. The doublet in Jeremiah 11:20 and 20:12 serves to frame the section that includes the prophet's confessions. The doublet in MT Jeremiah 16:14–15 and 23:7–8 has one occurrence placed in a judgment context (16:14–15) and another in a salvation context (Jer 23:7–8). In the former instance, the emphasis is on the stricter judgment that the people must endure (the land of the north versus Egypt). In the latter, the emphasis is on the greater salvation in store for the people (a new exodus versus the original exodus; cf. Isa 43:18–19). It is interesting to note, however, that LXX Jeremiah has verses 7–8 of chapter 23 at the very end of the chapter in a judgment context. Likewise, the doublet in Jeremiah 23:19–20 and 30:23–24 features one occurrence in a judgment context (the judgment of false prophets [23:19–20]) and one in a salvation context (the vindication of the faithful [30:23–24]). The balance of these contexts fits well with the programmatic text of Jeremiah 1:10.

The recognition formula ("acknowledge that I am the LORD") occurs numerous times throughout Ezekiel 5–39 both in contexts of judgment and in contexts of salvation.[46] Just as in the original exodus from Egypt, God intends to make himself known as Yahweh—the God who is present with his people (see Exod 3:12–15; 6:2, 7, 29; 7:5, 17; 8:22; 9:16; 10:2; 12:12; 14:4, 18; 16:12).[47] The ultimate manifestation of this is the appearance of God in his glory (40:34–35; 1 Kgs 8:10–11; Isa 6:4; Ezek 1:26–28; 43:4–5; Rev 21:3, 22–23). The statement "I am Yahweh" also appears multiple times throughout the Holiness Code of Leviticus 17–27,[48] a section known to

---

46. Ezekiel 5:13, 15, 17; 6:7, 10, 13, 14; 7:4, 9, 27; 11:10, 12; 12:15, 16, 20; 13:9, 14, 21, 23; 14:8–9; 15:7; 16:62; 17:21, 24; 20:5, 7, 12, 19, 20, 26, 38, 42, 44, 48; 21:5, 32; 22:16, 22; 23:49; 24:14, 24, 27; 25:5, 7, 11, 17; 26:6, 14; 28:22–24, 26; 29:6, 9, 16, 21; 30:8, 12, 19, 25, 26; 32:15; 33:29; 34:27, 30; 35:4, 9, 12, 15; 36:11, 23, 36, 38; 37:6, 13, 28; 38:23; 39:6–7, 22, 28.

47. See Rolf Rendtorff, *The Canonical Hebrew Bible*, trans. David E. Orton (Leiden: Deo, 2005), 39–40.

48. Leviticus 18:2, 4–6, 21, 30; 19:2–4, 10, 12, 14, 16, 18, 25, 28, 30–32, 34, 36–37; 20:7–8, 24, 26; 21:8, 12, 15, 23; 22:2–3, 8–9, 16, 30–33; 23:22; 24:22; 25:17, 55; 26:1–2, 44–45.

be very influential for Ezekiel.[49] Thus, the repetition of the recognition formula in Ezekiel not only maintains a motif within the book but also establishes intertextual relationships with the Pentateuch.

Seam Work

Compositional seams are a very effective means of bringing together smaller pieces of literature to form larger ones, thereby establishing a reading order and generating a meaning that would not exist in the individual parts separately. The best example of this kind of compositional activity among the Latter Prophets is the Book of the Twelve.[50] As noted in the discussion of the programmatic passage of the Twelve (Hos 3:4–5), the three criteria for identifying the seam work that connects the books of the Twelve to one another are distinctiveness, development of the program, and citation from Jeremiah. This top layer of the composition of the Twelve creates a new network in which to understand the old prophecies so that the prophecies continue to speak to future generations of readers.

Table 8: The Seams of the Twelve

	Distinctiveness	*Program*	*Jeremiah*
Hos 14:9; Joel 1:2–3	Wisdom language in prophetic books	Reading strategy for the Twelve	Hos 14:9 cites Jer 9:12a
Joel 3:16a; Amos 1:2a	Same text inserted at end of Joel and beginning of Amos[51]	The Day of the LORD	Joel 3:16a and Amos 1:2a cite Jer 25:30b
Amos 9:11–15; Obad 1–5, 17–21	Message of restoration (Amos 9:11–15) in a book of judgment	Edom represents nations included in God's kingdom (Amos 9:12; Obad 19, 21)	Obad 1–5 cites from Jer 49:9, 14–16
Obadiah; Jonah	Juxtaposition: Obad functions like a seam between Amos and Jon	Nineveh is to Jon what Edom was to Amos-Obad (Jon 1:2; 3:2; 4:11)	Obad 1–5 cites from Jer 49:9, 14–16

49. See Lyons, *From Law to Prophecy*.
50. For a full discussion of the seams of the Twelve, see Shepherd, *Commentary on the Book of the Twelve*, 23–26, and the commentary on the individual passages.
51. See also Joel 3:18a and Amos 9:13b.

	Distinctiveness	*Program*	*Jeremiah*
Jon 4:2b; Mic 7:18–20	Citation from Exodus 34:6–7	Judgment and restoration	Mic 3:12 (the middle verse of the Twelve) cites Jer 26:18 in a later form
Mic 7:18–20; Nah 1:2b–3a	Separate hymn (Mic 7:18–20) and insertion into acrostic (Nah 1:2b–3a)	Citation from Exodus 34:6–7 (judgment and restoration)	Mic 3:12 (the middle verse of the Twelve) cites Jer 26:18 in a later form
Nah 1:2–8; Hab 3:3–15	Poems at the beginning and the end serve as bookends	Judgment of the wicked and deliverance of the righteous in the last days	Hab 2:13–14 cites Jer 51:58 and Isa 11:9
Hab 2:20b; 3:16b; Zeph 1:2–3, 7a, 15	Distinctive language ("hush"; "day of distress")	The Day of the LORD	Zeph 1:2 cites from Jer 8:13
Zeph 3:9–20; Hag	The restoration section of Zeph 3:9–20 stands apart from the previous messages of judgment in Zeph 1:1–3:8	The temple project in Haggai is now a picture of future restoration (cf. Ezek 34–39 and 40–48)	Zeph 3:17b cites MT Jer 32:41a (see also Zeph 3:20 and Jer 30:3)
Hag 2:20–23; Zech 1:2–6	Additional ending about Zerubbabel (Hag 2:20–23); added introduction to the visions (Zech 1:2–6)	Zerubbabel prefigures the Messiah (Hag 2:23; Zech 3:8; 6:12–13)	Hag 2:23 cites Jer 22:24; Zech 1:4 cites Jer 25:4–7
Zech 9:1; 12:1; Mal 1:1	These are the only three occurrences of this heading ("The Oracle of the Word of the LORD")	Eschatology and messianism (Zech 9:9–10; 12; 14; Mal 3:1)	According to Matt 27:9–10, Zech 11:13 is a citation from Jeremiah
Mal 4:4–6; Ps 1[52]	Mal 4:4–6 is not part of the six disputations in the book; Pss 1 and 2 form a separate introduction to the Psalter	The Day of the LORD	Ps 1 cites Jer 17:5–8

52. This is a canonical seam that connects the Prophets to the Writings (cf. Deut 34:5–12; Josh 1:1–9; see the introduction of this book).

PSALMS, JOB, AND PROVERBS

There are two basic approaches to the book of Psalms. One treats the book as an anthology of individual psalms whose primary context is a reconstructed historical setting. This approach keeps the psalms in the past in such a way that they are only artificially relevant to the modern reader. Another approach treats the book as a book so that the primary context for each individual psalm is the literary strategy of the Psalter as a whole. This approach recognizes the efforts of a composer above the level of the individual psalms to "update" the material by organizing and arranging the collections for the purpose of communicating an eschatological and messianic message. The former approach views the book as "the hymnbook of ancient Israel," while the latter views it as a prophetic book (see 1 Chr 25:1; Acts 2:30).

The major collections of psalms according to the superscriptions and content are as follows:[53] David (Pss 3–41),[54] Korah (Pss 42–49),[55] David (Pss 51–65), Asaph (Pss 73–83), Praise (Pss 95–100), Hallelujah (Pss 111–117), Ascent (Pss 120–134), David (Pss 138–145), and Praise (Pss 146–150).[56]

53. The fact that the LXX Psalter adds to the superscriptions found in the MT Psalter has suggested to many that all the superscriptions are non-original accretions. On the other hand, all textual witnesses to the Psalter have superscriptions in some measure. Thus, a sound, text-critical method cannot delete all the superscriptions based on a hypothetical projection. The merits of each reading must be weighed on a case-by-case basis.

54. Psalms 10 and 33 do not have David's name in the MT Psalter. Psalms 9 and 10 form a single alphabetic acrostic psalm and are presented as such in the LXX and in a few MT manuscripts. The LXX version of Ps 33 (LXX 32) adds a superscription with David's name. A few MT manuscripts combine Pss 32 and 33 to form a single psalm. Since Pss 9 and 10 are counted as one psalm in the LXX Psalter, the numbering of the following psalms is different (MT 11–113 = LXX 10–112). The LXX combines MT 114–115 into a single psalm (LXX 113) but then divides MT 116 into two psalms (MT 116:1–9 and 116:10–19 = LXX 114 and 115). From this point the numbering continues to be one off (MT 117–146 = LXX 116–145) until the LXX divides MT 147 into two psalms (MT 147:1–11 and 147:12–20 = LXX 146 and 147). The last three psalms are perfectly aligned (MT 148–150 = LXX 148–150). The LXX Psalter has an additional Psalm 151, but the superscription states that the psalm is "outside the number" of the canonical Psalter.

55. Psalms 42 and 43 form a single psalm (see Pss 42:5, 11; 43:5).

56. The repetition of material within these collections is difficult to explain on the model of the Psalter as a collection of individual psalms (see Pss 14 and 53; 40:12–17 and 70; 57 and 60 [together] and 108; 115:5–8 and 135:15–18; see also Ps 18 and 2 Sam 22; Ps 77:17–20 and Hab 3:10–15; Pss 95 and 106 and 1 Chr 16). Such repetition would have to be dismissed as an accident of literary growth. On the other hand, the model of the Psalter as a composition provides a way to explain the repetitions as meaningful contributions to their respective contexts.

These collections have now been arranged into five books (Book 1: Pss 1–41; Book 2: Pss 42–72; Book 3: Pss 73–89; Book 4: Pss 90–106; Book 5: Pss 107–150), presumably on the model of the five books of the Torah (see Ps 1). Gerald Wilson has observed a general movement in the Psalter from a concentration of petition psalms in Psalms 1–89 to a concentration of praise psalms in Psalms 90–150, a movement that coincides with a focus on the Davidic kingship in Psalms 1–89 and a focus on the divine kingship in Psalms 90–150.[57] The earliest psalm according to its superscription is Psalm 90, which is attributed to Moses. The latest psalms presuppose the Babylonian exile (e.g., 137) or even the return from Babylon (e.g., 126). Thus, the person responsible for the final composition of the Psalter must have done his work in the postexilic period.

The five books of the Psalter are clearly demarcated by the doxologies that conclude the first four books (Pss 41:13; 72:18–20; 89:52; 106:48),[58] but these are only the formal indicators of the Psalter's composition. The psalms that lie along the seams of these books reveal the theological message of the Psalter's macrostructure that consequently influences interpretation of the lower levels of the text. Psalms 40–41, 72, 89, and 110 are all strategically placed at these junctures not because everything that they say is messianic but because they each have something to contribute to the textual portrait of the Messiah that the composer wants to paint. Each of these psalms is cited as a messianic psalm in the New Testament, but the citations of these psalms in the New Testament does not make them messianic.[59] Rather, the messianic shaping of the Psalter itself has influenced the interpretive decisions of the New Testament authors.

Psalms 1 and 2, which lack superscriptions, form a separate introduction to the Psalter (see b. Ber. 9b–10a, which notes the inclusio in Pss 1:1a and 2:12b).[60] Psalm 1 contrasts the blessed person (verses 1–3) with the

---

57. Gerald H. Wilson, "Psalms and Psalter: Paradigm for Biblical Theology," in *Biblical Theology: Retrospect and Prospect*, ed. Scott J. Hafemann (Downers Grove, IL: InterVarsity, 2002), 100–110.

58. There is also a collection of praise psalms (Pss 146–150) at the end of the fifth book that concludes the Psalter as a whole.

59. See Ps 40:6–8 and Heb 10:5–10; Ps 41:9 and John 13:18; Ps 72:10–11, 15 and Matt 2:11 and Rev 21:26; Ps 89:50–51 and 1 Pet 2:21; 4:14; Ps 110:1 and Matt 22:44 (Matt 26:64; Mark 12:36; 14:62; Luke 20:42–43; 22:69; Acts 2:34–35; Heb 1:13); Ps 110:4 and Heb 5:6 and 7:17, 21.

60. See Robert L. Cole, *Psalms 1 and 2: Gateway to the Psalter* (Sheffield: Sheffield Phoenix, 2013).

wicked (verses 4–6) and depicts the blessed person as one whose trust in the LORD manifests itself when he "murmurs" (i.e., reads aloud quietly) in the text of the Torah (i.e., the Pentateuch) day and night (cf. Josh 1:8). The "Torah" here is not simply the "law" given at Mount Sinai but the book of the Torah (i.e., the Pentateuch). Whereas the law given at Sinai was cause for great fear (Exod 20:18–21; Deut 5:23–27), the book of the Torah is something in which the blessed person delights because of its message about the new covenant, justification by faith, and the hope of the Messiah. Such a person will be like a tree planted by streams of water—a tree that produces fruit at the right time (cf. Jer 17:5–8). That is, this person is blessed precisely because the Torah is his or her constant source of spiritual nourishment. After Psalm 1 draws attention to the Torah, which remains the focus throughout the Psalter (e.g., Pss 77–78; 105–106; 135–136), Psalm 2 guides the readers to see what they should find in the text of the Torah, namely, the Messiah (see Ps 2:1–2 and Acts 4:25–26; Ps 2:7 and Acts 13:33 [Heb 1:5; 5:5]; Ps 2:9 and Rev 12:5).[61]

Psalms 1 and 2 form the first of three couplets distributed throughout the Psalter that combine a Torah psalm with a messianic psalm.[62] The second couplet features Psalm 18 (messianic) and Psalm 19 (Torah). Psalm 18 is another version of the psalm in 2 Samuel 22, and with it come the messianic expectations associated with the role of 2 Samuel 22 in the book of Samuel (see above the discussion of the Former Prophets). Psalm 19 divides into two parts: 19:1–6 and 19:7–14. The first half states that the sky is declaring the glory of God, but there are no words in the sky to explain this (see RSV, NET). This sets up the second half of the psalm where the reader finds that the words of the Torah are available. These words are more desirable than any pleasure that the temptation of sin has to offer. The psalm concludes with a prayer that appears to refer back to Psalm 1:2b ("and in his Torah he murmurs [*yehgeh*] day and night"): "May the words of my mouth and the murmuring [*hegyon*] of my heart be acceptable before you, O LORD my rock and my redeemer" (Ps 19:14). In other words, as long as the psalmist murmurs in the Torah day and night, then the murmuring of his heart will be acceptable to the LORD. The final couplet of the Psalter appears in Psalm 118 (messianic) and Psalm 119

---

61. See Brevard S. Childs, *Introduction to the Old Testament as Scripture* (Philadelphia: Fortress, 1979), 516; Christoph Rösel, *Die messianische Redaktion des Psalters: Studien zu Entstehung und Theologie der Sammlung Psalm 2–89* (Stuttgart: Calwer, 1999).

62. See James L. Mays, "The Place of Torah-Psalms in the Psalter," *JBL* 106 (1987): 3–12.

(Torah). Psalm 118 is a thanksgiving psalm that takes up the theme of the new exodus (see Exod 15:2; Isa 12:2; Ps 118:14) and speaks of the triumphal entry of the messianic king (Ps 118:22–26; cf. Zeph 3:14–15; Zech 2:10–11; 9:9–10; Ps 24:7–10; Matt 21:1–11; 23:39; John 12:12–19). It also contributes to the messianic stone imagery of the Hebrew Bible (Ps 118:22; cf. Isa 8:14–15; 28:16; Zech 3:9; 4:7, 10; Dan 2:34–35, 44–45; see also Matt 21:42–44; Rom 9:30–33; 1 Pet 2:1–10). Psalm 119 is by far the longest of the Torah, a 176-verse alphabetic acrostic poem with eight verses devoted to each letter of the twenty-two-letter Hebrew alphabet. The psalm uses the same synonyms for the Torah found in Psalm 19. It is essentially an extended prayer that the LORD would keep the psalmist devoted to the Torah even in the face of persecution for his faith (see, e.g., Ps 119:18, 23). These couplets (1 and 2; 18 and 19; 118 and 119) complement the already messianic structuring of the five books of the Psalter.

Turning now to the book of Job, perhaps the most important compositional feature of the work is the relationship between its narrative framework (Job 1–2; 42) and the poetic speeches that form the bulk of its content (chapters 3–41). In particular, the prologue of Job 1–2 makes the reader privy to information that Job himself never learns within the book (i.e., the conversations between the LORD and the adversary angel in Job 1:6–12; 2:1–6). This creates a fascinating dynamic in which the reader privileged with such information is able to watch the main character respond to situations without knowing why terrible things are happening to him. In the end, however, it is not the reader's knowledge that Job needs to learn. Rather, it is the example of Job that instructs the reader in how to affirm the trustworthiness of the LORD despite not having an explanation for suffering.

Job is introduced to the reader as a God-fearing man (Job 1:1, 8; 2:3), a quality that comes to define what biblical wisdom is (28:28; Prov 1:7; 9:10; Eccl 12:13), but Job's fear of the LORD is put to the test when the adversary angel questions whether Job fears God for his own sake (Job 1:9–11; 2:4–5). God accepts the challenge and grants the adversary permission to take all that belongs to Job (1:12), including Job's health (2:6). Judging from his responses in Job 1:20–22 and 2:9–10, Job initially passes the test, but the piety expressed by Job in the opening chapters quickly fades into the background when he lashes out in chapter 3 and curses the day of his birth (cf. Jer 20:14–18). This outburst breaks the silence of Job's three friends who have come to visit him (Job 2:11–13).

The dialogues of Job 3–27 are arranged in a series of three sets of alternations between Job and each of his three friends Eliphaz, Bildad, and Zophar (Job 3–11; 12–20, 21–27), although Zophar is missing from the last set. The speeches of Job's friends begin politely but then increase in severity as their words are met with resistance from Job. Each of the friends appeals to a different authority to address Job's situation. Eliphaz appeals to private revelation (4–5); Bildad appeals to tradition (8); and Zophar tries to use Job's own words against him (11). Their conventional wisdom assumes that the righteous are blessed while the wicked are cursed (15:20–35; 18:5–21; 20:5–29), and thus they firmly believe that Job's suffering is due to a hidden sin that he must confess in order to be restored.[63] On the other hand, Job insists that the righteous sometimes suffer too (21:7–16; 27:13–23). He does not claim complete sinlessness for himself, but he does disagree with the thought that he is currently suffering because of a specific sin that he refuses to confess. Thus, Job wants his day in court with God so that he may be vindicated (9). This section of the book features hymnic material rich with biblical theology (5:9–13; 9:5–10; 12:13–25; 26:7–14), but the characters misapply this theology in all sorts of ways.

At this juncture in the book's composition, neither Job nor any of his three friends represents the right response to Job's suffering. In the midst of his terrible ordeal, Job has lost sight of the fear of the LORD that once characterized him (Job 1:1). Therefore, the author inserts a poem in chapter 28 that redirects the reader to the biblical definition of wisdom. This poem marks the transition to the second half of the book wherein Job relearns the fear of the LORD. According to the first part of the poem, there are precious items like silver, gold, iron, and bronze that humankind is able to find in the earth (28:1–11), but the question remains, "But as for wisdom, where can it be found" (28:12a)? "And wisdom, from where does it come" (28:20a)? It is hidden (28:21), but God understands its way and knows its place (28:23), and he has revealed it to humankind: "Look, the fear of the Lord, that is wisdom, and turning aside from evil is understanding" (28:28; cf. Prov 1:7; 9:10; Eccl 12:13; see also Deut 4:6; 31:13; Ps 19:9). In other words, biblical wisdom is something that is defined theologically. The proper response to Job's situation is not the conventional wisdom of the three friends, nor is it Job's quest for self-vindication. Rather, it is to fear and trust the Lord despite not knowing why things are the way they are (see Prov 3:5–7). The Lord has revealed enough of himself to show his trustworthiness.

---

63. The book's negative evaluation of this conventional wisdom serves as a corrective against overreading some of the sayings about the righteous and the wicked in the book of Proverbs in an absolute sense.

The second half of the book features three monologues from Job (Job 29–31), Elihu (32–37), and God (38–41). Job reminisces about the old days before his suffering when he was a respected man in his community (29). He then contrasts that former situation with his present state of affairs in which he finds himself the object of ridicule as one whose suffering yields suspicion of great guilt (30–31). When the three friends have no response for this final speech from Job (32:1), a new character named Elihu steps forward with the longest speech in the book.[64] While some commentators consider Elihu to be nothing more than a brash young man who merely repeats the words of the three friends, Elihu himself sees a clear difference between what he has to say and what has already been said (32:14). Indeed, Elihu does not seek to prove that Job's suffering is the result of a hidden sin of which he needs to repent (see 33:32). Rather, he takes issue with the fact that Job has sought to justify himself rather than God (32:2; 33:13; 34:10; 36:3; cf. Job 4:17; 9:2). That is, Job's efforts to vindicate himself have made God look like the bad guy. This concern that Elihu has is then echoed in God's speech: "Would you condemn me in order that you might be righteous" (40:8b)? Such continuity between Elihu's speech and God's speech suggests that Elihu is right. Elihu's final comments about the wonders of God in Job 37:14–24 make a nice segue into the first part of God's speech in chapter 38.

When God finally responds to Job from the storm (Job 38:1), he does not answer any of Job's questions or meet any of Job's demands. He does not vindicate Job. Rather, he reveals himself afresh to Job as the creator of the world who providentially oversees everything from the tops of the mountains to the depths of the ocean floors. His speech reminds Job of what Job has forgotten—the fear of the LORD. Once the fear of the LORD is restored to Job, he no longer requires an explanation for his suffering. He simply repents (40:3–5; 42:1–6). Thus, the book of Job is not a theodicy or philosophical treatise on the problem of evil. It is a lesson in true, biblical wisdom, which is the fear of the LORD.

The epilogue concludes the book with the LORD's rebuke of the three friends and his restoration of Job (Job 42:7–17). The adversary angel and Elihu are nowhere to be found. The adversary angel has lost the challenge. Despite the struggle to understand what was happening, Job never cursed God (1:11; 2:5, 9), and he was able to relearn the fear of the LORD even

---

64. The introductions in Job 34:1; 35:1; and 36:1 do not mark separate speeches. Rather, they indicate pauses in the same speech.

in the midst of his suffering prior to his restoration, showing devotion to God for his own sake even in the absence of God's visible blessings. As for Elihu, he was right. Therefore, Elihu does not become the object of the LORD's rebuke along with the three friends. His efforts to redirect Job to the righteousness of God have been affirmed by God's own speech.

The book of Proverbs, much like the book of Psalms, often suffers from mistreatment as a mere collection of disparate material, but the book shows clear signs of intentional design in its composition. There are seven major sections in the book, each distinctly marked with a heading (Prov 1–9; 10:1–22:16; 22:17–24:34; 25–29; 30; 31:1–9, 10–31). The first heading in Proverbs 1:1 ("The proverbs of Solomon, the son of David, the king of Israel") also doubles as a heading for the entire book, thus linking the book's wisdom to the story of Solomon's God-given wisdom (1 Kgs 3:16–28). The prologue in Proverbs 1:2–7 states that the purpose of the book is to know wisdom, the beginning of which is the fear of the LORD (cf. Prov 9:10).[65] That is, the purpose of the book is not to give the readers a proverb for every situation in life but to make the readers into wise persons who are able to apply their wisdom to every situation in life. Thus, it is important to resist the temptation to rearrange the content of the book topically. The book must be allowed to do its work in the readers according to its own presentation.

Chapters 1–9 feature a series of extended discourses addressed from a father to a son (Prov 1:8, 10; 2:1; 3:1, 21; 4:1, 10, 20; 5:1, 7; 6:1, 20; 7:1, 24; 8:32). According to the epilogue in chapter 9, these are intended to direct the reader to Lady Wisdom, who leads to life, and away from Lady Folly, who leads to death. Punctuating the discourses are three poems in which wisdom is personified as a woman (1:20–33; 3:13–20; 8).[66] Wisdom calls out to all those who might hear her (1:20–33), and those who find her are blessed (3:13–20). The climactic poem in Proverbs 8 includes an exegesis of Genesis 1:1–2:3 in which wisdom refers to herself as the "beginning," the one brought forth by the LORD as in childbirth yet already present to be the agent of creation (Prov 8:22–31; cf. Jer 10:12; 51:15; Ps 104:24; Prov 3:19).[67] The apostle Paul adopts the language of this text to describe

65. Since the fear of the LORD is wisdom according to Job 28:28, the fear of the LORD is not only the beginning of wisdom but also the middle and the end. Proverbs stresses that the fear of the LORD is the beginning of wisdom not because it is merely a place to start from which the reader must eventually depart but because the reader cannot start without it.

66. The Hebrew noun *hokmah* (wisdom) is grammatically feminine, requiring feminine pronouns and verbs for grammatical agreement.

67. See Michael B. Shepherd, *The Text in the Middle*, StBibLit 162 (New York: Lang, 2014), 9–11.

Christ as the "beginning," the firstborn of creation by whom all things were created (Col 1:15–20; cf. Matt 11:19; John 1:1–18; 1 Cor 1:24, 30; Rev 3:14; see also Sir 24). There will be an important echo of Proverbs 8:22–31 toward the end of the book of Proverbs.

With a few exceptions (e.g., Prov 16), the next several sections of the book move away from longer sections of related material to a format that features one individual proverb after another. Proverbs 10:1–22:16 is dominated by antithetical proverbs that contrast the wise and the foolish, the righteous and the wicked, and the rich and the poor.[68] The following section actually consists of two units labeled "the words of the wise" (22:17–24:22; 24:23–34). The proverbs found in these units bear a close resemblance to the Egyptian wisdom sayings of Amenemopet.[69] The final collection in the midsection of the book's composition presents proverbs of Solomon copied by the men of Hezekiah (25–29).

The last few sections of the book return to the more extended brand of discourse that characterized the book's opening chapters: the words of Agur (Prov 30), the words of Lemuel (31:1–9), and the alphabetic acrostic poem about the woman (31:10–31). The preface to Agur's numerical sayings creates a link to the wisdom poems in chapters 1–9: "Who has gone up to heaven and come down? Who has gathered the wind in his fists? Who has bound water in his cloak? Who established all the ends of the earth? What is his name, and what is the name of his son? Surely you know" (Prov 30:4; cf. John 3:13)! The answer to all the questions but the last is found in Proverbs 3:19. The LORD is the one who established all the ends of the earth, but he did so by means of wisdom. According to Proverbs 8:22–31, the LORD brought forth wisdom as in childbirth to be the agent of creation. Thus, the name of his son is wisdom (see again 1 Cor 1:24, 30). To know wisdom in the book of Proverbs is not only to know the fear of the LORD but also to know the Son of God by whom all things were created.

The words of King Lemuel in Proverbs 31:1–9 are those taught to him by his mother, and so they form a fitting transition to the celebration of the woman in Proverbs 31:10–31. It is only right that a book in which wisdom is personified as a woman should conclude with such a celebration. The He-

---

68. The heading "The proverbs of Solomon" (Prov 10:1) does not appear in the LXX, the Syr., and in some manuscripts of the Vulg. It is possible that the translators considered this heading to be redundant when compared with Prov 1:1. While the heading in 1:1 does set chapters 1–9 apart from the other sections, it is primarily a heading for the whole book, whereas Prov 10:1 designates the proverbs of Solomon proper. There are 375 proverbs in 10:1–22:16, equaling the numerical value of the name "Solomon."

69. See Pritchard, *Ancient Near Eastern Texts*, 421–25.

brew phrase *'esheth hayil* in Proverbs 31:10a is typically rendered as "virtuous woman" or "excellent wife" based on the understanding that "woman of strength" means a woman or wife of strong character (cf. Exod 18:21). Such character manifests itself in all the different things that she does with her hands (Prov 31:13, 16, 17, 19, 20, 31). This woman displays the very fear of the LORD that the book commends as the beginning of wisdom (31:30; see again 1:7; 9:10). On the other hand, the same phrase could mean "woman of wealth" or "valuable woman," which would fit nicely with the immediate description of her in Proverbs 31:10b as one whose value is far above that of jewels (cf. Prov 8:11). Yet another possibility is that the phrase means "woman of army" or "military woman." While this might seem like an unlikely option at first glance, there is much in the context to commend it.[70] Most English translations render Proverbs 31:11 to say that the heart of her husband trusts in her, and he does not lack "gain." The word translated "gain" is *shalal*, which is normally a term for plunder amassed from an enemy after a military victory in battle. According to most English translations of Proverbs 31:15, the woman gets up while it is still night (cf. Prov 31:18b) and provides "food" for her household, but the word translated "food" (*teref*) is normally a term for prey torn by a predator. Of course, none of this is intended to say that the woman is a literal warrior who goes off to fight in wars. Rather, the point is that this woman is to be celebrated for what she does just as a victorious warrior returning from battle would be celebrated (see, e.g., 1 Sam 18:6–7). Far from being a blueprint to follow or a litmus test to pass, the poem is a celebration of the woman. There are no commands or instructions here for the woman. Indeed, the only imperative in the passage is a masculine plural imperative directed to the men, commanding them to give to the woman from the fruit of her hands so that her works might praise her in the city gates (Prov 31:31).

The final acrostic poem in Proverbs 31:10–31 not only looks back to the earlier parts of the book of Proverbs but also looks forward canonically to the following five books of the Megilloth (Ruth, Song of Songs, Ecclesiastes, Lamentations, and Esther), each of which gives an example of either a Proverbs 31:10–31 woman or the fear of the LORD wisdom that the Proverbs 31:10–31 woman displays. Judging from a comparison of MT Proverbs 24–31 and LXX Proverbs, which has chapters 24–31 in a different

70. See Tremper Longman III, *Proverbs*, BCOTWP (Grand Rapids: Baker Academic, 2006), 539–48.

arrangement (24:1–22; 30:1–14; 24:23–34; 30:15–33; 31:1–9; 25–29; 31:10–31), it appears likely that Proverbs 31:10–31 was one of the last pieces added to the composition of the book.[71] In both Hebrew editions of the book (MT and LXX Hebrew source), Proverbs 31:10–31 maintains its position at the end despite the radical rearrangement of chapters 24–31. This suggests that the poem was added after the completion of both editions. If so, then there is a very good possibility that the poem was added for compositional reasons and also for canonical reasons—that is, to connect Proverbs to the following collection of the Megilloth.

THE MEGILLOTH

The Megilloth (festival scrolls) are the books read during the major festivals according to later Jewish tradition: Ruth (Pentecost), Song of Songs (Passover), Ecclesiastes (Tabernacles), Lamentations (Temple Destruction), and Esther (Purim). These books each have their own individual integrity, but there are also compositional and canonical reasons why they appear together in this order after the book of Proverbs. Interpreters sometimes have difficulty understanding the contribution of these books to the canon individually, but their collective contribution is much easier to grasp. These are the only five books in the Hebrew canon that have a feminine singular subject. It is thus no coincidence that they follow the poem about the woman in Proverbs 31:10–31 and feature explicit verbal links back to that poem. There is also an extended play on the name Ruth (female companion) that runs throughout these five books.

Table 9: The Megilloth

	Festival	*Feminine*	*Prov 31:10–31*	*Ruth*
Ruth	Pentecost	Ruth	Ruth 3:11	Ruth 1:4
Song of Songs	Passover	Shulammite	Song 6:9	Song 1:9, 15
Ecclesiastes	Tabernacles	Qoheleth	Eccl 12:13	Eccl 1:14, 17
Lamentations	Temple	Daughter Zion	Lam 3:22–27	Lam 1:2
Esther	Purim	Esther	Esth 5:1–7	Esth 1:19

71. See Otto Eissfeldt, *The Old Testament: An Introduction*, trans. Peter R. Ackroyd (New York: Harper and Row, 1965), 472.

The central figure in the book of Ruth is none other than Ruth (*ruth*), who is the ideal "female companion" (*re'uth*). In the encounter between Ruth and Boaz in chapter 3, Boaz says to Ruth, "And now, my daughter, do not fear. All that you say I will do for you. For all the gate [*sha'ar*] of my people knows that you are a virtuous woman [*'esheth hayil*]" (Ruth 3:11). Boaz's description of Ruth draws from the first and last verses of the poem about the virtuous woman in Proverbs 31:10–31: "A virtuous woman [*'esheth hayil*], who can find? And far above jewels is her value" (31:10); "Give to her from the fruit of her hands so that her works might praise her in the gates [*she'arim*]" (31:31). This identifies Ruth as a real-life, concrete example of a wise woman who is to be celebrated according to Proverbs 31:10–31. The conclusion to the book of Ruth shows that King David is a descendant of Ruth (Ruth 4:18–22; see also Matt 1:1–17). This means that Ruth is the ancestor not only of the wise King Solomon (1 Kgs 3:16–28) but also of the one who is greater than Solomon (Matt 12:42; Luke 11:31). The Proverbs 31 woman of wisdom is the progenitor of the very embodiment of wisdom, Christ.

The focus of the song of Songs is not on the man but on the woman. This is evident from the three descriptions of the woman (Song 4:1–7; 6:4–9; 7:1–10) as compared to the single description of the man (5:10–16). It is also evident from the repetition of the woman's wisdom in the refrains of the book (see 2:7; 3:5; 8:4; see also 2:16; 6:3; 7:10). The parallelism of the concluding line to the second description of the woman in Song of Songs 6:9b bears a striking resemblance to that of Proverbs 31:28:

Her sons rise up and call her blessed; her husband, and he praises her. (Prov 31:28)

Daughters see her and call her blessed; queens and concubines, and they praise her. (Song 6:9b)

The Song of Songs woman is yet another example of a Proverbs 31 woman. Like "Ruth" (*ruth*), the Song of Songs woman is an ideal "female companion" (*re'uth*). Throughout the book, the male lover refers to her as his "female companion" (*ra'yah*) (Song 1:9, 15; 2:2, 10, 13; 4:1, 7; 5:2; 6:4).

The Vanity of Vanities (Eccl 1:2; 12:8) follows the Song of Songs, but the book of Ecclesiastes does not feature an actual female figure. Thus, in order to maintain the continuity with the other books of the Megilloth, the featured speaker of the book has the title *qoheleth* (meaning preacher, teacher, or convener), which is a grammatically feminine singular participle in the Hebrew language. The final reflection on the words of this speaker in the epilogue of Ecclesiastes 12:9–14 commends the fear of God to the reader (12:13). The fear of the LORD is not only the beginning of wisdom in the book of Proverbs (Prov 1:7; 9:10) but also a quality possessed by the Proverbs 31 woman: "Charm is deceit, and beauty is vanity; a woman with the fear of the LORD, she is the one who will be praised" (31:30). Since there is no female figure in the book of Ecclesiastes, there is also a creative link to the words for "Ruth" (*ruth*) and "female companion" (*re'uth* and *ra'yah*) found in Ruth and Song of Songs. There is a homonym *re'uth* (striving), which looks and sounds the same as *re'uth* (female companion). This word shows up several times in the first half of Ecclesiastes when the speaker talks about how all is vanity and "striving" after wind (Eccl 1:14, 17; 2:11, 17, 22, 26; 4:4, 6, 16; 6:9).

The "female" subject in the book of Lamentations is variously known as Daughter Zion, Daughter Jerusalem, or Daughter Judah, which are terms for the people of Jerusalem and Judah (Lam 1:6, 15; 2:1–2, 4–5, 8, 10, 11, 13, 15, 18). Daughter Zion must relearn the fear of the LORD (Prov 31:30) in the wake of the devastation of Judah and Jerusalem, much the same way that Job relearns the fear of the LORD in the midst of his personal tragedy.[72] Nowhere is this displayed better than in the climactic words of Lamentations 3:22–27 from the voice of the representative speaker. Here the confession is that the faithful LORD is the spiritual "portion" of the people. What was once the privilege of the priestly tribe of Levi due to their lack of a land portion (Num 18:20; Deut 10:9) is now the privilege of everyone due to the loss of all the land. All of Daughter Zion's "male companions" (*re'im*) have abandoned her (Lam 1:2), but the LORD remains faithful to the end.

When King Ahasuerus is advised to depose Queen Vashti for her insubordination in the story of Esther 1, it is suggested that she be replaced by her "female companion" (*re'uth*) who is better than she is (Esth 1:19). Indeed, when Esther emerges as Vashti's replacement, she is not only "good of appearance" (*tovath mar'eh*) like Vashti (1:11) but also "beautiful of form" (*yephath to'ar*) (2:7). Like Ruth, Esther finds favor in the eyes of all who see her (Ruth 2:13; Esth 2:15). It is difficult to pinpoint one moment in the narrative of the book where Esther displays the qualities of the Proverbs 31 woman, but certainly her willingness to risk her life for the well-being of

---

72. The composer of Lamentations artfully portrays this with a series of alphabetic acrostic poems in Lam 1–4 and a final twenty-two-line prayer in Lam 5.

her family and her people stands out (Esth 5:1–7). According to Proverbs 31:23, the husband of a virtuous woman is known in the city gates when he sits with the elders of the land. Mordecai is not Esther's husband, but he does obtain a prominent position in the community in large part due to Esther's willingness to go before the king (Esth 8:15–16; 10:2–3).

DANIEL, EZRA-NEHEMIAH, AND 1-2 CHRONICLES

The last three books of the Hebrew Bible conclude the canon by looking back to Moses and the Prophets in order to look forward. The book of Daniel offers an eschatological interpretation of Jeremiah's prophecy of seventy years (Dan 9:1–2, 24–27; see LXX Jer 25:9, 11).[73] Ezra-Nehemiah features a reading and interpretation of the Torah (Ezra 7:6, 10; 8–9) in the context of a community that has returned from a literal period of seventy years in Babylon (Jer 29:10). This reading shows what the people have yet to become despite suffering the consequences of the broken covenant relationship. The books of 1–2 Chronicles, which form a single composition in the Hebrew Bible, present a comprehensive account of biblical history from Adam (1 Chr 1:1) to the decree of Cyrus (2 Chr 36:22–23), focusing in particular on the books of Samuel and Kings. According to the interpretation of Jeremiah's prophecy of seventy years in Daniel 9:1–2, 24–27, the decree of Cyrus is the beginning of the countdown to the coming of the Messiah and the defeat of the final enemy (cf. Ezek 38–39). Thus, these three books at the conclusion of the Hebrew canon are in many ways the final deposit of all that has been formulated up to this point.

The composition of the book of Daniel involves the interplay of material in two different languages: Hebrew (Dan 1:1–2:4a; 8–12) and Aramaic (2:4b–7:28). This situation has led to theories about how all or part of the Hebrew sections originally existed in Aramaic, or about how all or part of the Aramaic section originally existed in Hebrew. Various attempts to explain why the book came to be the way that it is have not been confirmed by the fragments of Daniel discovered among the Dead Sea Scrolls. The

73. See Michael B. Shepherd, *Daniel in the Context of the Hebrew Bible*, StBibLit 123 (New York: Lang, 2009), 95–99. The placement of the book of Daniel next to the book of Esther juxtaposes two figures, Mordecai and Daniel, who achieve high status in the setting of a foreign royal court much like Joseph in the Genesis narratives. Like Joseph, Daniel in particular is filled by the Spirit in order to interpret visions and dreams (Dan 4:8–9, 18; 5:11, 14; cf. Gen 41:38).

interpreter's task is thus to explain what the compositional relationship between the Hebrew and Aramaic sections in the extant form of the book is. The Hebrew sections appear to provide an interpretive framework for understanding the Aramaic section. While Daniel 1:1–2:4a provides an introduction to the major characters (Nebuchadnezzar, Daniel, and the three friends) and themes (divine providence over the kingdoms of the world), Daniel 8–12 answers the questions raised but left unanswered in Daniel 2:4b–7:28. For instance, Daniel 2:38 informs the reader that Babylon is the first of the four kingdoms represented by the four parts of the statue in chapter 2 and by the four beasts in chapter 7, but nowhere in the Aramaic section does the reader learn about the second, third, and fourth kingdoms, although there is a hint in Daniel 5:28 that the kingdom of the Medes and Persians is the second kingdom. It is not until the Hebrew text of chapter 8 that the reader finds out that the second and third kingdoms are those of the Medes and Persians and the Greeks, and it is not until the Hebrew text of chapter 9 that the reader finds out that the fourth kingdom is not a historical kingdom but a final, eschatological enemy. The vision of chapters 10–12 then takes the reader back through the whole sequence of kingdoms one last time. Chapter 12 explains why Daniel and his three friends are able to face the fiery furnace and the lions' den in the Aramaic stories of chapters 3 and 6 with such confidence in their God. They have a hope in the resurrection. The final word to Daniel in Daniel 12:13 provides guidance to the reader for what to do with what has been learned from the book: "And as for you, go to the end ["to the end" is lacking in the LXX]; and you will rest, and you will stand to your allotment at the end of the days" (cf. Isa 8:16–18; Hab 3:16–19).

The Aramaic section (Dan 2:4b–7:28) also has its own internal structure. Chapters 2 and 7 are parallel to one another; chapters 3 and 6 are parallel to one another; and chapters 4 and 5 are parallel to one another. This forms a chiastic arrangement of the material. The outer parts of this structure highlight the sequence of kingdoms via the four parts of the statue (2) and the four beasts (7). According to Daniel 2:28 (see also 10:14), this sequence culminates "in the end of days" with the defeat of the final enemy and the establishment of the messianic kingdom (2:34–35, 44–45; 7:9–14, 23–27; cf. Gen 49:1, 8–12; 24:7–9, 14, 17; Isa 2:1–5; Ezek 38:14–17). The innermost parts of the structure (Dan 4 and 5) state the thesis of the book that the kingdom belongs to God who gives it to whomever he pleases (4:17, 25; 5:21 [lacking in the OG]; cf. Jer 27:5–6). This thesis is reiterated in the small poetic units that dot the narratives of the Aramaic section

(Dan 2:20–23; 4:1–3 [lacking in the OG], 34–35; 6:26–27). For now, God removes kings and raises up kings (2:21), but he will ultimately establish an everlasting kingdom in accordance with the terms of the covenant with David (2 Sam 7:13, 16; Dan 2:44; 4:3, 34; 6:26; 7:14, 27).

The book of Ezra-Nehemiah is a single composition in the Hebrew Bible and not two separate ones, although the books are divided in English Bibles. It is a combination of third-person narratives about the postexilic community and first-person memoirs from Ezra and Nehemiah. The work may be outlined according to its accounts of three different returns from Babylonian exile. The first return took place sometime after the decree of Cyrus (ca. 539 or 538 BCE) under the leadership of Zerubbabel and Joshua (Ezra 1–6). The second return occurred in 458 BCE under the leadership of Ezra (7–10), and the third return happened in 445 BCE under Nehemiah's leadership (Neh 1–7). The conclusion to the book focuses on the reading and interpretation of the Torah (8–9) and the response of the people to it (10–13).

While there are many details in these accounts, the primary macrostructural item of interest is the repetition of the list of returnees in Ezra 2 and Nehemiah 7. This repetition sets up a contrast between what happens in Ezra 3 and what happens in Nehemiah 8–9. In Ezra 3, the focus of the community is on the building of the altar for burnt offerings, the laying of the temple foundation, and the reestablishment of the cult. The people appear to be oblivious to the fact that the old covenant has long since been broken (Jer 11:10). The basis for such religious practice is no longer intact. In Nehemiah 8–9, however, the focus of the community shifts away from temple worship to the reading and interpretation of Scripture by the great Torah scholar Ezra (Ezra 7:6, 10). Ezra, a priest who finds himself indebted to the prophets (9:10–11), does not direct the people to the laws of the old covenant (Neh 9:13–14) but to the faith of Abraham (9:7–8), the gift of the Spirit (9:20), and the message of the prophets (9:30). This shift away from the temple to the teaching of the text of the Torah anticipates the later worship setting of the synagogue and the early church, where the community of faith does not gather around the altar but around the expert teaching of Scripture (e.g., 1 Tim 4:13). Unfortunately, the people in Nehemiah 10 miss the point of Ezra's exposition and decide to sign an agreement to become keepers of the law—a plan that fails miserably just as it did for their forefathers (Neh 13). It is important to note that Ezra's name is conspicuously absent from the document.

As noted in the section on literary form and genre in chapter 1, the Chronicler employs genealogies in 1 Chronicles 1–9 to make his way from

Adam to the death of Saul (1 Chr 10) and the reign of David. The remainder of the book focuses on the history of the Davidic monarchy in Judah known from Samuel and Kings. The relationship between the Chronicler and his primary source material in Samuel and Kings is not one of mere reproduction. Not all of Samuel and Kings reappears in Chronicles, and Chronicles includes large blocks of material not found in Samuel and Kings. When the Chronicler does adopt text from Samuel and Kings, he frequently adds, omits, or rearranges material. The design of this process of adoption is not to change or to distort the source but to explicate its meaning. In his rewriting of Samuel and Kings, the Chronicler introduces a form of commentary that manifests itself in postbiblical literature like the Hebrew book of Jubilees and the Aramaic Genesis Apocryphon (from the Dead Sea Scrolls), which are rewritten versions of parts of Genesis and Exodus from the last two centuries BCE.

Two of the most glaring omissions from Samuel and Kings in the book of Chronicles are the failures of David (2 Sam 11) and Solomon (1 Kgs 11), but such omissions are surely not intended to fool a readership that would already be familiar with these failures from Samuel and Kings. Rather, the Chronicler is taking a page out of the playbook of the Prophets when he presents an idealized kingdom united under David and Solomon. His purpose is not to revise the history but to reuse the history to cast an image of a future messianic kingdom (cf. 1 Kgs 4:25; Mic 4:4; Zech 3:10). For the Chronicler living in the postexilic period, there is no longer a Davidic king reigning on the throne. Therefore, his interest is not in documenting the history of the kings from the past to the present. He retells the history in such a way as to kindle hope in what the covenant with David still holds for the future (2 Sam 7:12–16; Zech 6:12–13; 1 Chr 17:11–14).

Also missing from the Chronicler's version of Kings are the accounts of the reigns of the kings of the northern kingdom of Israel. Precisely because the kings of the north all follow in the sins of Jeroboam (1 Kgs 12:25–33) and thus bear no relationship to the covenant with David and its hope for the future, the Chronicler devotes no space to the recounting of their history. This leaves room for extra material not found in the book of Kings about the kings of the southern kingdom of Judah. For example, the Chronicler's account of King Asa's reign is three chapters long (2 Chr 14–16), whereas the account in Kings is only part of one chapter (1 Kgs 15:9–24). The Chronicler's account of King Jehoshaphat's reign is four chapters long (2 Chr 17–20) compared to eleven verses in 1 Kings 22:41–51. The account of King Hezekiah's reign in 2 Chronicles 29–32 is roughly the same length as the corresponding versions of his reign in 2 Kings 18–20 and Isaiah 36–39, but only 2 Chronicles 32 runs parallel to some of the material in the accounts of Kings and Isaiah, condensing the material found in those accounts into a single chapter. The text of 2 Chronicles 29–31, which features Hezekiah's temple repairs and Passover celebration, is unique to the Chronicler. It begins with a play on the name of "Hezekiah" (*yehizqi-yyahu*), who opened the doors of the house of the LORD "and repaired them" (*wayehazzeqem*) (2 Chr 29:3)—a technique known from elsewhere in the Chronicler's work (e.g., 1 Chr 22:9).

The most substantial portion of continuous text found in Chronicles but not in Samuel and Kings is the extensive account of David's preparations for Solomon's temple (1 Chr 22–29). This section is motivated in part by 1 Kings 1:13, 30 where there is a reference to an oath taken by David that Solomon would be his successor to the throne. There is also a reference in 1 Kings 7:51 to Solomon depositing the holy things of David in the treasuries of the newly-built temple. Since there is no narrative in the book of Samuel about David's oath or about his preparations for Solomon's temple, the Chronicler is compelled to fill the gap.[74] At the same time, there was motivation to include this historical information from the Chronicler's own context, which had a keen interest in the building of the Second Temple and in the role of the priesthood in the postexilic period (Hag 1–2; Ezra 1–6).

In addition to the many pluses and minuses at various levels of the text of Chronicles vis-à-vis Samuel and Kings, there are also many examples in Chronicles of small-scale and large-scale rearrangement of material from Samuel and Kings. One example of large-scale rearrangement occurs in 1 Chronicles 11. The chapter begins with the account of the anointing of David at Hebron and the taking of the city of Jerusalem from the Jebusites in 2 Samuel 5:1–10 (1 Chr 11:1–9). The Chronicler adds the detail that Joab struck the Jebusites first and thus earned the right to become David's military commander (11:6)—a detail that does not appear in 2 Samuel 5. This prompts the Chronicler to put the list of David's mighty men right at the outset of his account of David's reign (1 Chr 11:10–47). The same list appears in 2 Samuel 23:8–39 toward the end of David's story where it is part

---

74. This is not the only place where this sort of thing happens. For instance, the account of Manasseh's reign in 2 Kgs 21 comes with the unresolved problem of the worst of all the Judean kings being allowed to reign for the longest period of time (fifty-five years). The Chronicler resolves this with his account of Manasseh's repentance (2 Chr 33:12–13), which in turn provides the impetus for the apocryphal work known as the Prayer of Manasseh.

of an appendix designed to show to the reader the restoration of David after the account of his downfall that began with his taking of Uriah's wife Bathsheba (2 Sam 11–18). David is now no longer willing to take what does not belong to him at the expense of someone else (23:17; 24:24). Both lists in 2 Samuel 23:8–39 and 1 Chronicles 11:10–47 include the name of Uriah as one of David's mighty men (2 Sam 23:39; 1 Chr 11:41), but only the book of Samuel has the story of David's failure (2 Sam 11). Another example of rearrangement occurs in 1 Chronicles 13–15 where the source material from the book of Samuel occurs in the following order: 2 Samuel 6:1–11 (1 Chr 13); 2 Samuel 5:11–26 (1 Chr 14); 2 Samuel 6:12–23 (1 Chr 15). This arrangement is driven in part by the sustained wordplay based on the root *prts* (to break through) (1 Chr 13:2, 11; 14:11; 15:13; cf. 2 Sam 5:20; 6:8).

This chapter has demonstrated that each book of the Hebrew Bible has a coherent compositional strategy that involves the interplay of a variety of different literary forms and genres. The following chapter will show that the New Testament authors draw extensively from this material for the formation of their documents.

THE MEANING OF THE BIBLE IN THE COMPOSITIONAL
STRATEGY OF THE NEW TESTAMENT | 4

Once again, the task here is not to provide an exhaustive or comprehensive account of the biblical books but to give readers a sense of how an understanding of the making of the Bible and its history of transmission and translation leads to comprehension of the Bible's meaning, primarily at the macrostructural level of the books. With the New Testament documents, however, there is an additional component that must be taken into consideration. There is a fixed canon of Hebrew Scripture to which the New Testament authors relate themselves. While the Hebrew Bible itself features an extensive system of intertextual relationships, such intertextuality is an integral part of the making of the Hebrew canon itself. The New Testament documents, on the other hand, are not part of the Hebrew canon even if they are part of the larger biblical canon. Thus, their exegetical relationship to the Hebrew Bible will form an important part of the following survey.

THE GOSPELS AND ACTS

Each of the Gospels explains the historical Jesus of Nazareth from the Hebrew Scriptures in its own unique and complementary way. Matthew's Gospel presents Jesus as "the son of David, the son of Abraham" known from the Hebrew Scriptures (Matt 1:1). Mark's Gospel presents him as "the Son of God" announced by the prophet Isaiah (Mark 1:1–3). Luke's Gospel presents him as the servant of the LORD (Luke 4:16–30) known from the servant songs of the book of Isaiah (Isa 42:1–7; 49:1–9; 50:4–11; 52:13–53:12; 61:1–8). The book of Acts, which is the second volume of the two-volume work Luke-Acts, is a continuation of Luke's Gospel (see

Acts 1:1; cf. Luke 1:1–4). John's Gospel indicates that its stated purpose is for its readers to believe that the Christ, the Son of God already revealed in the Hebrew Scriptures is the historical Jesus of Nazareth presented in the book (John 20:31).

Matthew's compositional technique is a familiar one to readers of the Hebrew Bible. Just as the poems of the Pentateuch and the speeches of the Former Prophets interpret the narratives that precede them and guide readers to their meaning, so Matthew alternates between narratives and discourses designed to give readers a proper understanding of the narratives: narrative (Matt 1–4), discourse (5–7), narrative (8–9), discourse (10), narrative (11–12), discourse (13:1–52), narrative (13:53–17:27), discourse (18), narrative (19–23), discourse (24–25), narrative (26–28). Matthew helps his readers to see the boundaries of the discourses by concluding each of them in similar fashion (7:28; 11:1; 13:53; 19:1; 26:1).

The first narrative section in Matthew 1–4 features a series of fulfillment quotations designed to explain the early life and ministry of Christ from the Hebrew Scriptures (1:22–23; 2:5–6, 15, 17–18; 3:3; 4:14–16). This aspect of the initial narrative is then addressed toward the beginning of the Sermon on the Mount (5–7), which is the first discourse section of the book: "Do not think that I have come to abolish the Law or the Prophets; I have not come to abolish but to fulfill" (5:17). Jesus has not come to replace the Hebrew Scriptures (Moses and the Prophets). Rather, he is the very one of whom the Hebrew Scriptures speak, and he has come to explain their true meaning—a meaning that has been obscured by the teachings of mainstream Judaism.

The second narrative section in Matthew 8–9 concludes with Jesus having compassion on the crowds because the people are like sheep without a shepherd (9:36). The following discourse in Matthew 10 then begins with Jesus sending the disciples to the lost sheep of the house of Israel (10:6). The third narrative section in Matthew 11–12 features key references to the kingdom of heaven (11:11–12; 12:25–28), which then become the focus of the parables of the kingdom in the following discourse of Matthew 13:1–52. The fourth narrative section in Matthew 13:53–17:27 anticipates the death and resurrection of Jesus (16:21–28; 17:22–23) and the subsequent formation of a community of Jesus's followers (16:13–20). The following discourse in Matthew 18 is all about this community of followers (see 18:15–20; cf. Matt 16:13–20). The fifth narrative section in Matthew 19–23 highlights Jesus's arrival in Jerusalem (21:1–11) but is clear that there is yet another, ultimate arrival of Jesus still to come in the future (23:39). This leads into the fifth and final discourse of Matthew 24–25 (the Olivet Discourse) in which Jesus's comments about the Jerusalem temple (24:1–2) prompt the disciples to ask about the sign of his coming and of the end of the age (24:3). Jesus's lengthy response includes reference to the sign of the Son of Man in the book of Daniel (24:15, 30) and a series of parables about preparation for his coming. The final narrative of the book is Matthew's account of Jesus's death and resurrection (26–28).

In Mark's Gospel of Jesus Christ as the Son of God (Mark 1:1), Jesus is explicitly declared to be the Son of God at his baptism (1:11), his transfiguration (9:7; cf. Deut 18:15), and his crucifixion (Mark 15:39; see also 5:7; 14:61–62). Matthew and Luke have close parallels to these declarations in their accounts of Jesus's baptism (Matt 3:17; Luke 3:22), transfiguration (Matt 17:5; Luke 9:35), and crucifixion (Matt 27:54; Luke 23:47). The importance of Mark's identification of the Son of God with the historical Jesus of Nazareth can hardly be overstated. According to the covenant with David, the son of David who comes to build the temple and reign over an everlasting kingdom is God's Son (2 Sam 7:14; cf. Ps 2:7).

The prologue to Luke's Gospel states that the purpose of the book is to provide an orderly account based upon collected eyewitness testimony in order that the reader might know the truth (Luke 1:1–4). Luke thus begins with the most detailed birth narrative of all the Gospels (1–2) before he comes to the baptism of Jesus (3) and the temptation of Jesus (4:1–15). His programmatic text in Luke 4:16–30 sets forth Jesus as the servant of the LORD from the book of Isaiah and prepares the reader for the lengthy narrative of Jesus's journey to Jerusalem in Luke 9:51–19:48. At the outset of this narrative, Jesus "sets his face" to go to Jerusalem (9:51). This resolve to go to the place of his suffering and death echoes the words of the servant of the LORD in Isaiah 50:7b: "Therefore, I set my face like flint, and I know that I will not be ashamed."

The emphasis that Luke places on the Hebrew Scriptures for his portrayal of Jesus may be seen in two passages that are unique to Luke's Gospel. The first is the story of the rich man and Lazarus in Luke 16:19–31. When the rich man and Lazarus go to their respective eternal destinations (the rich man to Hades and Lazarus to the bosom of Abraham), the rich man asks Abraham about the possibility of finding even the slightest relief in his place of torment. After he learns that there is no such relief, he asks Abraham to send Lazarus to warn his five living brothers so that they might avoid the same fate. Abraham responds that they have Moses and the Prophets. The rich man insists that his brothers would repent if someone were to come to them from the dead, but Abraham says, "If they do not listen to Moses and the Prophets, neither will they be persuaded if someone rises from the dead" (16:31). In other words, it is better to have the revelation of the Hebrew Scriptures than to have someone return from the dead to give a warning about the afterlife! The second passage in which this kind of emphasis on the Hebrew Scriptures occurs is the narrative of Jesus's encounter with the two disciples on the road to Emmaus (24:13–35). Before revealing his identity to these two disciples who are lamenting his death, Jesus rebukes them for not believing the prophetic Scriptures, Moses and the Prophets, which reveal the necessity of the Christ's suffering (24:25–27). The message of the gospel was there in the Hebrew Scriptures all along and required no special key to unlock its meaning. Thus, in the conclusion to Luke's Gospel, Jesus commissions the disciples to take this message of Moses and the Prophets and Psalms to all the nations (24:44–49). The message of the gospel is not simply the recounting of the events of Jesus's life, death, and resurrection. It is a matter of explaining the meaning of those events from the Hebrew Scriptures.

Jesus's statement in Luke 24:44 does not require readers to find a full revelation of Christ and the gospel in every verse or subunit of the Hebrew Bible. He says that all the things written about him in Moses and the Prophets and Psalms must be fulfilled, but he does not say how Moses and the Prophets and Psalms write about him. Readers must find this. As the survey of the Hebrew Bible in chapter 3 suggests, the full portrait of the Messiah emerges in the macrostructure of the compositions and not simply in the individual parts.

The second volume of Luke's two-volume work, the book of Acts, begins where the first volume ends (see Luke 24:48–49 and Acts 1:4, 8; see also Luke 24:50–53 and Acts 1:9–12), but it also ends in a manner similar to the first volume's ending. Luke's Gospel concludes with the main character, Jesus, teaching the gospel from Moses and the Prophets (Luke 24:25–27; 44–49). The book of Acts concludes with the main character of the second half of the book, the apostle Paul, teaching the gospel from Moses and Prophets (Acts 28:23–31; cf. Acts 13:13–52; 17:2–3; 24:14–15; 26:22–23). Luke, Paul's traveling companion (see Acts 16:10; Col 4:14; 2 Tim 4:11; Phlm 24), likely learned the importance of the Hebrew Scriptures from the apostle himself. The final chapter of Acts is not a premature ending or open-ended conclusion. It is the product of intentional literary design that shows the relationship of the church's good news about Jesus Christ to the Hebrew Scriptures. Luke wants his reader, the Roman official Theophilus

(Luke 1:3; Acts 1:1; cf. Acts 23:26; 24:3; 26:25), to know that Christianity is not some new, deviant religious sect to be viewed as a threat by the Roman authorities. Rather, the Christians are the true heirs of the Hebrew Scriptures.

The programmatic text in Acts 1:8 sets the trajectory for the book as a whole, anticipating the apostolic spread of the gospel in the following narrative from Jerusalem and from Judea and Samaria to the end of the earth (see Acts 8:1). For the book of Acts, the end of the earth is Rome (see 19:21; 28). Thus, despite expressing a desire elsewhere to go to Spain (Rom 15:24), Paul writes from house arrest in Rome in his letter to the Colossians that the gospel has been proclaimed in all creation under heaven (Col 1:23; cf. Rom 15:19). According to Paul, the apostles have fulfilled in the first generation of the church the commission given to them by Jesus (Matt 28:18–20). It is now the responsibility of each subsequent generation to do the same until Christ returns (24:14).

The major speeches in the book of Acts function like the poems of the Pentateuch, the speeches of the Former Prophets, and the discourses of Matthew to explain the narratives that they accompany (see Acts 2:14–36; 3:11–26; 7:1–53; 10:34–43; 13:13–41; 15:6–22; 17:22–31; 20:17–35; 22:1–21; 24:10–21; 26:1–23). These speeches all appeal to the Hebrew Scriptures in one way or another. For instance, Peter's speech in Acts 2:14–36 explains the coming of the Spirit at Pentecost from the prophecy in Joel 2:28–32 (see also Acts 3:11–26). Stephen's speech in Acts 7:1–53 and Paul's speech in Acts 13:13–41 both rehearse the narrative of the Hebrew Bible and serve to orient the persecution of the early church and the spread of the gospel to the Gentiles to the larger context of the textual world of the Hebrew Scriptures. The speeches in Acts 10:34–43 and 15:6–22 appeal to the Hebrew Scriptures to explain the inclusion of the Gentiles in God's kingdom. Paul's speeches before Felix (Acts 24:10–21) and Agrippa (26:1–23) refer to Moses and the Prophets; and even in his speeches in which the reference is not so explicit, the language of the Hebrew Scriptures is still present (see Acts 17:22–31; 20:17–35; 22:1–21).

John's purpose statement for his Gospel is among the clearest in the whole of the Bible (John 20:30–31; cf. 1 John 5:13), but English translations of John 20:31 typically do not represent the Greek syntax very well.[1] For example, the ESV says: "but these [signs] are written so that you may be-

1. See D. A. Carson, "Syntactical and Text-Critical Observations on John 20:30–31: One More Round on the Purpose of the Fourth Gospel," *JBL* 124 (2005): 693–714.

lieve that Jesus is the Christ, the Son of God, and that by believing you may have life in his name." This assumes that the subject of the content clause ("that Jesus is the Christ") is Jesus, which would mean that the historical Jesus of Nazareth in the book is the known entity about whom something new is being predicated—namely, that he is the Christ or the Messiah of the Hebrew Scriptures. The problem with this understanding is twofold. First, the Greek syntax features two nominative nouns joined by a linking verb, in which case normally the noun with the definite article is the subject regardless of the word order (see, e.g., Acts 18:5, 28; 1 John 2:22; 4:15; 5:1, 5). In John 20:31, this rule would make "the Christ" the subject of the content clause, yielding the following translation: "but these are written so that you may believe that the Christ, the Son of God, is Jesus, and that by believing you may have life in his name." In other words, the Christ of the Hebrew Scriptures is the known entity, and John wants his readers to believe that the Messiah whom they already know from their Bible is the historical Jesus of Nazareth whose appearance on the world stage is relatively recent. Second, throughout the Gospel John does not explain the Christ from Jesus. Rather, he explains Jesus from what is revealed about the Christ in the Hebrew Scriptures. When Philip finds Nathanael in John 1:45, he does not say that he has discovered Jesus of Nazareth through whom Moses and the Prophets may now be read. He assumes that someone is already known from Moses and the Prophets, and precisely because of this knowledge an identification can be made with the recently discovered Jesus from Nazareth: "We have found the one of whom Moses in the Law wrote, and the Prophets, Jesus the son of Joseph who is from Nazareth" (cf. John 5:46).

Each part of John's Gospel has a contribution to make to the fulfillment of the author's purpose as stated in John 20:30–31. If readers find that their interpretation of a particular passage has nothing to do with the purpose statement, then that is an indication that they have veered off course and must now revise the interpretation. This is especially true of the signs, which are explicitly intended to lead the reader to the belief that the Christ is Jesus. Thus, the wedding at Cana in John 2:1–11 portrays Jesus in a setting that is reminiscent of the abundance and celebration of the messianic kingdom in biblical prophecy (see Gen 49:12; Amos 9:14; see also Rev 19:5–10). The account of the temple cleansing in John 2:13–22 draws upon Psalm 69:9.[2] The healings in John 4:43–54 and 5:1–9 reveal Jesus to

2. Here it is important to distinguish between psalm and Psalter. Psalm 69 as an in-

be the servant of the LORD as depicted in Isaiah 53:4 (cf. Matt 8:14–17; see also the healing in John 9). The feeding of the five thousand in John 6:1–15 shows Jesus to be the prophet like Moses (John 6:14; 7:40, 52; Acts 3:22; 7:37; see Deut 18:15, 18; 34:10; cf. Exod 16; Num 11; John 6:22–71).[3] The final sign in John 11 is the raising of Lazarus, which foreshadows Jesus's resurrection at the end of the book and the resurrection of all believers at the end of the age (see Isa 53:12; Dan 12:1–2; Rev 20). The intersection of these signs with the well-known "I am" statements of the book makes the match between the Messiah of the Hebrew Scriptures and the historical Jesus of Nazareth very evident for the reader (John 6:35; 8:12; 10:7, 11; 11:25; 14:6; 15:1). Jesus is the light of the world (John 8:12; see Isa 42:6; 49:6), the good shepherd (John 10:11; see Jer 23:5–6; Ezek 34:23–31), and the one who makes the branches of the vineyard bear the fruit of righteousness (John 15:1; see Isa 5:1–7; 9:6–7; 11:3–5; 27:2–6; 53:11; 56:1; 60:21; 61:3).

THE PAULINE EPISTLES

The apostle Paul's epistles are unapologetically dependent upon the Hebrew Scriptures for their content, as one might expect from a man trained by Gamaliel (Acts 22:3). Romans and Galatians are good initial examples of this dependence. In the opening verses of the salutation in his letter to the Romans, Paul introduces himself as an apostle set apart to the gospel of God, "which he proclaimed beforehand through his prophets in the holy Scriptures" (Rom 1:1–2). Paul does not claim originality in his proclamation of the gospel. He firmly believes that the gospel is already revealed in the Bible he possesses. This is also the way Paul's letter to the Romans ends: "To the one who is able to establish you according to my gospel and the proclamation of Jesus Christ according to the revelation of what was previously undisclosed, kept silent in ages past but now manifested and made known to all the nations through the prophetic Scriptures according to the command of the eternal God for the obedience of faith—to the only wise God, through Jesus Christ, to whom be the glory forever, amen"

dividual psalm does not appear to be a messianic psalm, but it has been included within the Psalter for messianic purposes. This means that certain features of the psalm apply to the Messiah, while others do not (e.g., Ps 69:5).

3. Some interpreters consider the walking on the water in John 6:16–21 to be one of the signs. The parallel account in Mark 6:45–52 features an allusion to Exod 33:22 and 34:6 (Mark 6:48; see John 1:14).

(16:25–27). In this concluding doxology, Paul acknowledges the undisclosed nature of the gospel prior to the formation of the Hebrew Bible; but now that the canon of prophetic Scriptures is complete, the message of the gospel and the textual portrait of the Messiah are there for all to see. Thus, Paul says, "But now apart from the law the righteousness of God is manifested, being attested by the Law and the Prophets, the righteousness of God through faith in Jesus Christ to all those who believe" (3:21–22). Apart from the works of the law of the old covenant, the Hebrew Scriptures (Moses and the Prophets) now with one voice bear witness to the gospel of justification by faith in Christ.

The programmatic text for Paul's letter to the Romans (Rom 1:16–17) features a citation of Habakkuk 2:4b ("but the one who is righteous by faith will live"). This text is then supported in the main body of the letter (Rom 4:3) by the corresponding citation of Genesis 15:6 ("Abraham believed God, and it was reckoned to him as righteousness"). These two texts from Moses and the Prophets form the basis for Paul's doctrine of justification by faith and thus aid his efforts to address Jewish-Gentile relations in the Roman church in light of that doctrine. In Paul's letter to the Galatians, the lead text cited is Genesis 15:6 (Gal 3:6), which is then supported by Habakkuk 2:4b (Gal 3:11) in order to offset the specific wording of Leviticus 18:5 quoted in Galatians 3:12 ("the one who does these things will live by them"). Here the doctrine of justification by faith combats the teaching of the Judaizers. The life offered in Leviticus 18:5 is only a hypothetical one (see Ezek 20; Matt 19:16–22; Rom 7:7–25; 10:5–13).

As with Romans and Galatians, most of Paul's epistles may be paired or grouped with other epistles for one reason or another. The epistles written to the same church (1–2 Cor; 1–2 Thess) or to the same individual (1–2 Tim) make for natural pairings. The letters to Timothy may be further grouped with the letter to Titus (see 1 Tim 3 and Titus 1) as the pastoral epistles. Ephesians and Colossians are cognate epistles. Much of the content in Colossians seems to have been borrowed and reworked for Ephesians. This leaves Philippians and Philemon as the only two letters that stand alone in terms of their material, although they are typically grouped with Ephesians and Colossians as the so-called prison epistles. The book of Acts provides a narrative context for much of what readers find in Paul's letters (see Acts 13–28).

Paul's letters to the Corinthians include a series of clearly delineated topics that the apostle addresses: divisions in the church (1 Cor 1–4), sexual immorality (5–6), marriage (7), Christian liberty (8–11), spiritual gifts

(12–14), resurrection (15), giving (16), boasting (2 Cor 1:12, 14; 5:12; 7:4, 14; 8:24; 9:2, 3; 10:8, 13, 15, 16; 11:10, 12, 16–18, 30; 12:1, 5, 6, 9), and commendation (3:1; 4:2; 5:12; 6:4; 7:11; 10:12, 18; 12:11). Even in the midst of this topic-driven discussion, Paul states that the gospel he proclaims is "according to the Scriptures" (1 Cor 15:3–4). Likewise, Paul's correspondences with the Thessalonians are heavily influenced by the eschatology of the Hebrew Scriptures, especially the book of Daniel (1 Thess 1:10; 2:19; 3:13; 4:15; 5:1–1, 23; 2 Thess 1:3–12; 2:1–12; see also 2 Pet 3:16). Indeed, even in the prison epistles (Ephesians, Philippians, Colossians, and Philemon), which seem on the surface to be the least dependent upon the Hebrew Scriptures, there is nevertheless a great deal of influence (e.g., Eph 4:8, 25, 26; 5:31; 6:2, 3; Phil 2:10–11; Col 1:15–20; Phlm 8–16 [Deut 23:16–17; Prov 30:10]).

In Paul's letters to Timothy, to which his letter to Titus may be compared, the overarching purpose is that Timothy might know "how it is necessary to behave in the house of God, which is the church of the living God, the pillar and support of the truth" (1 Tim 3:14–15). First and foremost, Timothy is to devote himself "to the public reading of Scripture, to encouragement, to teaching" (1 Tim 4:13; 2 Tim 4:1–2). Timothy's devotion in this regard is to be singular (2 Tim 2:3–4, 15). This is because the holy Scriptures that Timothy has known since his youth (i.e., the Hebrew Scriptures) are able to make him "wise for salvation through faith in Christ Jesus" (3:15). "All Scripture is God-breathed and beneficial for teaching, for rebuking, for correcting, for training in righteousness, in order that the man of God may be complete, equipped for every good work" (3:16–17). It is little wonder then that in his final extant letter before his death the apostle Paul is asking for the parchments, the scriptural books of the Hebrew Bible (4:13).

THE GENERAL EPISTLES AND REVELATION

The General Epistles (Hebrews, James, 1–2 Peter, 1–3 John, Jude) and Revelation conclude the New Testament in most modern English Bibles. The prologue to the letter or homily (Heb 13:22; cf. Acts 13:15) to the Hebrews begins by saying that the God who spoke formerly in many parts and in many ways to the forefathers by the prophets has in these last days spoken to us by a Son (Heb 1:1–2). This is not intended to be a comparison or contrast between the Hebrew Bible and the Greek New Testament. It is not even a comparison or contrast between the old covenant and the new covenant. Rather, it is a simple juxtaposition of the way God spoke formerly through prophets and the way he has spoken more recently through the incarnation of the one who has the status of the Son of God. Since the Son of God has now ascended to the right hand of the Father (1:3), there is no longer any direct access to the latter way of speaking such as what the disciples enjoyed. The writer to the Hebrews must appeal to the prophetic Scriptures of the Hebrew Bible in order to make his case for the superiority of the Son of God.

As evidenced by the warning passages (Heb 2:1–4; 3:7–4:11; 5:11–6:12; 10:19–39), the epistle to the Hebrews is written to urge Jewish Christians to stay the course of their faith despite the persecution that they must face for it. The temptation for Jewish Christians in the first century CE was to turn back to the safe haven of the state-recognized religion of Judaism rather than endure opposition from both Jewish and Roman authorities for their Christian faith. This is why the author argues for the superiority of Christ. He is worth pursuing no matter the cost. Christ is superior to the angels; he is the ultimate man to whom all things will be subjected (1–2). He is superior to Moses and Joshua because he alone will bring lasting rest to the people of God (3–4). He is superior to Aaron because he is a priest according to the superior order of Melchizedek (5–7). In Christ, a superior covenant based on a better sacrifice has been made (8–10). It is important to note that the writer to the Hebrews demonstrates the superiority of Christ from the Hebrew Scriptures. He does not equate the Hebrew Bible with the religion of Judaism. He considers it to be genuine Christian Scripture. Thus, in order to prevent his readers from turning back to Judaism and in order to encourage them to continue in their Christian faith, he directs their attention to the Hebrew Scriptures. Nowhere is this more evident than in Hebrews 11, a chapter in which the author walks his readers through the narratives of the Pentateuch and the Former Prophets in order to commend to them the perseverance of faith found therein (12–13). They have not come to Mount Sinai but to Mount Zion, the new Jerusalem, and to the mediator of a new covenant (12:18–29). Therefore, the only response is to accept their heavenly Father's discipline (12:4–11) and to identify with the suffering of Christ, knowing that the city of God awaits them (13:12–16).

The evidence of influence from the Hebrew Scriptures continues to surface in the remainder of the General Epistles (e.g., Jas 2:8, 11, 23; 4:6; 1 Pet 1:16, 24–25; 2:6–10, 22; 3:10–12; 4:18; 5:5; 2 Pet 2; 1 John 3:11–18; Jude). Peter's reflections on the importance of these Scriptures are particularly striking: "Concerning which salvation prophets who prophesied about the grace to you searched and sought, seeking as to what person or what time the Spirit of Christ in them was making clear by testifying beforehand to the sufferings of Christ and the glories to follow, to whom it was revealed that not to themselves but to you they were ministering these things, which have now been proclaimed to you by those who preached the good news to you by the Holy Spirit sent from heaven, into which things angels desire to look" (1 Pet 1:10–12). The nature of biblical prophecy is not to predict names (e.g., Jesus of Nazareth) or times (e.g., the first century CE) but to provide a textual portrait of the Messiah (see 2 Pet 3), which then becomes a necessary means of explaining the Messiah when he arrives and matches the picture.

In 2 Peter 1:16–18, Peter reflects upon his experience during the transfiguration of Jesus (Matt 17:1–5; Mark 9:2–7; Luke 9:28–35). As real and as significant as that event was, it was not an experience that Peter had in common with his readers. Thus, he directs his readers to the publicly accessible prophetic word of the Hebrew Scriptures, to which they would do well to pay attention as to a light shining in a murky place until the day dawns and the morning star rises in their hearts (2 Pet 1:19; cf. Num 24:17). Scriptures are more than bare, uninterpreted events or subjectively explained personal experiences. They provide a sure interpretation of things precisely because they are not brought by the will of man but by prophets who were carried along by the Holy Spirit and who thus spoke from God (2 Pet 1:20–21). An event such as the crucifixion, for example, does not come with its own interpretation of its meaning. Eyewitnesses to the event might know that someone named Jesus died, but they would not necessarily know that he died for the sin of the world. It is the theological interpretation of the event revealed in the Scriptures that explains the substitutionary nature of Jesus's death (e.g., Isa 52:13–53:12).

The book of Revelation is more thoroughly saturated with language from the Hebrew Bible than any other New Testament document. At the same time, it is among the New Testament writings with the least number of explicit citations. Much like John's Gospel, in which the apostle explains his experience with Jesus from the Hebrew Scriptures, the book of Revelation is John's explanation from the Hebrew Scriptures of the visions that he has received. The visions themselves are real, but John needs a means of communicating them to his readers, and he finds that means in the language of his Bible.

The book of Revelation begins with elements of the type of salutation known from any other New Testament epistle (Rev 1:1–8). The programmatic text in Revelation 1:7 combines material from Daniel 7:13 and Zechariah 12:10 (cf. Matt 24:30) and sets the book's trajectory for the coming of Christ. Indeed, the books of Daniel and Zechariah will prove to be two of the most strategically influential books in the composition of Revelation. The book then divides into four major visions: (1) Revelation 1:9–3:22; (2) Revelation 4:1–16:21; (3) Revelation 17:1–21:8; and (4) Revelation 21:9–22:5. The first vision deals with current affairs in the churches, while the latter three address things to come (1:1, 19; 4:1). The book concludes with an epilogue in Revelation 22:6–21.

Key to the interpretation of the book of Revelation is an understanding of the apocalyptic genre, for which there are precursors in the books of Ezekiel, Zechariah, and Daniel. First of all, the apocalyptic genre does not communicate in a straightforward, literal manner like the prose of biblical narrative. If readers try to draw a straight line from the words of apocalyptic literature to real events, then their interpretation will fail miserably. Readers must recognize the figurative nature of the language and the use of symbols, metaphors, and other figures of speech to cast an image that is highly descriptive of real events in an indirect way. Any attempt to bypass this intermediary stage in reading will miss the author's intent in the verbal meaning of the text. The hermeneutical task is not to predict the events to which the book refers or to work out the logistics of those events. Such prediction relies on personal ingenuity, which makes interpretation of the book of Revelation seem very daunting to most readers. The task is to understand the textual images, and this is primarily done by understanding the texts from the Hebrew Bible upon which John draws to construct these images. In contrast to other types of literature in which predominantly figurative language occurs (e.g., poetry), the imagery of apocalyptic literature is often otherworldly. That is, it takes features of everyday life and combines them in unusual ways. The imagery is designed to transport the reader to the other side of world history.

The second thing to keep in mind when reading apocalyptic literature is to look in the text for the guidance of an angel or other interpreter to aid with the meaning of the visions (see, e.g., Dan 7–8; 10–12; Zech 1–6). Since the visions are symbolic, their meaning has to be revealed. It is also important to remember that apocalyptic literature tends to provide more than one vision or part of a vision to describe the same event. This allows the reader to see the same event from a variety of different angles. For instance, the second vision in Revelation 4–16 features the seals (6), the trumpets (8–9), and the bowls (15–16). The overlap among these three strongly suggests that they do not represent one long sequence of events but three different versions of the same tribulation. The interspersed chapters address issues related to this tribulation: the people of God (7 and 14), the apostle John (10), witness during the tribulation (11), and the enemy (12–13). Likewise, the sequence of the battle of Armageddon (16:16) followed by the Millennium (i.e., the messianic kingdom; 20:1–6) is reiterated by the sequence of the battle of Gog (20:7–10) followed by the new Jerusalem in the new creation (21:1–22:5).[4] To make this into one sequence would be to run contrary to the very prophetic literature upon which John depends.[5] The prophets always envision one final battle (Ezek 38–39; Joel 3; Zech 12; 14) followed by the messianic kingdom and new creation (Isa 11:1–10; 65:17–25).

Our discussion of the making and meaning of the Bible has now taken us from compositional techniques to transmission and translation of the literature and finally to interpretation of the individual books of the Bible. The final chapter looks at the Bible as a whole—the textual world of the Bible—and explores how the biblical authors interpret one another in a complex web of intertextual relationships.

4. Note also how the two parts of the same resurrection (Dan 12:1–2) are divided between Rev 20:1–6 and 20:11–15.

5. John deliberately depicts the battle of Armageddon in terms of the battle of Gog (Rev 19:17–18; cf. Ezek 39:17–20) and vice versa (Rev 20:8–9; cf. Zech 12:1–6, 9; 14:1–2). He also depicts the new creation in Rev 21:1–4 in terms of the messianic kingdom (see Isa 25:5–9; cf. Isa 2:1–5).

THE TEXTUAL WORLD OF THE BIBLE | 5

The textual world of the Bible is the world as constructed by the biblical authors in the tapestry of their compositions and in the intricate web of intertextual relationships that exist among those compositions. This world is not merely a lens through which to view the real world. It is also not merely a coping mechanism with which to deal with the real world. Rather, it defines and explains the real world. It is the biblical authors' theological representation of reality.[1] In traditional, precritical reading of the Bible, the historicity of the text is taken for granted, and the assumption is that the Bible forms one cumulative story from creation to new creation, thus absorbing all of history within its framework. This is possible due to the patterns of figuration established by the biblical authors. These patterns make past events (e.g., creation, exodus, covenant) into metaphors for future events (e.g., new creation, new exodus, new covenant). Thus, the biblical authors are able to take their readers from paradise to paradise lost and to paradise regained all within the breadth of their narrative.

The realism of the Bible requires readers to accept the biblical world as the real world. It is not possible to keep the Bible at arm's length or to remain neutral in response to its demands. Biblical realism also disallows spiritualization of the Bible's content. The new creation, for instance, is every bit as real as the original creation. In contrast to the disdain for the physical body found within Greek philosophy, the Bible affirms the basic goodness of creation and sees the ultimate manifestation of the redemption of the fallen world not in an abstract spiritual existence but in a bodily resurrection.

---

1. See Erich Auerbach, *Mimesis: The Representation of Reality in Western Literature*, trans. Willard R. Trask, 50th anniversary ed. (Princeton: Princeton University Press, 2003), 14–15.

What then should be the posture of the reader of the Bible? Should readers seek to find their own story in the Bible, or should they reorient themselves to the Bible's textual world?

> Far from seeking, like Homer, merely to make us forget our own reality for a few hours, it [the Bible] seeks to overcome our reality: we are to fit our own life into its world, feel ourselves to be elements in its structure of universal history.[2]

> Since the world truly rendered by combining biblical narratives into one was indeed the one and only real world, it must in principle embrace the experience of any present age and reader. Not only was it possible for him, it was also his duty to fit himself into that world in which he was in any case a member, and he too did so in part by figural interpretation and in part of course by his mode of life. He was to see his disposition, his actions and passions, the shape of his own life as well as that of his era's events as figures of that storied world.[3]

> Typology does not make scriptural contents into metaphors for extra-scriptural realities, but the other way around. It does not suggest, as is often said in our day, that believers find their stories in the Bible, but rather that they make the story of the Bible their story. . . . Intratextual theology redescribes reality within the scriptural framework rather than translating Scripture into extrascriptural categories. It is the text, so to speak, which absorbs the world, rather than the world the text.[4]

> For in Midrash the Bible becomes . . . a world unto itself. Midrashic exegesis is the way into that world; it does not seek to view present-day reality through biblical spectacles, neither to find referents of biblical prophecy in present-day happenings, nor to find referents to the daily life of the soul in biblical allegory. Instead it simply overwhelms the present; the Bible's time is important, while the present is not; and so it invites the reader to cross over into the enterable world of Scripture.[5]

2. Auerbach, *Mimesis*, 15.

3. Hans W. Frei, *The Eclipse of Biblical Narrative: A Study in Eighteenth and Nineteenth Century Hermeneutics* (New Haven: Yale University Press, 1974), 3.

4. George A. Lindbeck, *The Nature of Doctrine: Religion and Theology in a Postliberal Age* (Philadelphia: Westminster, 1984), 118.

5. James L. Kugel, "Two Introductions to Midrash," in *Midrash and Literature*, ed. Geoffrey Hartman and Sanford Budick (New Haven: Yale University Press, 1986), 90.

What these quotes suggest is that readers' own personal stories are not the primary frame of reference. Rather, it is the readers' responsibility to adopt the biblical story as their own and to subordinate everything else to it.

Protestant Christianity has a long history of emphasizing the personal testimony of the individual believer (i.e., life before conversion, conversion, and life after conversion), and rightly so (see, e.g., Acts 22:6–16; 26:12–18; Titus 3:3–7). This should not be to the exclusion of the biblical story shared by all believers, nor should the personal story have priority over the biblical one. Personal testimonies of religious conversion tend to sound very similar and often lack elements that are uniquely biblical or Christian. It is thus important for believers to see themselves as part of a larger community of faith and within the framework of the biblical narrative.

One way to illustrate the understanding of the world advocated here is to compare and contrast two important Protestant works of literature from the seventeenth century, Paul Bunyan's *Pilgrim's Progress* and John Milton's *Paradise Lost*. Bunyan's work has maintained popularity among a general readership largely due to the appeal of its focus on the personal faith journey of the individual believer, but this is also the basic weakness of its perspective. The primary frame of reference is the story of the Christian to which various and sundry biblical texts are attached. The biblical text is only there in the service of telling a story very different from its own.[6] Milton, on the other hand, has garnered critical acclaim for his poetic rendition of the biblical world. However much the reader may quibble about Milton's interpretation of certain biblical texts, he has clearly succeeded in recreating the textual world of the Bible as that which encompasses all of world history and as the primary frame of reference for all events. In other words, all things are subjected to the Bible itself and must find their place therein.

The text of Deuteronomy 26:5–9 provides an example of the sort of testimony that is common to all the people of God. In the immediate context of Deuteronomy 26:1–11, this passage is the creed, so to speak, that the worshiper is to recite upon bringing the offering of first fruits in the land of the covenant.

> And you will answer and say before the LORD your God, "My father was a wandering Aramean, and he went down to Egypt and sojourned there with a few people and became there a great nation, mighty and abundant. And the Egyptians treated us badly and afflicted us and put

6. See Frei, *Eclipse of Biblical Narrative*, 152–54.

on us hard labor. And we cried out to the LORD God of our fathers, and the LORD heard our voice and saw our affliction and our toil and our oppression. And the LORD brought us out of Egypt with a strong hand and with an outstretched arm and with great fear and with signs and with wonders, and he brought us to this place and gave to us this land, a land flowing with milk and honey."

This is a concise version of the kind of rehearsal of the biblical narrative that readers can find throughout the Hebrew Bible (Deut 6:20–25; 26:5–9; 32; Josh 24:1–15; Judg 2:1–5; 6:7–10; 10:11–15; 1 Sam 12:6–17; Isa 63:7–14; Jer 2:1–13; Ezek 20; Amos 2:6–16; Mic 6:1–8; Pss 78; 105; 106; 135; 136; Neh 9) and in the New Testament (Acts 7; 13:13–41; Heb 11).[7] Since this testimony is to be recited by every subsequent generation of the people of God, even those who did not experience the exodus from Egypt will refer to the exodus story as their own (note the use of the pronouns "my," "us," and "our"; cf. Josh 24:5–7). Any one part of the story of the people of God is part of the story for all the people of God past, present, and future. Thus, the apostle Paul can say to the church at Rome, "For whatever things were written before were written for our instruction in order that through the patience and through the encouragement from the Scriptures we might have hope" (Rom 15:4; cf. Hos 12:4; Rom 4:23–24; 1 Cor 9:10; 10:11; 1 Pet 1:12).

Closely related to the idea of prioritizing the textual world of the Bible is the practice of reading "the Bible for its own sake" (*torah lishma*).[8] Do believers really trust the way God has chosen to reveal himself in literary form according to the Bible's own arrangement and agenda, or do they think that the Bible should be reordered and supplemented to address issues that they have already predetermined to be important from tradition or culture or the news or social media or their personal lives? For example, the deeply personal situation of Hannah narrated in 1 Samuel 1 is not at all the main subject of her prayer in 1 Samuel 2:1–10. Rather, she focuses her attention on the coming of the Messiah revealed in the poems of the Pentateuch (1 Sam 2:10). Likewise, the seemingly all-important political situation described in Isaiah 7:1–2 is not the main focus of Isaiah's proph-

---

7. See Michael B. Shepherd, *The Textual World of the Bible*, StBibLit 156 (New York: Lang, 2013).

8. See Karin Hedner Zetterholm, *Jewish Interpretation of the Bible: Ancient and Contemporary* (Minneapolis: Fortress, 2012), 36.

ecy. He sees the conflict as an occasion to urge faith in the one who is yet to come in fulfillment of the covenant with David (Isa 7:14–16; 9:6–7; 11:1–10). Habakkuk's concern about the immediate historical crisis in his day (Hab 1) is redirected by a reorientation to the textual world of the Bible in the theophany of Habakkuk 3:1–15 such that he learns to wait upon the future work of God (3:17–19; cf. Isa 8:16–18; Dan 12:13).

There is a tendency to think that whatever activity people find to do must be made biblical or Christianized, but there is a distinct possibility that such activity is not worthwhile at all. The biblical authors must be allowed to dictate what is important and what is not. Consider Karl Barth's farewell to his students in Bonn prior to his expulsion from Nazi Germany in 1935:

> We have been studying cheerfully and seriously. As far as I was concerned it could have continued in that way, and I had already resigned myself to having my grave here by the Rhine! I had plans for the future with other colleagues who are either no longer here or have been away for a long time—but there has been a frost on our spring night! And now the end has come. So listen to my last piece of advice: exegesis, exegesis and yet more exegesis! Keep to the Word, to the scripture that has been given us.[9]

Such commitment to the exegetical task in the midst of extraordinary circumstances is rooted in a fundamental belief about the Bible, that "the biblical texts must be investigated for their own sake to the extent that the revelation which they attest does not stand or occur, and is not to be sought, behind or above them but in them. If in reply it is asked whether Christianity is really a book-religion, the answer is that strangely enough Christianity has always been and only been a living religion when it is not ashamed to be actually and seriously a book-religion."[10] Preoccupation with the details of the biblical text helps to drown out the competing voices. A tractate from the Babylonian Talmud (b. Menaḥ. 99b) relates a story in which the nephew of Rabbi Ishmael (second century CE) asks what the rule is with regard to studying Greek wisdom now that he has learned the whole of the Torah. Rabbi Ishmael responds by quoting

9. See Eberhard Busch, *Karl Barth: His Life from Letters and Autobiographical Texts*, trans. John Bowden (London: SCM, 1976; repr., Eugene, OR: Wipf & Stock, 2005), 259.
10. Karl Barth, *Church Dogmatics*, vol. 1.2 (Edinburgh: T&T Clark, 1958), 494–95.

Joshua 1:8, which says that the book of the Torah should not depart from one's mouth and that one should murmur in it day and night. He then says, "Go and search for an hour that is neither part of the day nor part of the night, and learn Greek wisdom in it."

Full embrace of the textual world of the Bible has direct implications for biblical application. Is it the reader's responsibility to generate application of the Bible, assuming that the original message of the Bible is in need of an update, or do the biblical authors put their texts together in such way that their meaning remains applicable for future generations of readers? The treatment of the books of the Bible in chapters 3 and 4 shows that the eschatology of the Bible keeps the message relevant so that an explanation of the Bible's meaning is at the same time an explanation of the Bible's application. Lest the reader think that eschatology is impractical, Peter's discussion of eschatology in 2 Peter 3:11 is clear that the hope that believers have in the last days has direct implications for holy living and godliness. When Paul says in 2 Timothy 3:16 that all Scripture is "beneficial for teaching, for rebuking, for correcting, for training in righteousness," he means that Scripture is beneficial the way that it is. It does not need to be made beneficial. This requires a process of contextualizing readers to the Bible rather than contextualizing the Bible to readers.[11]

Unfortunately, much of what passes for biblical application or "practical" Bible teaching is in fact application by addition. Preachers or teachers do not identify how the biblical text applies itself. Rather, they add their own application to the text and give the audience the impression that this addition to the text is the authoritative Word of God for them. If someone says that the Bible is practical, but then adds application to it, then that person does not really believe the Bible is practical. Such a person is like a husband who tells his wife that she is beautiful but then constantly tells

---

11. "Therefore, it is primarily the job of preachers and teachers to explain the text in the manner that it has been given and on its own terms. People do not need more to-do lists and clever outlines that fade away. They need a model for reading the Bible that teaches them to ask the right kind of exegetical questions so that they can read the Bible for themselves. They do not need a finished product (e.g., a sermon or a lesson) as much as they need to be brought into the workshop so that they too can learn the tools of the trade. A repackaged version of the Bible that caters to the concerns of the audience will not suffice. The people must be reoriented to the concerns of the biblical text. It is fine to make the text as accessible as possible, but ultimately the reader must come to it. The text of Scripture, like all things great and worthwhile, does not come to anyone on his or her own terms" (Michael B. Shepherd, *A Commentary on the Book of the Twelve: The Minor Prophets*, KEL [Grand Rapids: Kregel Academic, 2018], 512).

her how to improve her appearance. The model provided in passages like Deuteronomy 31:9–13 and Nehemiah 8–9 is that the biblical text is simply to be read and explained with trust in its enduring relevance—to provide a guided tour, so to speak. The clues to application are there if the reader will only be patient to wait on them (e.g., Deut 31:13; Dan 12:13; Rom 12:1–2; Eph 4:1). Otherwise, the reader is likely to miss what the author wants to teach and thus obscure the application that the author provides.

INTERTEXTUAL SELF-INTERPRETATION

In chapter 1, which discussed the making of the Bible, there were two sections on how the Bible is designed to interpret itself and to reward those who reread it. The first section discussed how this happens at lower levels of the text (microlevel self-interpretation). The second section took the discussion to higher levels of book composition and canon formation (macrolevel self-interpretation). Now in this final chapter the discussion turns again to the Bible's interpretation of itself with a special focus on the intertextual relationships across and between biblical books. This taps into an extensive system of citation and interpretation among the biblical authors, which is an essential part of the making of the Bible's textual world beyond the level of individual compositions. The following discussion is necessarily selective, but the examples have been chosen to illustrate how such relationships can play a major role in the development of biblical theology, specifically with regard to the kingdom of God and the divine-human covenants.

THE KINGDOM OF GOD

The textual world of the Bible is the world of the kingdom of God. While the biblical text is replete with material about the kingdom of God, this section will focus on texts across the biblical canon that develop the concept of the kingdom of God in explicit relationship to one another. The first series of texts features a narrative (Gen 1:1–2:3), a poem (Ps 8), and part of an epistle (Heb 2:5–9). The poem serves as a kind of bridge between the narrative and the epistle.[12] The interaction among these different literary

---

12. See Michael B. Shepherd, *The Text in the Middle*, StBibLit 162 (New York: Lang, 2014), 1–9, 107–9.

forms from different biblical compositions establishes the kingdom of God for the reader of the biblical canon and sets up the reader very well for encounters with other complementary or supplementary texts.

In the narrative of Genesis 1:1–2:3, the crowning act of God's creation is the creation of humanity (1:26–31). Everything that happens up to this point in the narrative is in preparation for this moment. God creates humanity in his image as his vice-regent. That is, he creates humanity with the capacity to receive the blessing of life and dominion in the land (1:26–28). When humanity is driven out of the land of blessing in Genesis 3:24, the story of the Bible becomes the story of if and how the blessing of life and dominion might be restored. Thus, given the importance of Genesis 1:26–28 to the narrative of Genesis 1:1–2:3 and to the biblical narrative as a whole, any exegete of Genesis 1:1–2:3 who does not highlight in particular the dominion granted to humanity is operating independently of the biblical text and its author.

The exegesis of Genesis 1:1–2:3 in the poetry of Psalm 8 is couched within the structure of a praise hymn: superscription (Ps 8:1), call to praise (8:1–2; cf. Matt 21:16), cause for praise (Ps 8:3–8), and conclusion (8:9). The main body of the psalm is the cause for praise, and this is where the exposition of the Genesis text occurs. The psalmist is true to the text of Genesis insofar as his primary focus is on the granting of dominion to humanity. He considers the works of God in the sky (8:3; cf. Gen 1:14–19; Ps 19:1) and marvels at God's remembrance of humanity (Ps 8:4; cf. Job 7:17–18) and at how he made humanity "lack little from God" (LXX: "a little lower than angels" or "lower than angels for a little while"), crowning humanity (as vice-regent) with glory and honor (Ps 8:5]).[13] God caused humanity to rule over the works of his hands; he put everything under humanity's feet (8:6–8; cf. Gen 1:26–28). The language of putting everything under humanity's feet (i.e., in subjection to humanity) here at the beginning of

---

13. The English translation of *'elohim* in Ps 8:5 should probably be "God" due to the fact that this word means "God" in Gen 1:1–2:3, which is the very text that the psalmist is exegeting. There are several reasons why the LXX translates *'elohim* in this verse as "angels." The first is that *'elohim* can mean "angels" (e.g., Hos 12:3–4; Ps 97:7), although it normally means "God" or "gods." The second is that the ancient Jewish interpretation of the first-person plural, "Let us make humankind," in Gen 1:26 was that it referred to God and the angels (but see Gen 1:27), even though there are no angels in the text of Gen 1:1–2:3 (see Jub. 2:2; cf. Isa 6:1–2, 8). The third reason is that angelology was a topic of interest during the time of the making of the Greek translations of the Hebrew Bible.

Book 1 has an important connection within the Psalter to Psalm 110:1 at the beginning of Book 5, which envisions David's Lord, the Davidic Messiah, sitting at the right hand of the LORD until the LORD makes the Messiah's enemies into a footstool for his feet (cf. Matt 22:41–46; 1 Cor 15:27).

The citation of Psalm 8:4–6, minus Psalm 8:6a, in Hebrews 2:6–8 comes in the midst of the author's argument for the superiority of the Son of God to angels. He thus cites the Greek version of Psalm 8:5, which says that God made humanity "a little lower than angels" (or "lower than angels for a little while"). This citation is not an implicit claim about the correctness of the Greek version's interpretation of *'elohim* in Psalm 8:5. The Greek version simply suits the argument that the writer to the Hebrews wants to make. Note how the writer introduces the citation very vaguely: "Somewhere someone has testified" (Heb 2:6). God put humanity not in the heavenly realm with the angels but in the earthly realm, and he crowned humanity with glory and honor (see 1 Cor 6:3). He put all things under humanity's feet. According to Hebrews 2:8, however, we do not currently see all things in subjection to humanity. In other words, Genesis 1:26–28 is not about "human flourishing" in the present. It is about the blessing of life and dominion in the land, a blessing that was subsequently lost (Gen 3:24) and is now in need of restoration.

While we do not currently see all things in subjection to humanity, we do see Jesus made a little lower than the angels (i.e., in the incarnation), crowned with glory and honor because of the suffering of death, in order that by the grace of God he might taste death for all (Heb 2:9). Jesus is the ultimate man under whose feet all things are placed (Ps 8:6; 1 Cor 15:27) because, as the writer to the Hebrews repeatedly notes elsewhere (Heb 1:13; 5:6; 7:17, 21), he is the Davidic Messiah of Psalm 110 whose enemies will be made into a footstool for his feet. The writer to the Hebrews has successfully made the inner-textual connection between Psalm 8 and Psalm 110. It is by means of the death of Jesus that the lost blessing of life and dominion is ultimately restored not to angels but to humanity (Heb 1:14; 2:16). The great medieval Jewish commentator Rashi (Rabbi Solomon ben Isaac) notes in his commentary on Genesis 1:1 that God's creation of the world gives him the right to give the land of blessing (i.e., the land of the covenant; see Gen 2:10–14; 15:18) to whomever he pleases. This is a theme that recurs throughout the biblical canon (see Jer 27:5–6; Dan 4:17, 25). According to the book of Daniel, God will ultimately give the land to the Son of Man (Dan 7:13–14; Matt 24:30; Rev 1:7) and to the saints of the Most High who will reign with him in his kingdom (Dan 7:18, 22, 27; Rev 5:10; 20:6).

There is no kingdom without a king, and the link to Psalm 110 taps into another series of intertextual relationships that bring the king into sharper focus.[14] In Psalm 110:4, the LORD calls the Davidic Messiah "a priest forever according to the order of Melchizedek" (see 11QMelch). This designation draws upon the narrative of Genesis 14 in which Abram defeats an invading coalition of kings with an army of 318 and thus rescues his nephew Lot.[15] In the wake of this victory, Abram is met by the grateful king of Sodom and also by the mysterious king of Salem named Melchizedek who is also priest of God Most High. Melchizedek brings out bread and wine and blesses Abram, and Abram gives to him a tenth of the spoils (Gen 14:18–20). Since Salem is the old name for Jerusalem (Ps 76:2), the presence of one who is both king and priest in what would eventually become known as the City of David (2 Sam 5:7) creates a category for a priestly order to which a Davidic king might belong.

In Hebrews 7, the author wants to make the case for the superiority of Christ's priesthood to that of Aaron and his sons from the tribe of Levi. The problem is that there is no such thing as a priesthood from the tribe of Judah, which is the tribe from which the Davidic Messiah comes (Heb 7:13–14). The writer to the Hebrews thus appeals to Genesis 14:18–20 (Heb 7:1–3) and Psalm 110:4 (Heb 7:17, 21; see also 5:6) in the course of his argument. He interprets the name "Melchizedek" ("my king is Zedek") to mean "king of righteousness" (see Gen 15:6), and he interprets the phrase "the king of Salem" (*melekh shalem*) in Genesis 14:18 to mean "king of peace" (*melekh shalom*) (Heb 7:2; see Gen 15:15a, 16b). He also draws upon the narrative effect of Melchizedek's mysterious entry and exit to say that he was "without father, without mother, without genealogy, having neither beginning of days nor end of life" (Heb 7:3). The lack of any background information about Melchizedek and the absence of any development of his character in the biblical story allows for a comparison to be made to the Son of God who is actually eternally preexistent (John 1:1) and who actually remains a priest forever. This is an important analogy for the writer to the Hebrews. Unlike Aaron or any of his

---

14. See Shepherd, *Text in the Middle*, 25–27.

15. Three hundred eighteen is the numerical value of the name Eliezer (God is help) in Gen 15:2b.

sons, Jesus always lives to make intercession for his people (Heb 7:25; cf. Heb 7:8, 16) and is thus a guarantor of a better covenant (7:22). Indeed, this aspect of Melchizedek's appearance in the biblical narrative is already the basis for the statement about the eternal Messiah in Psalm 110:4: "You are a priest forever according to the order of Melchizedek" (Heb 5:6; 7:17, 21; cf. 2 Sam 7:13, 16; Dan 7:14; see also 1 Sam 2:35; 13:14; Zech 6:12–13).[16] Furthermore, since Abram gave a tenth of the spoils to Melchizedek (Gen 14:20b), it was as if Abram's descendant Levi (and Levi's descendants, including Aaron and his sons) paid a tithe to Melchizedek. According to the writer to the Hebrews, this shows that the priestly order of Aaron is inferior to that of Melchizedek (Heb 7:4–10).[17]

The chapters that come between Hebrews 1–2 (the superiority of Christ to the angels) and Hebrews 5–7 (the superiority of Christ to Aaron) in Hebrews 3–4 (the superiority of Christ to Moses and Joshua) also feature an interesting set of intertextual relationships. After noting that Christ is as a son over God's house, while Moses was a servant in God's house (Heb 3:1–6; see Num 12:7), the author cites from the second half of Psalm 95 (Heb 3:7–11, 15; 4:3, 7) in order to make the case that a future rest remains for the people of God in Christ—a rest that neither Moses nor Joshua was able to give them (Heb 4:8–9; cf. Josh 11:22; 13:1; Judg 1:27–33). The second half of Psalm 95 appears to depend upon the story of the water from the rock in Exodus 17 because of its references to the place name "Massa" and to the "testing" of the LORD that took place there (Exod 17:2, 7; Ps 95:8–9). On the other hand, the exposition of Psalm 95 in Hebrews 3–4, which warns against unbelief (Heb 3:12, 18–19; 4:2–3, 6, 11), appears to have its basis in the parallel story of the water from the rock in Numbers 20, which is part of the faith theme of the Pentateuch (see Num 20:12).

16. Whereas the author of Hebrews understands the one Messiah to occupy both the office of king and the office of priest, the Qumran sectarian documents speak of a separate Messiah of Aaron (see Lawrence Schiffman, *Reclaiming the Dead Sea Scrolls: The History of Judaism, the Background of Christianity, the Lost Library of Qumran* [New York: Doubleday, 1995], 317–28).

17. Just as Christ is king and his people reign with him (Rev 5:10; 20:6), so Christ is high priest and his people form a priesthood (Exod 19:6; Isa 61:6; 66:21; 1 Pet 2:9; Rev 1:6; 5:10; 20:6). Likewise, Christ is the prophet like Moses (Deut 18:15, 18; 34:10; John 6:14; Acts 3:22; 7:37) and his people are prophets in the sense that they are filled by the Spirit (Joel 2:28; see Num 11:29; Mic 3:8).

THE COVENANTS

A "covenant" (*berith*) in the Bible is a "self-binding obligation" (see *TLOT* 1.256–266).[18] While there are examples of "covenants" between human parties, which might be better characterized as "agreements" or "treaties," the focus of the present section is on the major divine-human covenants in the Bible and their interrelationships. In particular, the covenant with David in 2 Samuel 7 will serve as an excellent example of a text built on other texts while spawning its own series of inner-biblical readings. The careful presentation of these covenants within the biblical compositions resists the tendency among theologians to isolate and systematize them and encourages readers to understand them within their given literary setting.

The biblical covenants are often described in terms foreign to modern readers or in terms alien to the biblical context. For instance, unconditional covenants are compared to ancient Near Eastern land grant treaties, while conditional covenants are compared to ancient Near Eastern suzerain-vassal treaties. Such comparisons are not particularly helpful due to the fact that they are essentially explanations of the unknown from the unknown. Likewise, theological debates about whether there is one covenant with different administrations or multiple covenants with different dispensations do little to illuminate the role that the covenants play in the respective compositions in which they appear.[19] Rather, they impose a historical grid on the texts in order to arrange the material according to a predetermined scheme. Thus, the idea that there is one covenant with multiple administrations downplays the substantive differences between the covenants and redefines the "making" of different covenants in the biblical texts as renewals of the same covenant relationship. On the other hand, the idea that there are multiple covenants with different dispensations ignores the overlap among the covenants and seeks to separate them chronologically in order to assign them different purposes. It will become apparent in the following survey that the different covenants in the Bible are coexisting and complementary covenants designed to achieve the same

18. See John H. Sailhamer, *The Meaning of the Pentateuch: Revelation, Composition and Interpretation* (Downers Grove, IL: InterVarsity, 2009), 433.

19. The textual variation between "the covenant" and "the covenants" in witnesses to the Greek text of Rom 9:4 is likely not a choice between one covenant (with different administrations) and multiple covenants (with different dispensations) but a choice between reference to the one Sinai or Mosaic covenant (i.e., the old covenant) and reference to the multiple biblical covenants.

end: the restoration of the lost blessing of life and dominion in the land. Each covenant has a unique contribution to make to the achievement of this goal.

The first order of business is to determine whether there is already a covenant in the account of Genesis 2—a covenant with Adam. It has long been suggested by some that the stipulation in Genesis 2:17, which prohibits the tree of knowledge, constitutes a covenant relationship. The difficulty, of course, is that there is no formal account of the making of a covenant in the narrative, nor does the term "covenant" appear anywhere in the text. To this it is usually responded that the term "covenant" also does not appear in the account of the making of the covenant with David in 2 Samuel 7. The difference, however, is that there are multiple texts elsewhere that refer to 2 Samuel 7 as a covenant (e.g., 2 Sam 23:5; Ps 89:3, 28, 34, 39; 2 Chr 13:5; 21:7). Is there a passage that refers to Genesis 2 as a covenant? Proponents of a covenant with Adam argue that Hosea 6:7 is such a passage.

Hosea 6:7 has been understood in at least three ways in the history of interpretation, each of which turns on the meaning of the Hebrew word *'adham*. According to those who argue for a covenant with Adam, the text should be translated, "And they, like Adam [*ke'adham*], transgressed a covenant; there they acted treacherously against me." In other words, the people of Israel have transgressed the Mosaic covenant in the land of Israel ("there"; see Hos 6:10) just like Adam transgressed the covenant that God made with him in the Garden of Eden. Given the lack of evidence for such a covenant in Genesis 2 and elsewhere, it is reasonable to ask whether this is most likely to be the way that the text of Hosea 6:7 is intended to be read. Granted that this interpretation is possible, is it the best or most plausible option on the scale of probability? Others have suggested that Hosea 6:7 should be rendered as follows: "And they, at Adam [*be'adham*], transgressed a covenant; there they acted treacherously against me." This requires a change from the preposition *k* (like) to the preposition *b* (at)— two commonly confused letters in transmission of ancient Hebrew manuscripts. It is argued that the place name "Adam" (see Josh 3:16) fits better in context with the following clause, which refers to a place by means of the adverb "there" (but see Hos 6:10). The problem is that there is no account of a covenant transgressed at Adam. This must be judged to be the least likely of the available options.

The third option is to understand *'adham* in its most common sense as "humankind": "And they, like humankind [*ke'adham*], transgressed a covenant; there they acted treacherously against me." Despite all of the privileges granted to the people of Israel, they are no different from the rest of fallen humanity in their inability to maintain fidelity to a covenant relationship. This interpretation is not only the most straightforward one in the immediate context but also the one that creates the fewest problems. If readers adopt the view that Hosea 6:7 refers to a covenant with Adam, then they are left with the unresolved difficulty of a lack of a sign for this covenant—something that the other divine-human covenants all have (Gen 9:12; 17:11; Exod 31:13). Furthermore, all the other covenants are designed to restore the lost blessing of life and dominion in the land. There is no need for this yet in the Garden of Eden. A covenant with Adam is unnecessary. The interpretation of Hosea 6:7 that identifies a comparison of Israel to humankind in general avoids these problems.

The first major divine-human covenant in the Bible is the covenant with Noah (Gen 9:1–17). This is a covenant for all humanity. After the failure of humanity in Genesis 3 and the subsequent expulsion from the land of blessing, there are questions about whether God will choose to restore humanity and about how he might choose to do so. Despite the fact that God is under no obligation to restore humanity, it becomes apparent that covenant is his chosen means to bring about the desired restoration. After the entrance of death into the world (2:17; 4–5), the judgment of the world via the flood (6–7), and the remaking of the land (8), God confirms a covenant with Noah by revisiting his earlier words. According to the original blessing in Genesis 1:28, God blessed humanity and said, "Be fruitful and multiply and fill the land and subdue it, and rule over the fish of the sea and over the flying creatures of the sky and over every living creature that creeps on the land." This language is clearly echoed in God's words to Noah. According to Genesis 9:1–2, God blessed Noah and his sons and said, "Be fruitful and multiply and fill the land, and the fear of you and the terror of you will be on every living creature of the land and on all the flying creatures of the sky, over everything that creeps on the ground and over all the fish of the sea; into your hand are they given" (see also 9:7). Likewise, just as God granted food in Genesis 1:29–30, so he grants food in Genesis 9:3. The sign of the covenant with Noah is the rainbow (9:12–17)—a reminder after the rainfall that God would not destroy life on earth again by means of a flood of water (but see 19:24; 2 Pet 3). This covenant with Noah is an unconditional covenant relationship. It is an "everlasting covenant" (*berith 'olam*) (Gen 9:16).

The next major covenant is the covenant with Abra(ha)m (Gen 15). It is not a replacement of the covenant with Noah. Rather, there is every indication that the two covenants coexist and complement one another. Just as Noah was called from the ark (8:16), so Abram is called from the land of the Chaldeans to go to the land of blessing (12:1). Just as the covenant with Noah was designed to restore the lost blessing of Genesis 1:28 to all humanity (9:1–2), so the covenant with Abra(ha)m will restore the blessing to all the families of the earth through Abra(ha)m and his seed (12:2–3, 7; 15:18 [cf. Gen 2:10–14]; 18:18; 22:18; 26:4; 28:14; Jer 4:2; Ps 72:17; Gal 3:16). Thus, the covenant with Abra(ha)m is a more specific version of the covenant with Noah. God calls Abram out of the context of the nations descended from the sons of Noah (Gen 10–11) to give him a great "name" and to restore the lost blessing to all the nations specifically through him and his descendants. It is important to note that God does not call Abram and his descendants to be the sole people of God. Rather, he calls them to be the means of restoring the lost blessing of life and dominion in the land to the whole world, primarily through the coming of the Messiah. The conception of the people of God from the very beginning of the biblical narrative is that of a people from all the nations.[20] The story of the fate of Israel is thus the story of the fate of the world. However it goes for believing descendants of Abraham, so it goes for believing Gentiles. However it goes for unbelieving descendants of Abraham, so it goes for unbelieving Gentiles. Faith, not ethnicity, is what determines membership among the people of God (John 1:12–13).

After the call of Abram in Genesis 12:1–3, the account of the making of the covenant with Abram occurs in Genesis 15 as a prophetic vision of the future of the people of God. The boundaries of the land of the covenant granted to Abram's seed (15:18) correspond to those of the Garden of Eden (2:10–14). Genesis 17 is the confirmation of the covenant, and this is where "Abram" (exalted father) becomes "Abraham" (*'avraham*), which sounds like the Hebrew phrase *'av hamon goiim* (father of a multitude of nations) (17:5; Neh 9:7–8). Abraham is the "father of all who believe" (= *'av lekhol*

---

20. This relieves the theologian of the perceived need to construct a relationship between Israel and the church. According to one system, Israel was once the people of God, and now the church is the people of God. According to another system, Israel was once the people of God, and now the church is the people of God, but there are special promises only for Israel that God must honor in the eschaton. The problem with both these systems is the idea that Israel was once the sole people of God to the exclusion of the nations. This was never the intention, nor was there ever a separate plan for Israel. The unique role of Israel is in the restoration of the blessing to all the nations through the coming of Abraham's (and subsequently David's) messianic seed (Matt 1:1).

hamma'aminim) from all the nations (Rom 4:11). From Abraham and Sarai (later renamed Sarah) will come nations and kings of peoples (Gen 17:16; see also 49:10), and their people will be an assembly of nations (28:3; 35:11; 48:4). The sign of the covenant with Abraham is physical circumcision (17:9–14), which marks the organ that passes the seed of Abraham from generation to generation. Those who choose not to observe the sign of the covenant are cut off from the covenant community, but the covenant itself is an unconditional, "everlasting covenant" (*berith 'olam*) like the covenant with Noah (17:13; see 15:12–21). The intervening chapters of Genesis 13–14 and 16, in which Abram gives his nephew Lot the land option (13:8–9) and then attempts to build a family through his wife's Egyptian handmaid Hagar (16), pose potential threats to the covenant relationship. The apostle Paul sees this for what it is—an allegory about two covenants (Gal 4:21–5:1). The unconditional covenant with Abraham represents freedom ("the above Jerusalem"). Hagar represents the conditional covenant made at Sinai and the bondage it brings ("the present Jerusalem").

The Sinai or Mosaic covenant is a parenthesis in the series of biblical covenants due to the fact that it is the only conditional and thus temporary divine-human covenant. It is an "everlasting covenant" (*berith 'olam*) only in the sense that the time of its breaking is undefined and unknown at the outset (Exod 31:16). The conditions for the Mosaic covenant relationship are clearly laid out in Leviticus 26 and Deuteronomy 28. Only if these conditions are met will the people enjoy the blessing of life and dominion in the land (Lev 18:5). Thus, given the sinful nature of the people, this sort of relationship is doomed to failure from the beginning, and it appears to be intentionally designed to do nothing more than expose the sin of the people and to show the need for a new covenant relationship based on divine faithfulness. The prospect of obtaining the blessing by keeping the law given at Sinai is only a hypothetical one (see Ezek 20:25).

The Sinai covenant is not a replacement of the covenant with Abraham (see Gal 3:17). Rather, when the Israelites come to Sinai in the narrative of Exodus 19, they are called to keep the covenant that God made with the patriarchs (19:5). The law was added secondarily because of the people's transgression (Gal 3:19; see again the discussion in chapter 3) and thus became the basis for the terms of the covenant in Exodus 24.[21] The sign of the Sinai covenant is the Sabbath (Exod 31:12–17). It is a reminder that God

---

21. The priestly covenant (Num 18:19) is embedded within the Sinai covenant. It has

is the one who has set apart the people, just as he set apart the Sabbath day. Nevertheless, the account of the golden calf in Exodus 32 illustrates well the fact that this covenant relationship will not last. Already at Sinai the covenant is broken, yet this fractured relationship remains the context in which the people interact with God until the full consequences of their failure manifest themselves in the Babylonian exile (see Lev 26:33; Deut 28:36, 64; 29:28).

The model for understanding how such a broken relationship could remain in effect to any extent is provided in Exodus 34. God says that he is "making a covenant" (*koreth berith*) again (Exod 34:10), and the terms of this covenant are essentially the same as the ones set forth in Exodus 20–24 (see also 34:10–26). The expression "cutting a covenant" in Exodus 34:10 is the Hebrew idiom for the making of a covenant. It does not mean "renewing a covenant," an expression that would require a *piel* participle of the root *hdsh* (renew) with *berith* (covenant) as its object (cf. the renewal of the kingdom in 1 Sam 11:14). The expression for covenant renewal does not appear in Hebrew literature until the Qumran sectarian documents (see *DCH* 3:164).

The last two covenants—the Davidic covenant (2 Sam 7) and the new covenant (Jer 31:31–34)—are already anticipated in the composition of the Pentateuch. Jacob's prophecy about the last days in Genesis 49 looks forward to the coming of a messianic king from the tribe of Judah (Gen 49:8–12), and the text of Deuteronomy 29:1 introduces the words of a covenant "apart from" (*millevadh*) the covenant that was made at Horeb/Sinai—a covenant in which God circumcises the hearts of the people (Deut 30:6). Thus, while the Pentateuch does not have narrative accounts of the making of the Davidic covenant or the new covenant, all five major divine-human covenants in the Bible are already present in some form within the first book of the Bible, the book of Moses. The Davidic covenant and the new covenant are very closely linked to the covenant with Abraham and to one another. The one who comes in accordance with the covenant with David is the one who establishes the new covenant (Isa 42:6; 49:8; 55:3).

The account of the making of the covenant with David in 2 Samuel 7:1–17 comes in the context of the narrative of David's rise to power as king of Israel (1–10). It follows the stories of David's capture of the city of Je-

---

no meaning or function or life of its own apart from the terms of the Sinai covenant. Its fate is linked to that of the Sinai covenant.

rusalem (5) and his transportation of the ark of the covenant to the city (6), which set the stage for the expression of David's desire to build there for the LORD a temple that would house the ark of the covenant—a desire that the prophet Nathan initially affirms (7:1–3; cf. Ps 132:1–10). The LORD, however, has other plans, and he sends Nathan back to David with the words of a "prophetic vision" (2 Sam 7:4–5, 17; Ps 89:19; cf. Gen 15:1). He has never required such a temple from his people (2 Sam 7:6–7), and it would not be David's role to build one. David's role would be that of a warrior king to establish the borders of the land (1 Kgs 5:17; 1 Chr 22:7–8). This would enable his son Solomon to focus on the construction of the temple during peacetime (1 Chr 22:9–10). Nevertheless, David would make extensive preparations for Solomon's temple (22–29). David wanted to build a "house" (i.e., temple) for the LORD, but the LORD would build a "house" (i.e., dynasty) for him (2 Sam 7:11).

There are several key verbal links between the covenant with David and the covenant with Abra(ha)m: (1) Just as God said that he would make Abram's "name" great (Gen 12:2), so he says that he will make a great "name" for David (2 Sam 7:9); (2) Just as God said that he would give the "land" of blessing to Abram's seed (Gen 12:7; 15:18), so he says to David that he will give a "place" to his people (2 Sam 7:10); (3) Just as God said that he would give Abram "seed" (Gen 15:4–5), so he says that he will give David "seed" (2 Sam 7:12). In both cases, the "seed" is both a plurality of descendants and an individual offspring who will come from that plurality. These links indicate that the two covenants are both working toward the same end and that the latter serves to specify something about the former.

Two of the big questions surrounding the covenant with David are, on the one hand, how the terms of the covenant will apply to the multiple sons of David, and, on the other hand, how they will apply to the one son of David. Second Samuel 7:11 indicates that the LORD will build a "house" (i.e., dynasty) for David, but what follows in 2 Samuel 7:12–15 focuses on a single son of David who will build the temple and reign over an everlasting kingdom. This cannot be true of every son of David who reigns on the throne. Rather, the text has in view a unique son of David who will have a special relationship with the LORD: "As for me, I will become his father; and as for him, he will become my son" (7:14a; cf. Pss 2:7; 89:26; Rom 1:4). Such language may have been common for other ancient Near Eastern monarchs, but in the Bible, it is limited to David and this particular son of David. Second Samuel 7:14b then appears to illustrate this relationship with something that is common to all father-son relationships: "whom, in his committing iniquity, I will rebuke with a rod of men and with blows of sons of man" (see Heb 5:8). Modern English translations tend to render the first part of this as a temporal clause ("when he commits iniquity"), which would presuppose that the son of David will commit iniquity (e.g., ESV, NET, NIV). The ancient versions, however, interpret the same Hebrew construction as conditional ("if he commits iniquity"), which would mean that the scenario is only hypothetical (see LXX, Tg. Jon., Vulg.; see also Luther, KJV).

The inner-biblical readings of the covenant with David are devoted to answering the above two questions about the application of the terms of the covenant to the sons of David and to the son of David. Both David and Solomon believe Solomon to be the son of David who will build the temple, and they believe that the terms of the covenant apply conditionally to the sons of David (1 Kgs 2:4; 3:14; 6:12; 8:25; 9:4–5; 1 Chr 22:13; but see 2 Sam 23:1–7). The author of Kings, however, shows that the kingdom of Solomon does not last (1 Kgs 11–12), and this leads to the end of the Davidic monarchy (2 Kgs 24–25). Is this because Solomon and his sons did not keep the terms of the covenant, or is it because Solomon was not after all the son of David who would build the temple and reign over an everlasting kingdom? The resounding answer from the other biblical authors is both. The terms of the covenant do apply conditionally to the sons of David who reign on the throne from Solomon to Zedekiah, but the covenant is unconditional in its application to the one messianic son of David who is yet to come and build his temple and reign forever.

When the Latter Prophets take up the language of the Davidic covenant, they see the hope of a new, ideal David in the future (e.g., Isa 9:6–7; 11:1–10; Ezek 34:24–25; Hos 3:5; Mic 5:2), and they put no condition on the fulfillment of this hope. Whereas 2 Samuel 7:12 says, "When your days are fulfilled, and you lie with your forefathers, I will raise up [*hiphil* of *qum*] your seed after you who will go out from you, and I will establish his kingdom," Jeremiah 23:5 says, "Look days are coming, the prophetic utterance of the LORD, and I will raise up [*hiphil* of *qum*] for David a righteous Branch, and a king will reign and act wisely and perform justice and righteousness in the land" (cf. Isa 4:2; 11:1). This use of the *hiphil* of *qum* from 2 Samuel 7:12 also appears in the messianic prophecies of Jeremiah 30:9 and Ezekiel 34:23.

The text of Zechariah 6:12–13, which is what the prophet Zechariah is to say to Joshua the high priest about the man whom Joshua's symbolic act of wearing a crown represents, cites from Jeremiah 23:5 and 2 Samuel 7:13: "Look, a man, Branch is his name, and from his place will he sprout, and he will build the temple of the LORD [lacking in the Syr.]; and he is the one who will build the temple of the LORD [lacking in the LXX]." The messianic title "Branch" comes from Jeremiah 23:5 (see also Zech 3:8), and the statements about the building of the temple come from 2 Samuel 7:13. Both the Syriac, which deletes the last clause of Zechariah 6:12 ("and he will build the temple of the LORD"), and the Septuagint, which deletes the first clause of Zechariah 6:13 ("and he is the one who will build the temple of the LORD"), are the result of reading the two clauses as redundant repetition, but the two clauses are not identical in the Hebrew text. The clause at the beginning of Zechariah 6:13, which features the fronted pronoun *hu'* (he), more closely matches the syntax of 2 Samuel 7:13. In 2 Samuel 7:13, the sense of the fronting is to say, "He [rather than you, David] is the one who will build a house for my name." In Zechariah 6:13, the sense of it is to say: "and he [rather than Solomon] is the one who will build the temple of the LORD." From the postexilic perspective of the prophet Zechariah, both Solomon and the history of the Davidic monarchy are things of the past, and only the messianic hope of the covenant with David lies ahead.

Psalm 89 is arguably the most extensive treatment of 2 Samuel 7 in the Hebrew Bible (see Ps 89:1–4, 19–37). The text presents a poetic version of the prophetic vision that came to David through Nathan and clearly articulates that the terms of the covenant with David apply conditionally to the sons of David (Ps 89:30–32; cf. 2 Sam 7:14), but then the LORD speaks of his unconditional covenant loyalty: "But as for my covenant loyalty, I will not break [nonn Mss, Syr.: remove] it from him" (Ps 89:33; cf. 2 Sam 7:15). To whom does the singular pronoun "him" refer? If it refers to David (Ps 89:20–28), then the question becomes one of how the LORD can maintain covenant loyalty to David if the terms of the covenant apply to the sons of David conditionally. In other words, if and when the sons of David break the covenant, how does the covenant relationship with David endure? On the other hand, it is possible that the pronoun "him" refers to the seed of David (89:4, 29), not in the collective sense but in the individual sense. That is, the terms of the covenant apply unconditionally to the one messianic son of David who is yet to come. Even if the pronoun "him" refers to David, the only way left for the LORD to show enduring faithfulness to David after the failure of the sons of David is to raise up the messianic son of David to reign over an everlasting kingdom. It is precisely this distinction between the conditional application to the sons of David and the unconditional application to the son of David that the voice in Psalm 89:38–51 is struggling to understand. It is the voice of one of the sons of David who sees the impending demise of the Davidic monarchy that the sons of David have brought upon themselves. This is incomprehensible to him because he mistakenly thinks that the terms of the covenant apply to the sons of David unconditionally. For the reader of the psalm, however, it is clear that those terms only apply unconditionally to the new David as depicted in the Prophets.

Psalm 132 also appears to distinguish between the conditional application of the terms of the Davidic covenant to the sons of David and the unconditional application of those same terms to one particular son of David. Psalm 132:12 says, "If your sons keep my covenant and my testimonies that I teach them, also their sons forever will sit on your throne." Alternately, Psalm 132:17–18 says, "There [i.e., in Zion] will I cause to sprout a horn [Tg. Jon.: a glorious king] for David; I have arranged a lamp for my anointed one [or, my Messiah]. His enemies will I clothe with shame, and upon him his crown will shine [LXX, Syr.: my consecration will blossom]" (cf. 1 Sam 2:10; 2 Sam 23:5; 1 Kgs 11:36; Isa 4:2; Jer 23:5; Ezek 29:21; Zech 3:8; 6:12; Luke 1:69).

The book of Daniel returns to the sole focus on the one messianic son of David found in the Prophets. According to 2 Samuel 7:13b, the LORD will establish the throne of the son of David forever. Thus, Daniel's interpretation of Nebuchadnezzar's dream in Daniel 2 looks beyond the history of the Davidic monarchy to the last days (Dan 2:28; cf. Gen 49:1, 8–12; Num 24:7–9, 14, 17; Isa 2:2–5; Jer 30:8–9, 21, 24; Ezek 38:14–17; Hos 3:5; Dan 10:14). The dream itself culminates with the image of a stone that strikes the statue of gold, silver, bronze, and iron and clay and then becomes a great mountain that fills the whole earth (Dan 2:34–35; cf. Isa 8:14–15; 28:16–17; Zech 3:8–10; Ps 118:22; Matt 21:33–46; Rom 9:33; 1 Pet 2:4–10). Daniel's interpretation of this indicates that it represents an everlasting kingdom that will never be destroyed (Dan 2:44–45). The parallel vision of Daniel 7 culminates with the destruction of the four beasts and the presentation of the Son of Man before the Ancient of Days (7:1–14). The Son of Man is the messianic son of David who receives an everlasting kingdom (7:14; see also Matt 24:30; Rev 1:7). In full restoration of the lost blessing of life and dominion in the land (Gen 1:26–28), the Davidic Messiah will reign, and the saints will reign with him (Dan 7:14, 18, 27; cf. Isa 32:1; Jer 3:15; 23:4–6; Mic 5:2–6; Rev 1:6; 5:9–10; 20:6). There is no condition set on this. It is an unconditional prophecy.

The Chronicler's version of the covenant with David in 1 Chronicles 17 reveals the interest of someone living in the postexilic period whose only hope in the future lies not in the conditional application of the terms of the covenant to the sons of David but in the unconditional application of those terms to the messianic son of David. In 2 Samuel 7:16, God says to David through Nathan, "And your house [dynasty] will endure, and your kingdom, forever before you; your throne will be established forever." Here the emphasis is on David's dynasty, kingdom, and throne, despite the fact that the focus of the previous verses in 2 Samuel 7:12–15 has been on the everlasting kingdom of the son of David. For the Chronicler, however, the time of David's dynasty, kingdom, and throne has passed. Only the everlasting kingdom of the son of David remains: "And I will cause him to endure in my house [i.e., temple] and in my kingdom forever, and his throne will be established forever" (2 Chr 17:14). Here the emphasis is on the endurance of the future son of David in God's house and in God's kingdom. It is the throne of the son of David that will be established forever.

The sign of the covenant with David is not explicit in 2 Samuel 7 the way that the signs of the covenants with Noah, Abraham, and Moses are made explicit in their respective contexts. If indeed there is a sign for this covenant, the best that the reader can do is to infer it from the terms of the covenant. Since the Davidic seed is undoubtedly a central feature of the covenant, it is possible that the son of David himself is the sign of the covenant. According to the prophecy about the Davidic Messiah in Isaiah 11:1–10, nations will seek the root of Jesse who stands as a "banner" for peoples (Isa 11:10, 12; cf. Gen 49:10; Hos 3:5). Targum Jonathan calls this banner a "sign" (cf. Isa 66:19). Thus, in John 12:32 Jesus says, "And as for me, if I am lifted from the earth, I will draw all to myself" (see also John 3:14–17, which compares the lifting up of the Son of Man to the lifting of the "banner" in Num 21:8–9). Likewise, the sign of the coming of Christ and of the end of the age (Matt 24:3) is said to be the coming of the Son of Man in Daniel 7:13–14 (Matt 24:30) who will reign over an everlasting kingdom in accordance with the covenant with David, an "everlasting covenant" (*berith 'olam*; 2 Sam 23:5).

The new covenant is the covenant "apart from" (*millevadh*) the covenant that was made at Horeb/Sinai (Deut 29:1). It is not a renewal of the Sinai covenant. The LORD had not yet given the people a heart to know, eyes to see, or ears to hear under the old covenant (Deut 29:4).

Thus, the old covenant was broken (Jer 11:10), and the new covenant now makes it obsolete (Heb 8:13). Indeed, the opening statement about the new covenant in Jeremiah 31:31–32 is that it is not like the covenant that God made with the people when he brought them out of Egypt— the very covenant that they broke. Rather, in the new covenant, the hearts of the people are circumcised (Deut 10:16; 30:6; Jer 4:4; 9:25–26; Rom 2:28–29; Col 2:11) and God's instructions are written not ineffectively on tablets of stone (Exod 31:18) but effectively on the hearts of the people themselves (Jer 31:33–34; 32:39). This transformation is wrought by the Spirit of God (Ezek 11:19–20; 18:31; 36:26–27). The new covenant is an unconditional, "everlasting covenant" (*berith 'olam*; Isa 61:8; Jer 32:40; Ezek 37:26). The sign of the covenant is circumcision of the heart (Deut 30:6), which is the spiritual version of the sign of the Abrahamic covenant (i.e., physical circumcision of the flesh). This new covenant is established by the Davidic Messiah (Isa 42:6; 49:8; 55:3; Ezek 37:25–26; Luke 22:20).

Table 10: The Covenants

Covenant	Conditional or Unconditional	Sign
Noahic (Gen 9:1–16)	Unconditional	Rainbow
Abrahamic (Gen 15)	Unconditional	Circumcision of flesh
Mosaic (Sinai) (Exod 24)	Conditional	Sabbath
Davidic (2 Sam 7:1–17)	Unconditional	Son of David
New (Jer 31:31–34)	Unconditional	Circumcision of heart

The life of the Christian and the life of the church are inextricably linked to a healthy understanding of the making and meaning of the Bible. The biblical authors invite both the individual believer (Pss 1; 19; 119) and the community of faith (Neh 8–9) to enter the textual world of the Bible. A Christian without Scripture is like a tree without water, and a church without Scripture fails to build up the body of Christ to be a witness to the gospel both near and far (Eph 4:11–16; 1 Tim 4:11–16). The intricacies of the Bible and the Bible's rich history of interpretation are more than enough to keep believers occupied for a lifetime, and there is no better way to live a life of faith than to be busy with the details of God's word. In order for this to happen, however, churches must not put limits on the education of its members. Pastors must be equipped and supported as experts in the teaching of the Bible in its original languages, and church leaders must make available every kind of excellent and high-quality resource to the membership for the people to grow as much as they can. The result will be a new breed of Christian churches—churches shaped not by tradition alone or by the changing trends of culture but by the study of Scripture itself.

GLOSSARY

Aleppo Codex: a codex of the Masoretic Text (the traditional, rabbinic text of the Hebrew Bible) from the medieval period

Alexandrian Text: conservative text of the Greek New Testament associated with the church in Alexandria, Egypt

Alexandrinus: a fifth-century CE codex of the Greek Bible

anthropomorphism: attribution of human characteristics to God

Antiochene Greek Translation: ancient Greek translation of the Hebrew Bible that bears witness to the Old Greek

apocalyptic: a type of literature characterized by otherworldly imagery, visions of things to occur on the other side of history, and angelic guides to interpretations of visions

Apocrypha (hidden): ancient literature produced by Jews mostly in Hebrew or Aramaic but later preserved by Christians in translation; once considered "hidden" until the present time or "sealed" until the appropriate time, but later deemed inappropriate for public worship yet valuable for exegesis of the Bible

apodictic laws: simple commands or prohibitions that apply absolutely in every circumstance

Aquila: produced a woodenly literal revised Greek version in the second century CE

Babylonian Talmud: a major body of rabbinic literature from around 600 CE

Byzantine Text: also known as the majority text or the received text, a text of the Greek New Testament associated with the church of Asia Minor and characterized by expanded and conflated readings

Caesarean Text: text of the Greek New Testament that combines features of the Alexandrian and Western texts

Cairo Codex: a codex of the Masoretic Text (the traditional, rabbinic text) of the Prophets from the medieval period

canon of Scripture: sometimes defined as a closed list of authoritative books but also as an arrangement of scriptural books that have mutually influenced each other

case laws: laws that only apply if the stated conditions of the situation are met

chiastic: arranged in inverse order

compositional analysis: examines how the parts of a literary work fit into the whole

Dead Sea Scrolls: ancient biblical and non-biblical scrolls in Hebrew, Aramaic, and Greek from a series of discoveries in the Judean wilderness near the Dead Sea beginning in 1947

Deuteronomistic History: according to the German scholar Martin Noth, a single literary complex that includes Deuteronomy and the Former Prophets (Joshua, Judges, 1–2 Samuel, and 1–2 Kings)

dispensation: system of order

dynamic equivalency: freer, more thought-for-thought translation technique

exegesis: the process by which an interpreter draws out the meaning of a text; the opposite of eisegesis (reading something into a text)

formal equivalency: literal or word-for-word translation technique

Former Prophets: the books of Joshua, Judges, 1–2 Samuel, and 1–2 Kings

gematria: practice of assigning numerical value to the letters of words

grammar and syntax: analysis of the form and arrangement of words

hermeneutics: interpretation

Hesychius: name to which an unknown recension of the Septuagint (third century CE, Egypt) was attributed by Jerome

historical criticism: studies the hypothetical prehistory of literature and reconstructs the events to which the literature refers

homoioarchton: accidental error in which a scribe or translator skips from the beginning of one section of text to a similar beginning of another section of text, thereby omitting the intervening text

homoioteleuton: accidental error in which a scribe or translator skips from the end of one section of text to a similar ending of another section of text, thereby omitting the intervening text

intertextuality: what happens between texts (e.g., citation, allusion, etc.)

Jerome: church father from the fourth century CE who produced the Latin Vulgate

kaige: a tradition of revising the original Greek or Old Greek translations of the Hebrew Bible toward the proto-MT (first century BCE and first century CE); best represented by the B text of Judges (Vaticanus), the revised sections of 2 Samuel and 2 Kings, the Greek Minor Prophets Scroll from Naḥal Ḥever, and the Megilloth

Latin Vulgate (Vulg.): Latin translation of the Bible from the church father Jerome

Latter Prophets: the books of Isaiah, Jeremiah, Ezekiel, and the Twelve (Hosea–Malachi)

Leningrad Codex: a codex of the Masoretic Text (the traditional, rabbinic text of the Hebrew Bible) from the medieval period

Masoretic Text (MT): the traditional, rabbinic Hebrew text of the Bible with consonants, vowels, accents, and marginal notes

Megilloth (festival scrolls): the books of Ruth, Song of Songs, Ecclesiastes, Lamentations, and Esther

merism: a figure of speech in which two contrasting parts refer to the whole

New Perspective on Paul: movement within New Testament studies concerned with understanding the writings of the apostle Paul in light of ancient Jewish sources

Old Greek (OG): the original Greek translation of any book of the Hebrew Bible other than the Pentateuch (Genesis–Deuteronomy)

Old Latin: ancient Latin translation of the Septuagint

Origen: church father from the third century CE who produced the Hexapla, which contained the following: the Hebrew text (proto-MT), a Greek transliteration of the Hebrew text, Aquila, Symmachus, the Septuagint, and Theodotion

paradigmatic: involves signs that can replace each other

Pentateuch (five-part book): a Greek term for the five books of Moses (Genesis–Deuteronomy), otherwise known as the Torah (instruction) in Hebrew

programmatic passage: a text placed near the beginning of a literary work to set the trajectory for the work as a whole

Pseudepigrapha (falsely ascribed): ancient literature produced by Jews mostly in Hebrew or Aramaic but later preserved by Christians in translation; falsely ascribed to ancient authors yet valuable for exegesis of the Bible

Qumran: site of an ancient settlement in the Judean wilderness near the Dead Sea and close to the eleven caves where many of the Dead Sea Scrolls were discovered

Samaritan Pentateuch (SP): the ancient Hebrew version of the Pentateuch (Genesis–Deuteronomy) used by the Samaritan community

semantics: the study of word usage, range of meaning, and field of meaning (i.e., how a word compares and contrasts with other words in the same semantic field)

Septuagint (LXX): originally a term for the ancient Greek translation of the Pentateuch (Genesis–Deuteronomy) made by the "seventy" or seventy-two translators according to the legend of the Letter of Aristeas, but now commonly used as a term for the Greek version of the Hebrew Bible

Sinaiticus: a fourth-century CE codex of the Greek Bible

source language: language from which a translation is made

Symmachus: produced a revision of the old Antiochene Greek translation in the second century CE

syntagmatic: involves a sequence of signs

Syriac Peshitta (Syr.): the "simple" translation of the Hebrew Bible into the ancient Aramaic dialect of Syriac

target language: language into which a translation is made

Targum: ancient Aramaic translation and commentary of the Hebrew Bible

textual criticism: establishes the text that stood at the beginning of the transmission process

Theodotion: the closest heir to the kaige revised Greek translation tradition

theophany: manifestation of God

Torah (instruction): a term that could be used for the five books of Moses or for the Hebrew Bible as a whole

Vaticanus: a fourth-century CE codex of the Greek Bible

Western Text: primarily known from Codex D or the Bezan Codex (fifth-century CE) and associated with the church in Rome; a very expansive text of the Greek New Testament designed to provide clarification and explanation

SELECTED BIBLIOGRAPHY

Abegg, Martin, Jr., Peter Flint, and Eugene Ulrich. *The Dead Sea Scrolls Bible: The Oldest Known Bible Translated into English for the First Time*. New York: HarperCollins, 1999.

Auerbach, Erich. *Mimesis: The Representation of Reality in Western Literature*. Translated by Willard R. Trask. 50th anniversary ed. Princeton: Princeton University Press, 2003.

Bar-Efrat, Shimon. *Narrative Art in the Bible*. London: T&T Clark, 2004.

Barr, James. *The Concept of Biblical Theology: An Old Testament Perspective*. Minneapolis: Fortress, 1999.

Barth, Karl. *Church Dogmatics*. Vol. 1.2. Edinburgh: T&T Clark, 1958.

Beckwith, Roger T. "Formation of the Hebrew Bible." Pages 39–86 in *Mikra: Text, Translation, Reading and Interpretation of the Hebrew Bible in Ancient Judaism and Early Christianity*. Edited by Martin Jan Mulder and Harry Sysling. Philadelphia: Fortress, 1988. Repr., Peabody, MA: Hendrickson, 2004.

Berlin, Adele. *Poetics and Interpretation of Biblical Narrative*. Winona Lake, IN: Eisenbrauns, 1994.

Black, Matthew. *An Aramaic Approach to the Gospels and Acts*. 3rd ed. With an introduction by Craig A. Evans and an appendix by Geza Vermes. Oxford: Oxford University Press, 1967. Repr., Peabody, MA: Hendrickson, 1998.

Blenkinsopp, Joseph. *Prophecy and Canon: A Contribution to the Study of Jewish Origins*. Notre Dame: University of Notre Dame Press, 1977.

Bruns, Gerald. "Midrash and Allegory." Pages 625–46 in *The Literary Guide to the Bible*. Edited by Frank Kermode and Robert Alter. Cambridge, MA: Belknap, 1987.

Buisch, Pauline Paris. "The Rest of Her Offspring: The Relationship between Revelation 12 and the Targumic Expansion of Genesis 3:15." *NovT* 60 (2018): 386–401.

Bullinger, E. W. *Figures of Speech Used in the Bible: Explained and Illustrated*. London: Eyre and Spottiswoode, 1898. Repr., Grand Rapids: Baker, 1968.

Busch, Eberhard. *Karl Barth: His Life from Letters and Autobiographical Texts*. Translated by John Bowden. London: SCM, 1976. Repr., Eugene, OR: Wipf & Stock, 2005.

Carson, D. A. "Syntactical and Text-Critical Observations on John 20:30–31: One More Round on the Purpose of the Fourth Gospel." *JBL* 124 (2005): 693–714.

Chapman, Stephen B. *The Law and the Prophets: A Study in Old Testament Canon Formation*. FAT 27. Tübingen: Mohr Siebeck, 2000.

Chen, Kevin. "Wisdom Is Worth a Thousand Laws: Legal Insufficiency and Exception as Intentional Compositional Strategy in the Pentateuch." Pages 37–59 in *Text and Canon: Essays in Honor of John H. Sailhamer*. Edited by Robert L. Cole and Paul J. Kissling. Eugene, OR: Pickwick, 2017.

Childs, Brevard S. *The Book of Exodus: A Critical, Theological Commentary*. OTL. Louisville: Westminster John Knox, 1974.

———. *Introduction to the Old Testament as Scripture*. Philadelphia: Fortress, 1979.

———. *Isaiah: A Commentary*. OTL. Louisville: Westminster John Knox, 2000.

Christensen, Duane L. "Num 21:14–15 and the Book of the Wars of Yahweh." *CBQ* 36 (1974): 359–60.

Cole, Robert L. *Psalms 1 and 2: Gateway to the Psalter*. Sheffield: Sheffield Phoenix, 2013.

Comfort, Philip Wesley, and David P. Barrett. *The Text of the Earliest New Testament Greek Manuscripts*. 2 vols. 3rd ed. Grand Rapids: Kregel Academic, 2019.

Daniel, Andrew Glen. "The Translator's Tell: Translation Technique, Verbal Syntax, and the Myth of Old Greek Daniel's Alternate Semitic *Vorlage*." *JBL* 140 (2021): 723–49.

Driver, S. R. *Notes on the Hebrew Text and the Topography of the Books of Samuel*. 2nd ed. Oxford: Oxford University Press, 1912.

Eisenstein, Sergei M. *The Film Sense*. Translated and edited by Jay Leyda. San Diego: Harcourt Brace & Company, 1942.

Eissfeldt, Otto. *The Old Testament: An Introduction*. Translated by Peter R. Ackroyd. New York: Harper and Row, 1965.

Ellis, E. Earle. "The Old Testament Canon in the Early Church." Pages 653–90 in *Mikra: Text, Translation, Reading and Interpretation of the Hebrew*

Bible in Ancient Judaism and Early Christianity. Edited by Martin Jan Mulder and Harry Sysling. Philadelphia: Fortress, 1988. Repr., Peabody, MA: Hendrickson, 2004.

Feldman, Louis H., James L. Kugel, and Lawrence H. Schiffman, eds. *Outside the Bible: Ancient Jewish Writings Related to Scripture*. Vol. 1. Philadelphia: The Jewish Publication Society, 2013.

Fishbane, Michael. *Biblical Interpretation in Ancient Israel*. Oxford: Clarendon, 1985.

Flesher, Paul V. M., and Bruce Chilton. *The Targums: A Critical Introduction*. Waco, TX: Baylor University Press, 2011.

Floyd, Michael H. "New Form Criticism and Beyond: The Historicity of Prophetic Literature Revisited." Pages 17–36 in *The Book of the Twelve and the New Form Criticism*. Edited by Mark J. Boda, Michael H. Floyd, and Colin M. Toffelmire. ANEM 10. Atlanta: Society of Biblical Literature, 2015.

Fokkelman, J. P. *Reading Biblical Narrative: An Introductory Guide*. Translated by Ineke Smit. Louisville: Westminster John Knox, 1999.

Fox, Michael V. *Proverbs: An Eclectic Edition with Introduction and Textual Commentary*. The Hebrew Bible: A Critical Edition 1. Atlanta: Society of Biblical Literature, 2014.

———. "The Redaction of the Greek Alpha-Text of Esther." Pages 207–20 in *"Sha'arei Talmon": Studies in the Bible, Qumran, and the Ancient Near East Presented to Shemaryahu Talmon*. Edited by Michael Fishbane and Emanuel Tov with the assistance of Weston W. Fields. Winona Lake, IN: Eisenbrauns, 1992.

Frei, Hans W. *The Eclipse of Biblical Narrative: A Study in Eighteenth and Nineteenth Century Hermeneutics*. New Haven: Yale University Press, 1974.

Gunkel, Hermann. *An Introduction to the Psalms: The Genres of the Religious Lyric of Israel*. Completed by Joachim Begrich. Translated by James D. Nogalski. Macon, GA: Mercer University Press, 1998.

Hendel, Ronald. *Steps to a New Edition of the Hebrew Bible*. TCSt 10. Atlanta: Society of Biblical Literature, 2016.

Hirsch, E. D., Jr. *Validity in Interpretation*. New Haven: Yale University Press, 1967.

Horbury, William. *Jewish Messianism and the Cult of Christ*. London: SC, 1998.

Janzen, J. Gerald. *Studies in the Text of Jeremiah*. Cambridge: Harvard University Press, 1973.

Kaiser, Walter C., Jr. "Exodus." Pages 335–561 in *Genesis–Leviticus*. Edited by

Tremper Longman III and David E. Garland. EBC. Rev. ed. Grand Rapids: Zondervan, 2005.

Koorevar, Hendrik J. "Chronicles as the Intended Conclusion to the Old Testament Canon." Pages 207–35 in *The Shape of the Writings*. Edited by Julius Steinberg and Timothy J. Stone. Siphrut: Literature and Theology of the Hebrew Scriptures 16. Winona Lake, IN: Eisenbrauns, 2015.

Köstenberger, Andreas J., L. Scott Kellum, and Charles L. Quarles. *The Cradle, the Cross, and the Crown: An Introduction to the New Testament*. Nashville: B&H Academic, 2009.

Kreuzer, Siegfried, ed. *Introduction to the Septuagint*. Translated by David A. Brenner and Peter Altmann. Waco, TX: Baylor University Press, 2019.

Kugel, James L. *The Idea of Biblical Poetry: Parallelism and Its History*. New Haven: Yale University Press, 1981. Repr., Baltimore: The Johns Hopkins University Press, 1998.

———. "Two Introductions to Midrash." Pages 77–104 in *Midrash and Literature*. Edited by Geoffrey Hartman and Sanford Budick. New Haven: Yale University Press, 1986.

Kynes, Will. "Reading Job following the Psalms." Pages 131–45 in *The Shape of the Writings*. Edited by Julius Steinberg and Timothy J. Stone, 131–45. Siphrut: Literature and Theology of the Hebrew Scriptures 16. Winona Lake, IN: Eisenbrauns, 2015.

Levenson, Jon D. *Esther: A Commentary*. OTL. Louisville: Westminster John Knox, 1997.

Levey, Samson H. *The Messiah: An Aramaic Interpretation, The Messianic Exegesis of the Targum*. Cincinnati: Hebrew Union College Press, 1974.

Lindbeck, George A. *The Nature of Doctrine: Religion and Theology in a Postliberal Age*. Philadelphia: Westminster, 1984.

Longman, Tremper, III. *Proverbs*. BCOTWP. Grand Rapids: Baker Academic, 2006.

Lundbom, J. R. "Baruch, Seraiah, and Expanded Colophons in the Book of Jeremiah." *JSOT* 36 (1986): 89–114.

Lyons, Michael A. *From Law to Prophecy: Ezekiel's Use of the Holiness Code*. LHBOTS 507. London: T&T Clark, 2009.

Mackie, Timothy P. *Expanding Ezekiel: The Hermeneutics of Scribal Addition in the Ancient Text Witnesses of the Book of Ezekiel*. FRLANT 257. Göttingen: Vandenhoeck & Ruprecht, 2015.

Mays, James L. "The Place of Torah-Psalms in the Psalter." *JBL* 106 (1987): 3–12.

McConville, J. G. *Deuteronomy*. ApOTC 5. Downers Grove, IL: IVP Academic, 2002.

Meyer, Jason C. *The End of the Law: Mosaic Covenant in Pauline Theology.* NAC Studies in Bible & Theology 6. Nashville: B&H Academic, 2009.

Nihan, Christopher. "The 'Prophets' as Scriptural Collection and Scriptural Prophecy during the Second Temple Period." Page 67–85 in *Writing the Bible: Scribes, Scribalism and Script.* Edited by Philip R. Davies and Thomas Römer. Durham: Acumen, 2013.

Noonan, Benjamin J. "Abraham, Blessing, and the Nations." *HS* 51 (2010): 73–93.

Noth, Martin. *The Deuteronomistic History.* Sheffield: JSOT, 1981.

Parke-Taylor, Geoffrey H. *The Formation of the Book of Jeremiah: Doublets and Recurring Phrases.* SBLMS 51. Atlanta: Society of Biblical Literature, 2000.

Pritchard, James B., ed. *Ancient Near Eastern Texts Relating to the Old Testament.* 3rd. ed. Princeton: Princeton University Press, 1969.

Rabin, Chaim. "Hebrew and Aramaic in the First Century." Pages 1007–37 in *The Jewish People in the First Century.* Vol. 2. Edited by S. Safrai and M. Stern. CRINT 1. Philadelphia: Fortress, 1976.

Rendtorff, Rolf. *The Canonical Hebrew Bible.* Translated by David E. Orton. Leiden: Deo, 2005.

Robinson, Maurice A., and William G. Pierpont. *The New Testament in the Original Greek: Byzantine Textform.* Southborough, MA: Chilton Book Publishing, 2005.

Rofé, A. "The End of the Book of Joshua according to the Septuagint." *Henoch* 4 (1982): 17–36.

Rösel, Christoph. *Die messianische Redaktion des Psalters: Studien zu Entstehung und Theologie der Sammlung Psalm 2–89.* Stuttgart: Calwer, 1999.

Sailhamer, John H. "Biblical Theology and the Composition of the Hebrew Bible." Pages 25–37 in *Biblical Theology: Retrospect and Prospect.* Edited by Scott J. Hafemann. Downers Grove, IL: InterVarsity, 2002.

———. "Hosea 11:1 and Matthew 2:15." *WTJ* 63 (2001): 87–96.

———. *Introduction to Old Testament Theology: A Canonical Approach.* Grand Rapids: Zondervan, 1995.

———. *The Meaning of the Pentateuch: Revelation, Composition and Interpretation.* Downers Grove, IL: InterVarsity, 2009.

———. *The Pentateuch as Narrative: A Biblical-Theological Commentary.* Grand Rapids: Zondervan, 1992.

Schiffman, Lawrence. *Reclaiming the Dead Sea Scrolls: The History of Judaism, the Background of Christianity, the Lost Library of Qumran.* New York: Doubleday, 1995.

Schmitt, Hans-Christoph. "Redaktion des Pentateuch im Geiste der Prophetie." *Vetus Testamentum* 32 (1982): 170–89.

Schniedewind, William M. *The Word of God in Transition: From Prophet to Exegete in the Second Temple Period.* JSOTSup 197. Sheffield: Sheffield Academic, 1995.

Seeligmann, Isac Leo. *The Septuagint Version of Isaiah and Cognate Studies.* FAT 40. Tübingen: Mohr Siebeck, 2004.

Seitz, Christopher R. *Prophecy and Hermeneutics: Toward a New Introduction to the Prophets.* STI. Grand Rapids: Baker Academic, 2007.

———. "The Prophet Moses and the Canonical Shape of Jeremiah." *ZAW* 101 (1989): 3–27.

———. "Two Testaments and the Failure of One Tradition History." Pages 195–211 in *Biblical Theology: Retrospect and Prospect.* Edited by Scott J. Hafemann. Downers Grove, IL: InterVarsity, 2002.

Shepherd, Michael B. *A Commentary on Jeremiah.* KEL. Grand Rapids: Kregel Academic, 2023.

———. *A Commentary on the Book of the Twelve: The Minor Prophets.* KEL. Grand Rapids: Kregel Academic, 2018.

———. *Daniel in the Context of the Hebrew Bible.* StBibLit 123. New York: Lang, 2009.

———. "Is the Septuagint the Christian Bible?" *TrinJ* 41 (2020): 149–64.

———. "The New Exodus in the Composition of the Twelve." Pages 120–36 in *Text and Canon: Essays in Honor of John H. Sailhamer.* Edited by Robert L. Cole and Paul J. Kissling. Eugene, OR: Pickwick, 2017.

———. "Targums as Guides to Hebrew Syntax." *Them* 47.1 (2022): 49–59.

———. *The Text in the Middle.* StBibLit 162. New York: Lang, 2014.

———. *Textuality and the Bible.* Eugene, OR: Wipf & Stock, 2016.

———. *The Textual World of the Bible.* StBibLit 156. New York: Lang, 2013.

———. *The Twelve Prophets in the New Testament.* StBibLit 140. New York: Lang, 2011.

Steinberg, Julius, and Timothy J. Stone. "The Historical Formation of the Writings in Antiquity." Pages 1–58 in *The Shape of the Writings.* Edited by Julius Steinberg and Timothy J. Stone. Siphrut: Literature and Theology of the Hebrew Scriptures 16. Winona Lake, IN: Eisenbrauns, 2015.

Steiner, Richard C. "Four Inner-Biblical Interpretations of Genesis 49:10: On the Lexical and Syntactic Ambiguities of עַד as Reflected in the Prophecies of Nathan, Ahijah, Ezekiel, and Zechariah." *JBL* 132 (2013): 33–60.

Sternberg, Meir. *The Poetics of Biblical Narrative: Ideological Literature and the Drama of Reading.* Bloomington: Indiana University Press, 1985.

Tal, Abraham. "Is There a Raison d'Être for an Aramaic Targum in a Hebrew-Speaking Society?" *REJ* 160 (2001): 357–78.

Teeter, David Andrew. *Scribal Laws: Exegetical Variation in the Textual Transmission of Biblical Law in the Late Second Temple Period.* FAT 92. Tübingen: Mohr Siebeck, 2014.

Tigay, Jeffrey H. *The Evolution of the Gilgamesh Epic.* Philadelphia: University of Pennsylvania Press, 1982. Repr., Wauconda, IL: Bolchazy-Carducci, 2002.

Toorn, Karel van der. *Scribal Culture and the Making of the Hebrew Bible.* Cambridge: Harvard University Press, 2007.

Tov, Emanuel. *The Greek and Hebrew Bible: Collected Essays on the Septuagint.* VTSup 72. Atlanta: Society of Biblical Literature, 2006.

———. *The Text-Critical Use of the Septuagint in Biblical Research.* 3rd ed. Winona Lake, IN: Eisenbrauns, 2015.

———. *Textual Criticism of the Hebrew Bible.* 3rd ed. Minneapolis: Fortress, 2012.

Troyer, Kristen de. *The Ultimate and the Penultimate Text of the Book of Joshua.* CBET 100. Leuven: Peeters, 2018.

Ulrich, Eugene. *The Dead Sea Scrolls and the Origins of the Bible.* Grand Rapids: Eerdmans, 1999.

VanderKam, James, and Peter Flint. *The Meaning of the Dead Sea Scrolls: Their Significance for Understanding the Bible, Judaism, Jesus, and Christianity.* New York: HarperCollins, 2002.

VanderKam, James C. "The Festival of Weeks and the Story of Pentecost in Acts 2." Pages 185–205 in *From Prophecy to Testament: The Function of the Old Testament in the New.* Edited by Craig A. Evans. Peabody, MA: Hendrickson, 2004.

Westermann, Claus. *Basic Forms of Prophetic Speech.* Translated by Hugh Clayton White. Philadelphia: Westminster, 1967. Repr. with new foreword by Gene M. Tucker. Louisville: Westminster John Knox, 1991.

Wilson, Gerald H. "Psalms and Psalter: Paradigm for Biblical Theology." Pages 100–110 in *Biblical Theology: Retrospect and Prospect.* Edited by Scott J. Hafemann. Downers Grove, IL: InterVarsity, 2002.

Zetterholm, Karin Hedner. *Jewish Interpretation of the Bible: Ancient and Contemporary.* Minneapolis: Fortress, 2012.

INDEX OF SUBJECTS

INDEX OF SCRIPTURE AND OTHER ANCIENT SOURCES

RABBINIC WORKS

Babylonian Talmud

b. Baba Batra